CREATIVE
HOMEOWNER®

KITCHENS

PLAN ■ REMODEL ■ BUILD

CREATIVE HOMEOWNER®, Upper Saddle River, New Jersey

EDITORIAL DIRECTOR: Timothy O. Bakke
PRODUCTION MANAGER: Kimberly H. Vivas

SENIOR EDITOR: Fran J. Donegan
COPY EDITOR: Bruce Wetterau
ASSISTANT EDITOR/PHOTO
   RESEARCHER: Sharon Ranftle
EDITORIAL ASSISTANT: Jennifer Ramcke
TECHNICAL CONSULTANTS: Cecilia Herr, CKD,
   Former Director of Professional Programs,
   National Kitchen and Bath Association, 2000–02;
   Charles L. Rogers, Technical Training Consultant,
   Technical Skills Development Services
INDEXER: Schroeder Indexing Services

ART DIRECTION/LAYOUT: David Geer
COVER: Brad Simmons Photography,
   Clarke Barre (design)
ILLUSTRATIONS: Ian Worpole, Vincent Babak
   (pp. 86–93), Clarke Barre (p. 169)

Manufactured in the United States of America

Current Printing (last digit)
10 9 8 7

Kitchens: Plan, Remodel, Build
Library of Congress Control Number: 2001090755
ISBN: 1-58011-049-5

CREATIVE HOMEOWNER®
A Division of Federal Marketing Corp.
24 Park Way, Upper Saddle River, NJ 07458
Web site: **www.creativehomeowner.com**

Safety

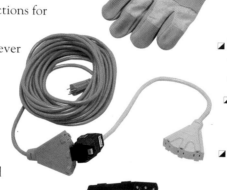

Although the methods in this book have been reviewed for safety, it is not possible to overstate the importance of using the safest methods you can. What follows are reminders—some do's and don'ts of work safety—to use along with your common sense.

☑ Always use caution, care, and good judgment when following the procedures described in this book.

☑ Always be sure that the electrical setup is safe, that no circuit is overloaded, and that all power tools and outlets are properly grounded. Do not use power tools in wet locations.

☑ Always read container labels on paints, solvents, and other products; provide ventilation; and observe all other warnings.

☑ Always read the manufacturer's instructions for using a tool, especially the warnings.

☑ Use hold-downs and push sticks whenever possible when working on a table saw. Avoid working short pieces if you can.

☑ Always remove the key from any drill chuck (portable or press) before starting the drill.

☑ Always pay deliberate attention to how a tool works so that you can avoid being injured.

☑ Always know the limitations of your tools. Do not try to force them to do what they were not designed to do.

☑ Always make sure that any adjustment is locked before proceeding. For example, always check the rip fence on a table saw or the bevel adjustment on a portable saw before starting to work.

☑ Always clamp small pieces to a bench or other work surface when using a power tool.

☑ Always wear the appropriate rubber gloves or work gloves when handling chemicals, moving or stacking lumber, working with concrete, or doing heavy construction.

☑ Always wear a disposable face mask when you create dust by sawing or sanding. Use a special filtering respirator when working with toxic substances and solvents.

☑ Always wear eye protection, especially when using power tools or striking metal on metal or concrete; a chip can fly off, for example, when chiseling concrete.

☑ Never work while wearing loose clothing, open cuffs, or jewelry; tie back long hair.

☑ Always be aware that there is seldom enough time for your body's reflexes to save you from injury from a power tool in a dangerous situation; everything happens too fast. Be alert!

☑ Always keep your hands away from the business ends of blades, cutters, and bits.

☑ Always hold a circular saw firmly, usually with both hands.

☑ Always use a drill with an auxiliary handle to control the torque when using large-size bits.

☑ Always check your local building codes when planning new construction. The codes are intended to protect public safety and should be observed to the letter.

☑ Never work with power tools when you are tired or when under the influence of alcohol or drugs.

☑ Never cut tiny pieces of wood or pipe using a power saw. When you need a small piece, saw it from a securely clamped longer piece.

☑ Never change a saw blade or a drill or router bit unless the power cord is unplugged. Do not depend on the switch being off. You might accidentally hit it.

☑ Never work in insufficient lighting.

☑ Never work with dull tools. Have them sharpened, or learn how to sharpen them yourself.

☑ Never use a power tool on a workpiece—large or small—that is not firmly supported.

☑ Never saw a workpiece that spans a large distance between horses without close support on each side of the cut; the piece can bend, closing on and jamming the blade, causing saw kickback.

☑ When sawing, never support a workpiece from underneath with your leg or other part of your body.

☑ Never carry sharp or pointed tools, such as utility knives, awls, or chisels, in your pocket. If you want to carry any of these tools, use a special-purpose tool belt that has leather pockets and holders.

Contents

6

Introduction

Dreams & Schemes

Planning a new kitchen is a challenging, exhilarating, exhausting task. But it's well worth the effort. Although remodeling a kitchen is one of the most costly home improvements, it's also one of the most rewarding. You gain a new kitchen that is more efficient and attractive than the old one, and a new kitchen is also a strong selling point should you put your house up for sale.

Begin by Deciding What You Want

Many people know exactly what they want in their new kitchen. But if your plan isn't clear in your mind, ask yourself the following questions. Your answers will get you started on planning your new kitchen.

- What do you like about your existing kitchen?
- What do you want to change?
- What do you do in your kitchen apart from fixing meals?

Remodeling a kitchen is certainly an enormous task, but it is also one of the most rewarding home improvement projects.

Organize Information

To keep track of all the decisions and details involved in planning and remodeling your kitchen, set up a scrapbook, folder, or file box. Keep kitchen photos clipped from magazines and newspapers, product brochures, articles about new trends or products, physical samples and color swatches of surface materials, notes from visits to showrooms, and all of your ideas and sketches. It might be helpful to sort your information into categories.

Paperwork. You should be able to put your hands on what you need:

- Calendar for scheduling and keeping a record of progress.
- Shopping lists with prices, warranties, serial numbers, receipts, and the like.
- Telephone directory of all subcontractors, suppliers, and service representatives.
- Contracts, permits, and inspection approvals.

Layout and Traffic Patterns. The arrangement of work spaces and appliances, and the flow of traffic through the kitchen greatly influence how tasks are performed.

Appliances. Choose among a number of appliance styles and features. Appliances should be placed so that they function most efficiently and conveniently, so the choices you make will affect the entire plan.

Storage. You need enough of the right kind of storage to provide a place for dry goods, perishables, dishes and flatware, pots and utensils, linens, cleaning supplies, garbage, recyclables, and anything else you want to keep in the kitchen.

Lighting. Plan on providing good overall lighting in the room, as well as task lighting that illuminates specific work areas.

Surfaces. Colors and textures help define your style. A kitchen's walls, floor, and countertops should be attractive, functional, and easy to clean.

Organization is key to the success of a kitchen remodeling. Create separate files for each element of the project.

- Who does the cooking in your house?
- How do family members interact when they cook?
- Is a typical meal heat and serve? Full-course from scratch? Something else?
- How do you entertain?
- Is your kitchen a family and company gathering place?
- What other tasks would you like to do in the kitchen? Pay bills? Homework? Use a computer? Do laundry?
- What decorating style do you want in your new kitchen?

Create a layout that suits your lifestyle and will help you prepare meals efficiently and safely.

How to Use this Book

Remodeling your kitchen may seem daunting at first, but the project will begin to appear more manageable when you realize that it consists of a series of smaller projects. *Kitchens: Plan, Remodel, Build* is intended to guide you through the entire process. The book will help you

- Analyze your existing kitchen and set your sights on the kitchen you would like to have.
- Choose the right materials, products, and appliances for your needs.
- Plan a layout that suits your lifestyle and the space available.
- Define your style with color, texture, lighting, and details.
- Decide what you can handle yourself, and where you might need the services of a professional.

The organization of the book allows you to plan and remodel an entire kitchen yourself. Or you can simply pick the sections that apply to your particular situation.

Your personal style will emerge in the look of your kitchen. Do you prefer homey, country rooms (left) or the clean lines of a contemporary design (above)? Or something else?

The Planning Chapters

Chapters 1 through 4 will help you plan your new kitchen. They provide information on appliances, finishes, and the latest kitchen trends. There are also sections that guide you through the layout process and help you pick a personal style for your new kitchen. Even if you will be working with a kitchen designer, these four chapters will give you a head start in the design and planning process.

The How-To Chapters

Chapters 5 through 8 provide the nuts and bolts of kitchen remodeling. Through a series of step-by-step photographs you will learn how to do everything from safely tearing down a wall to hooking up a dishwasher. The information is designed for do-it-yourselfers, but if a contractor works on your kitchen, these chapters will provide the information you need to check his work.

To keep you from getting in over your head, there is a project rating system. A level of difficulty for each project is indicated by one, two, or three hammers.

Guide to Skill Level

Look for these estimates of job difficulty.

Easy, even for beginners.

Challenging. Can be done by beginners who have the patience and willingness to learn.

Difficult. Can be handled by most experienced do-it-yourselfers who have mastered basic construction skills. Consider consulting a specialist.

Many different skills are needed for a kitchen remodeling. Decide what you want to do yourself, and seek help for the rest.

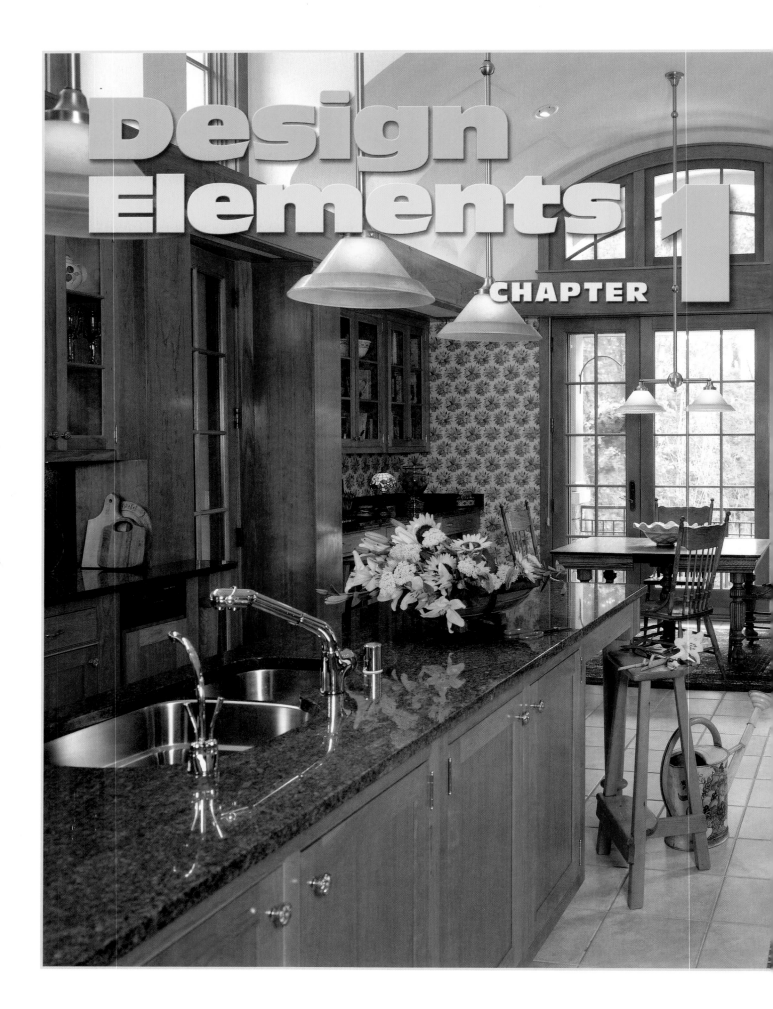

Design Elements

CHAPTER 1

Whether you typically prepare gourmet cuisine or simple fare, you'll want your new kitchen to allow you to function smoothly and at your best. The following pages present ideas that will make putting together a meal easier, cleaning up the mess quicker, and storing equipment and supplies more efficient.

If you've ever become exasperated looking for the right pot in a crowded cabinet, you'll appreciate today's myriad cabinet and storage options. Along with new cabinets, you might want to match the right appliances to your family's needs and habits. If you can't make major changes in these two costly areas, you can improve the look of your old kitchen with new surfaces—countertops, flooring, and wallcovering. Upgrading the lighting makes the space brighter and more efficient. Whatever the scope of your renovation, taking steps to improve the room's design will turn kitchen time into quality time.

Cabinets

While it's true that cabinets help define the style and create the environment of a kitchen, their main job is to store the many items involved in preparing, serving, and cleaning up after meals. They must be durable enough to withstand thousands of openings and closings over years of use.

Regardless of the type and style of cabinets you choose, insist on quality construction. Good cabinets feature dovetail and mortise-and-tenon joinery and solidly mortised hinges. The interiors are well finished, with adjustable shelves that are a mini-

Choose from a variety of possible cabinet finishes. Choices range from natural looks to glaze finishes (right) and painted finishes (below).

Framed cabinets—those with a full frame across the face of the cabinet box—are often used in traditional kitchens.

mum of ⅝ inch thick to prevent bowing under heavy loads. The drawers in good cabinets roll on ball-bearing glides, and they support at least 75 pounds when open.

Construction Styles and Options

There are basically two construction styles for kitchen cabinetry: framed and frameless. You can buy inexpensive ready-made cabinets directly from a retailer's stock in finished form, in unfinished form, or as knockdowns. These will usually be framed cabinets. If you prefer, choose more expensive semi-custom and custom-made cabinets. You can get custom cabinets from a large manufacturer, or have them built to your room's specifications by a carpenter or cabinetmaker.

Framed. Framed cabinets—or traditional-style cabinets—have a full frame across the face of the cabinet box. This provides a means of securing adjacent cabinets together and strengthens wider cabinet boxes with a center rail. Hinges may be either visible or hidden, and the front frame may or may not be visible around doors and drawers when they are closed.

Frameless. Frameless cabinets—also known as European-style cabinets—are built without a face frame. Close-fitting doors cover the entire front of the box, or they may be set into the box opening. Hinges are typically hidden. Both domestic and European manufacturers offer frameless cabinets. Prices can be high and delivery times lengthy if you want features that an import dealer does not have in stock.

Semi-custom cabinets are available with a variety of options, including refrigerator panels that match the cabinets.

Manufacturing Styles

Unless you have the time and skill to build the cabinets yourself or you can hire someone else to do it, you'll have to purchase them in one of three ways: stock, semi-custom, or custom. Prices vary from category to category, and even within each category.

Stock. Stock cabinets are literally in stock where they are sold or are quickly available by order. They are made in limited styles and colors, but in a wide variety of standard sizes that you can assemble to suit your kitchen space. The quality of stock cabinets may be fair, good, or excellent, depending on the manufacturer and price. Materials may be solid wood (hard or soft) and plywood, wood and parti-cleboard, wood and hardboard, or all particleboard. They may be carefully jointed and doweled or merely nailed and glued together. Stock cabinets also come in steel and in several types of plastic, either in part or entirely. The quality of cabinets made from these materials also varies from exquisite to barely adequate. Stock cabinets range in price from inexpensive to moderately costly.

You can save some money by buying unfinished stock cabinets and staining or painting them yourself. You can save even more by purchasing knockdown cabinets, which are shipped flat to lower the costs of packing and delivery. Knockdowns are sometimes unfinished as well.

Semi-Custom. Like stock cabinets, semi-custom cabinets are available only in specific sizes, but there are many more finishes, colors, styles, options, and special features to chose from than you will find with stock cabinets. The extras aren't added to the cabinets until you place the order, so there will be a wait for delivery. Times vary, but expect to wait three to six weeks for delivery.

Custom. Custom cabinets are built to the measurements of a particular project. Because custom cabinets are made from scratch, delivery may take from 4 to 16 weeks. The delivery delay rarely causes a problem because the preparation work for a new kitchen also takes time. But place your order well in advance of the date you will need your cabinets. Custom cabinets are almost always delivered completely finished, like fine furniture, whereas some stock cabinets may be bought unfinished. Prices for custom cabinets run from moderate to very expensive.

Carpenter-Built. If you have the time, some carpentry skills, and a work area, you can save money by constructing cabinets to your own specifications. Or you can hire a carpenter to build them. This won't be a money saver, of course, but will give you great leeway in your design.

Custom touches improve any design. The carved corbel (left) is an option offered by a cabinet manufacturer. The pantry and built-in (below) increase storage.

HOW-TO

See "Installing Wall Cabinets," page 200

See "Installing Base Cabinets," page 202

1 Design Elements

Storage

The type of storage in a kitchen is almost as important as the amount. Some people like at least a few open shelves for displaying attractive china or glassware; others want absolutely everything tucked away behind doors.

What are your storage needs? The answer depends partly on your food shopping habits and partly on how many pots, pans, and other pieces of kitchen equipment you have or would like to have. A family that goes food shopping several times a week and prepares mostly fresh foods needs more refrigerator space, less freezer capacity, and fewer cabinets than a family that prefers packaged or prepared foods and makes only infrequent forays to the local supermarket.

Planning

To help clarify your needs, mentally walk yourself through a typical meal and list the utensils used to prepare food, where you got them, and your progress throughout the work area. And don't limit yourself to full-scale meals. Much kitchen work is devoted to preparing snacks, reheating leftovers, and making lunches for the kids to take to school.

Order cabinets that suit your storage needs. Mentally walk through a typical day in the kitchen to find what works best.

Food Preparation. During food preparation, the sink and stove come into use. Some families rely heavily on the microwave for reheating. Using water means repeated trips to the sink, so that area might be the best place to keep a steamer, salad spinner, and coffee and tea canisters, as well as glassware and cups. Near the stove you may want storage for odd-shaped items such as a fish poacher or wok. You can hang frequently used pans and utensils from a convenient rack; stow other items in cabinets so that they do not collect grease.

During the Meal. When the food is ready, you must take it to the table. If the eating space is nearby, a work counter might turn into a serving counter. If the dining space is in another room, a pass-through facilitates serving.

After the Meal. When the meal ends, dishes must go from the table to the sink or dishwasher, and leftovers to storage containers and the refrigerator. Now the stove and counters need to be wiped down and the sink scoured. When the dishwasher finishes its cycle, everything must be put away.

Storage Checklist

- *Do you like kitchen gadgets?*

  Plan drawer space, countertop sorters, wall magnets, or hooks to keep these items handy near where you often use them.

- *Do you own a food processor, blender, mixer, toaster oven, electric can opener, knife sharpener, juicer, coffee maker, or coffee mill?*

  If you're particularly tidy, you may want small appliances like these tucked away in an appliance garage or cupboard to be taken out only when needed. If you prefer to have frequently used machines sitting on the counter, ready to go, plan enough space, along with conveniently located electrical outlets.

- *Do you plan to store large quantities of food?*

  Be sure to allow plenty of freezer, bin, and shelf space for the kind of food shopping you do.

- *Do you intend to do a lot of freezing or canning?*

  Allow a work space and place to stow equipment. Also plan adequate storage for the fruits of your labor—an extra stand-alone freezer, a good-sized food safe in the kitchen, or a separate pantry or cellar.

- *Do you bake often?*

  Consider a baking center that can house your equipment and serve as a separate baking-ingredients pantry.

- *Do you collect pottery, tinware, or anything else that might be displayed in the kitchen?*

  Soffits provide an obvious place to hang small objects like collectible plates. Eliminating soffits provides a shelf on top of the wall cabinets for larger lightweight objects like baskets. Open shelving, glass-front cupboards, and display cabinets are other options.

- *Do you collect cookbooks?*

  If so, you'll need expandable shelf space and perhaps a bookstand.

Personal Profile of You and Your Family

- *How tall are you and everyone else who will use your kitchen?*

  Adjust your counter and wall-cabinet heights to suit. Multilevel work surfaces for special tasks are a necessity for good kitchen design.

- *Do you or any of your family members use a walker, leg braces, or a wheelchair?*

  Plan a good work height, knee space, grab bars, secure seating, slide-out work boards, and other convenience features to make your kitchen comfortable for all who will use it.

- *Are you left- or right-handed?*

  Think about your natural motion when you choose whether to open cupboards or refrigerator doors from the left or right side, whether to locate your dishwasher to the left or right of the sink, and so on.

- *How high can you comfortably reach?*

  If you're tall, hang your wall cabinets high. If you're petite, you may want to hang the cabinets lower and plan a spot to keep a step-stool handy.

- *Can you comfortably bend and reach for something in a base cabinet?*

  Can you lift heavy objects easily and without strain or pain? If your range is limited in these areas, be sure to plan roll-out shelving on both upper and lower tiers of your base cabinets. Also, look into spring-up shelves designed to lift mixer bases or other heavy appliances to counter height.

- *Do you frequently share cooking tasks with another family member?*

  If so, you may each prefer to have your own work area.

Types of Storage

Storage facilities can make or break a kitchen, so choose the places you'll put things with care. Here's a look at a few alternatives:

Open versus Closed Storage. Shelves, pegboards, pot racks, cup hooks, magnetic knife racks, and the like put your utensils on view, which is a good way to personalize your kitchen. Here's an area where you can save some money, too. Open storage generally costs less than cabinets, and you don't have to construct and hang doors.

But open storage has drawbacks. For one thing, items left out in the open can look messy unless they are kept neatly arranged. Also, objects collect dust and grease, especially near the range. This means that unless you reach for an item almost daily, you'll find yourself washing it before, as well as after you use it.

Closed storage like under-counter pantries (above) keep items close to their point of use but out of sight. Glass-fronted cabinets (below) put items on display.

Speciality storage is key to a well-designed kitchen. A full-height pantry (left) can hold supplies for the long term. A revolving shelf (right) placed near the cooking center is a good place to store spices.

If extra washing and dusting discourages you from the idea of open storage but you'd like to put at least some objects on view, limit your displays to a few items. Another option is to install glass doors on wall cabinets. This handily solves the dust problem but often costs more than solid doors.

Pantries. How often you shop and how many groceries you typically bring home determine the amount of food storage space your family needs. If you like to stock up or take advantage of sales, add a pantry to your kitchen. To maximize a pantry's convenience, plan shallow, 6-inch-deep shelves so that cans and packages will never be stored more than two deep. This way, you'll easily be able to see what you've got on hand. Pantries range in size from floor-to-ceiling models to narrow units designed to fit between two standard-size cabinets.

Appliance Garages. Appliance garages make use of dead space in a corner, but they can be installed anywhere in the vertical space between wall-mounted cabinets and the countertop. A tambour (rolltop) door hides small appliances like a food processor or anything else you want within reach but hidden from view. This form of mini-cabinet can be equipped with an electrical outlet and even can be divided into separate sections to store more than one item. Customize an appliance garage any way you like. Reserve part of the appliance garage for cookbook storage, for example, or outfit it with small drawers for little items or spices.

Appliance garages with tambour doors keep countertop appliances in easy reach but out of sight when not in use.

Lazy Susans and Carousel Shelves. Rotating shelves like lazy Susans and carousels maximize dead corner storage and put items like dishes or pots and pans within easy reach. A lazy Susan rotates 360 degrees, so just spin it to find what you're looking for. Carousel shelves, which attach to two right-angled doors, rotate 270 degrees; open the doors, and the shelves swing out allowing you to reach items easily. Pivoting shelves are a variation on the carousel design and may or may not be door-mounted. In addition, units may be built into taller cabinets, creating a pantry that can store a lot in a small amount of space.

Fold-Down Mixer Shelf. A spring-loaded mixer shelf swings up and out of a base cabinet for use, then folds down and back into the cabinet when the mixer is no longer needed.

Slide-Outs and Tilt-Outs. Installed in base cabinets, slide-out trays and racks store small appliances, linens, cans, or boxed items, while slide-out bins are good for holding onions, potatoes, grains, pet food, or potting soil—even garbage or recycling containers. A tilt-out tray is located in the often-wasted area just below the lip of the countertop in front of the sink and above base cabinet doors.

HOW-TO

See "Installing Rollout Shelves," page 212

See "Installing Pullout Platforms," page 213

Pivoting Shelves. Door-mounted shelves and in-cabinet swiveling shelf units offer easy access to kitchen supplies. Taller units serve as pantries that hold a great deal in minimal space.

Pullout Tables and Trays. In tight kitchens, pullout tables and trays are excellent ways to gain eating space or an extra work surface. Pullout cutting boards come in handy near cooktops and microwaves. Pullout tea carts are also available.

Drawer Inserts. A drawer insert is a good way to keep packaged spices organized and easily accessible. Inserts are made for flatware and other items, too.

Tray Storage. A narrow base cabinet with horizontal slots is perfect for storing cookie sheets and trays on edge. Locate this in a baking center.

Pivoting shelves save you from stooping to retrieve items from the back of base cabinets.

Pullout trays provide extra work surfaces near cooking and baking centers.

Turn wasted space to valuable storage with pullout tray holders.

Customized Organizers. If you decide to make do with your existing cabinets, consider refitting their interiors with cabinet organizers. These plastic, plastic-coated wire, or enameled-steel racks and hangers are widely available at department stores, hardware stores, and home centers.

Some of these units slide in and out of base cabinets, similar to the racks in a dishwasher. Others let you mount shallow drawers to the undersides of wall cabinets. Still others consist of stackable plastic bins with plenty of room to hold kitchen sundries.

Beware of the temptation to overspecialize your kitchen storage facilities. Sizes and needs for certain items change, so be sure to allot at least 50 percent of your kitchen's storage to standard cabinets with one or more movable shelves.

Recycling Storage. Slide-out shelves can hold two or three large containers for sorting recyclable materials. Some products also include bins for holding newspapers.

Herb and Spice Racks. Be aware that herbs and spices lose their flavor more rapidly when exposed to heat or sunlight, so don't locate a spice rack or shelving intended for storing herbs too close to the cooktop or a sunny window. Choose opaque con-

Glass-fronted drawers put pasta, beans, or rice on display, making them part of the kitchen's design.

tainers, or keep seasonings in a cool, closed cupboard or in a drawer outfitted with a rack so you can quickly reach what you need.

Wine Storage. Some contemporary kitchens show off bottles of wine in open racks and bins that hold as much as a couple of cases. If you regularly serve wine with meals, by all means keep a few bottles on hand—but bear in mind that the kitchen is far from the ideal place to store wine for any length of time.

The problem is that heat and sunlight are two of wine's worst enemies, which is why fine wines are stored in cellars. The temperature in a wine cellar should be about 55 to 60 degrees F, so if you'd like to age new vintages for a year or two, keep them in a cool, dark location, such as the basement or an attached climate-controlled garage, where the bottles won't be disturbed.

Cabinet Hardware

Door and drawer pulls and knobs not only serve a functional purpose, they also contribute to the overall look of your kitchen. When selecting hardware, make sure you can grip it easily and comfortably. If your fingers or hands get stiff easily or if you have arthritis, select C- or U-shaped pulls because they are easier to grab and hold on to. If you like a knob, try it out in the showroom to make sure it isn't slippery or awkward when you grab it. Knobs and pulls can be inexpensive if you stick to unfinished ones that you can paint in an accent color picked up from the tile or wallpaper. If you don't plan to buy new cabinets, changing the hardware on old ones can redefine their style. The right knob or pull can suggest any one of a number of vintage looks or decorative styles.

Create a recycling center with units that hold tall containers, or pair tall containers with flat newspaper storage.

Food Preparation

Preparing food requires fire and ice. Luckily for us in the modern world, these are provided by a wide choice of functional and beautiful appliances: the ice by refrigerator/ freezers, of course, and the fire by cooktops and ovens.

Food-preparation centers require a range or cooktop (above) and a refrigerator (below). Note how the range, refrigerator, and sink are within easy reach of one another.

Refrigerators and Freezers

To estimate the refrigerator/freezer capacity your family needs, allow 12 cubic feet of total refrigerator and freezer space for the first two adults in your household, then add 2 more cubic feet for each additional member. Typically, a family of four would need a refrigerator/freezer with a capacity of 16 cubic feet. You must increase this capacity, however, if you prepare meals for the week in advance and keep them in the refrigerator or freezer. If your teenagers down a half-gallon of milk in a swallow, increase milk storage capacity. If you freeze produce from your garden for use out of season, increase your freezer space or consider buying an additional standalone freezer.

As you make a selection, be aware that the fuller a refrigerator or freezer is kept, the less it costs to run. This fact is a compelling reason not to buy a refrigerator or freezer too large for your household or for the amount of food you normally keep on hand, especially where electricity costs are high.

Refrigerator sizes vary by more than capacity. Many require a space that extends out beyond the full depth of a base cabinet and upward into the overhead cabinet space. In recent years, however, manufacturers have been offering 25-inch-deep freestanding models that do not protrude too far beyond the front edges of counters. Built-in 24-inch-deep designs further minimize the bulk of this massive

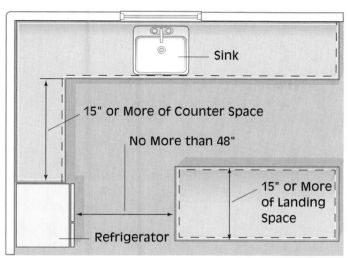

Plan adequate counter space near refrigerators. Island landing space should be no more than 48 inches away.

piece of kitchen equipment. Shallower refrigerators and freezers are wider than standard models, however, and often taller as well, so allocate kitchen space accordingly. Most conventional refrigerators come in one of these styles:

Top Freezer. The freezer and refrigerator sections are separate, usually with automatic defrosting. The freezer will maintain food for long periods of time.

Bottom Freezer. Similar in look to top-mounted freezer units, bottom mounts have a large freezer section under the main refrigerator area. The benefit: no need to bend down to look into the refrigerator.

Side-by-Side. A side-by-side offers the greatest access to both compartments and requires the least door-swing clearance in front. Side-by-side models are wider than up-and-down versions, and their narrow shelves may not handle bulky items, such as a large frozen turkey.

Modular Refrigerators. Modulars offer a departure from the vertical box we're used to. This concept allows refrigerator or freezer drawer units and cabinets to be located strategically throughout the kitchen—or house. The units are only 27 inches wide and are standard cabinet depth. They accept all types of paneling and handles, so they can blend in with cabinetry. Drawer units and cabinets may be individually temperature-controlled for optimal food storage—32 to 34 degrees F for vegetables, 38 degrees for milk, and 30 to 32 degrees for meats.

Undercounter-style refrigerators, freezers, and combination units may solve some design difficulties and provide for some specialized needs where tall units pose a problem.

Cool Options for Refrigerators

Today refrigerators can be loaded with options unheard of even a few years ago. As with any purchase, extras tend to drive up the price of the appliance, but many options can make your life easier or the appliance more efficient. Here are some to consider:

- Adjustable shelving
- Automatic ice maker
- Automatic defroster
- Wine rack
- Through-the-door water and ice dispenser
- Extra-deep door shelves for gallon jugs
- Zoned temperature controls
- Separate controls for crisper drawers
- Slide-out shelves
- Leak-proof shelves
- The ability to accept panels that match cabinets

Wine coolers keep your favorite vintages at optimal temperature.

Modular drawer units can be placed throughout the kitchen.

1 Design Elements

Cooking Center

The term "cooking center" may sound a bit grand, but with all of the options available, including restaurant-style ranges, modular cooktops, microwaves, and convection ovens, many home chefs want more than just a set of burners with an oven underneath.

As you begin to plan your cooking center, take yourself through the process of meal preparation in your household. Make a mental inventory of the range-top utensils you now have or plan to acquire.

Ranges

Until the late 1950s, the heart of every American kitchen was a "stove" that stood off by itself so heat would not damage nearby cabinets and countertops. Today the successors to the stove are drop-in or slide-in ranges that are insulated at the sides and rear so that they can fit flush against cabinets and other combustible surfaces. Like stoves, ranges include gas or electric burners on top and an oven/broiler below. The most common range styles are

- *Freestanding.* Typical freestanding models are 30, 36, or 40 inches wide. Both sides are finished.
- *High-Low.* A second oven, regular or microwave, on top provides extra capacity.
- *Drop-In.* Drop-ins look the most built-in but leave dead space beneath. They are usually 30 inches wide.
- *Slide-In.* The sides are not finished. Most are 30 inches wide; compact units are 20 or 21 inches wide.

Gas or Electric? Whether you choose gas or electric with which to cook depends in part on what's available locally. If natural gas is not available, appliance dealers can convert ranges to run on bottled liquid propane—but you'll need to arrange for regular delivery.

Many accomplished chefs prefer to cook with gas because gas burners heat up fast, cool quickly, and can be infinitely adjusted to keep food simmering almost indefinitely. Electric cooktops, on the other hand, are easier to clean. Also, new developments in cooktops, such as magnetic-induction cooking and smooth-top surfaces, are designed for electricity, not gas.

Although many people prefer gas for surface cooking, ovens are a different story. Electric ovens maintain more even temperatures than gas units.

Restaurant-style ranges look similar to commercial appliances but without the ventilation and clearance drawbacks.

Restaurant Ranges

True restaurant, or commercial-quality, ranges with heavy-duty burners deliver more heat more quickly than the usual kitchen range, and their ovens have superior insulation. Commercial-type cooking surfaces are made of cast iron, making them ideal for prolonged, low-intensity cooking. The sturdy appearance of a restaurant range appeals to serious cooks.

However, restaurant ranges are for restaurants. The tremendous heat that they generate will increase the risk of fire and injury in your home. Codes for installing this type of range are strict—some areas even prohibit the installation of commercial equipment for residential use. A commercial range also requires special venting and minimum clearances between it and adjacent cabinets or other combustible materials or surfaces.

As an option, you may want to consider a commercial-style range. They look like those used in restaurants, but more importantly they produce less heat—though more than standard ranges. They allow you to set flames as high as 15,000 Btu—30 to 50 percent higher than regular residential ranges—and to bring them down to 360 Btu (on some models) for low simmering. Some units come with the option of one high-flame burner (12,000 to 15,000 Btu).

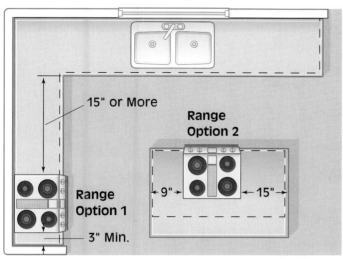

Plan adequate counter space near cooktops and ranges. Provide heat-proof surfaces in these areas.

Gas cooktops provide the precise temperature control many cooks desire.

Ceramic glass cooktops have smooth, easy-to-clean surfaces.

Cooktops

A surface cooking unit has top burners only and fits into the countertop. Most of the space underneath can be used for conventional storage.

Gas. Usually 30 or 36 inches wide, gas cooktops have brushed-chrome or porcelain-enamel finishes. If you think gas cooktops are difficult to keep clean, new sealed gas burners may be the answer, because the cooking surface is extended around the heating element. No more drip plates and no more escaping flames.

Electric. Conventional electric cooktops have coil or cast-iron disk burners. Disks heat more evenly than coils and are easier to clean.

Ceramic Glass. Also called a radiant-heat cooking surface, a ceramic top features electric coils directly under translucent glass, which transfers heat more efficiently to the cookware than do older, opaque, white ceramic surfaces. It also uses higher-wattage heating elements. The smooth, sleek appearance of ceramic glass cooktops appeals to contemporary tastes. The finish is scratch- and stain-resistant, but can be damaged by abrasive cleansers. You'll need flat-bottomed, heavy-gauge metal pans to heat food quickly and effectively with ceramic glass.

Halogen. Similar to ceramic glass cooktops, especially with regard to cookware and cleaning, halogen units combine resistant heating wires and halogen lamps that are located beneath a ceramic-glass cover to create heat.

Induction. This ceramic-glass cooking surface uses electromagnetic energy to heat the cookware, not the cooktop, making it safe because no heat is generated by a flame or coil. An induction cooktop is also easy to keep clean; because the surface remains relatively cool, spills don't burn and turn into a crusty mess that requires scrubbing.

Below the surface, the coils produce a high-frequency alternating magnetic field that flows through the cookware. Most of the heat from the cooktop is absorbed by the pan. Without a pan or utensil, the heating coil is de-energized and turns itself off. Induction cooktops require magnetic-responsive cookware, which means pots and pans for use with this appliance must be steel, porcelain-on-steel, stainless steel, or cast iron. Manufacturers of induction cooktops boast of its quick response—it can go from high heat to low heat instantly—and the precise temperature control.

HOW-TO

See "Installing a Gas Range," page 238

See "Installing an Electric Cooktop," page 239

Ovens

Ovens that are separate from cooktops can be located in a wall cabinet at a height that permits safe handling of heavy or awkward pans. The main features to consider, after making a choice between gas and electric, are the size of the oven's interior, whether you need one or two ovens, and what attachments are practical for your family. Most standard ovens, for instance, will hold a 20-pound turkey. But if your requirements are greater, shop for an oven that's more spacious.

Convection Ovens. You also may want to consider a convection oven. You'll pay more for a full-size convection oven, and because the heat source is outside the cooking cavity of a true convection oven, it won't broil. But here's what a convection unit does: It circulates heated air around the food, pulls the air out of the cooking cavity, reheats the air over a hot element, and returns the reheated air to the cavity. Because the convection system is closed, moisture is retained in the unit and therefore in the food. Cooked meats tend to be juicier and baked goods moister. Convection ovens bake and roast faster than conventional models at temperatures that are 25 to 75 degrees F lower, which saves energy. Because superheating the air over hot elements burns off odors, it's possible to bake dissimilar items, such as an apple pie and an onion/garlic casserole, at the same time without corrupting the flavor of either.

Microwave Ovens. Microwave units cut down cooking time for some foods to mere minutes. However, food cooked in a microwave oven often demands a certain amount of coddling and doesn't turn out the same as with traditional methods.

Even if you're not hooked on microwave cooking, you may want the convenience of quick reheating and defrosting. A microwave unit needn't be located in your primary cooking center, although some brands feature built-in range hoods that make them naturals for hanging over a range. Position the oven at about eye level, with 15 to 18 inches of counter space adjacent to or under it.

Fast-Cooking Ovens. Hybrid products that combine cooking technologies such as microwaves and radiant heat, fast-cooking ovens cut in half baking

Warming drawers keep food warm and moist until you are ready to serve. They range in size from 24 to 30 in.

Wall ovens are available with traditional gas or electric heating elements or with convection elements.

and roasting times for most foods. They are available as standalone ovens or as part of a range.

Warming Drawers. Another practical device is a warming drawer. They range in size from 24 to 30 inches wide and can keep food moist and warm for long periods of time. Most manufacturers make warming drawers to match other appliances in their lines, but you can outfit them with a trim finish that blends with the cabinetry, as well. Look for a model with adjustable temperature settings—from about 90 to 200 degrees F is a good range—flexible racks, automatic shutoff, and removable pans.

Ventilation hoods and fans not only remove unwanted moisture and odors, they can be a design element as well.

Sizing Ventilation Fans

No matter how attractive the hood may be, it is the fan in the system that actually takes the air out of the kitchen. Fans are sized by the amount of air they can move in cubic feet per minute (CFM). Here are some guidelines to help you size the ventilation fan to suit your needs: Multiply the recommended CFM below by the linear feet of cooking surface. Note: The length of the ductwork, the number of turns in the duct, and the location of the fan's motor also contribute to the size of the fan needed.

Ranges and Cooktops Installed against a Wall

Light Cooking: 40 CFM
Medium to Heavy Cooking: 100 to 150 CFM

Ranges and Cooktops Installed in Islands and Peninsulas

Light Cooking: 50 CFM
Medium to Heavy Cooking: 150 to 300 CFM

1 Design Elements

Ventilation

No discussion of cooking equipment is complete without addressing ventilation. Unvented grease, smoke, heat, and steam generated when you cook will take its toll on your new cabinets, countertops, floors, walls, and other surfaces, which will collect the residue along with germs and general grime.

The only efficient way to combat this residue and the stale cooking odors that linger is with an exhaust system. A fan over the range or cooktop is not enough. The most effective way to ventilate a kitchen is with a hooded system. The hood, which is installed directly over the cooking surface, captures the bad air as it heats and naturally rises. A fan expels the contaminants to the outside through a duct. A damper inside the hood closes when the system is turned off so that cold air can't enter the house from the outside. Don't try to save money by installing a ductless fan: Any system that isn't ducted to the outside is useless.

Although handsome hoods can create a focal point in the kitchen, most people don't regard ventilation as a glamorous feature. However, it is one of the most important—not only for preserving the good looks of your new room, but for your safety and health too. When installing a range hood, keep in mind that

manufacturers recommend a maximum distance of 24 to 30 inches between the cooktop and the bottom of the hood in order to get the best ventilation. The actual distance depends on the depth of the range hood. A 16-inch-deep hood should be no more than 24 inches above the cooktop; a 24-inch-deep hood can be installed the full 30 inches above the cooking surface. The width of the hood should overlap the cooking surface by about 3 inches on each side.

An alternative to a system that uses a hood is downdraft ventilation, which is often installed in conjunction with an island cooktop or grill. The vent is in the countertop and the fan is below it. Downdraft venting works by forcing the air above the burners through a filter, and then moving it out of the house via ductwork. This method is not as effective as a hooded system, but it is more effective than a ductless fan. Both hooded and nonhooded systems require a powerful fan. The more cooking you do, the more power you need.

HOW-TO See "Installing a Range Hood," page 148

Cleanup Center

The kitchen sink is the focal point in the cleanup center. This includes the sink, 18 to 24 inches of counter space on either side for dishes and food that you need to wash, a dishwasher, a waste-disposal unit (where local codes permit), and storage for glassware, frequently used utensils, detergents, colanders, and other sink accessories. The trash receptacle and recycling bins are also in the cleanup center; a trash compactor may be included here as well.

Because it's often located under a window and always tied to the plumbing system, the sink is one of the most fixed of kitchen fixtures. If you're thinking about moving your sink and dishwasher more than 60 inches from the current location, you'll probably have to rework vent and drain lines, and you might have to move a window as well. If cost containment is important to you, it's wise to begin your kitchen plan by trying to locate the sink at or near the place the old one occupies.

Where there's no window behind the sink, decide what you'll do with the wall space there. One choice is to integrate the space into a run of cabinets with units that are shorter than those on either side so that you'll have headroom. Another possibility is to install full-height cabinets only 6 inches deep. Whatever treatment you select, be sure your cleanup center includes adequate daytime and nighttime light falling directly onto the sink and adjacent counters.

Sinks

Sinks come in a great variety of sizes and shapes. Materials include stainless steel, pressed steel, cast iron, and the same solid-surfacing material used for countertops. Sinks of each material come in single-, double-, and triple-bowl models.

A single-bowl sink is large enough for soaking big pots and pans. Two-bowl sinks may have identical-size basins, or one may be smaller or shallower than the other. Three-bowl sinks include a small disposal basin at one side or between the larger bowls. These sinks usually require about 12 inches more counter space than a double-bowl unit.

Stainless-Steel Sinks. Stainless steel, made with nickel and chrome to prevent staining, continues to be a popular choice for sinks, although some homeowners complain about spotting. This kind of sink offers the greatest selection of bowl sizes and configurations. Choose 18-gauge stainless for a large sink or one with a disposer, lighter 20-gauge material for smaller sinks. Stainless steel also differs in grade, depending on the amount of nickel

Cleanup centers revolve around the main sink. To save money, locate the new sink where the old one stood.

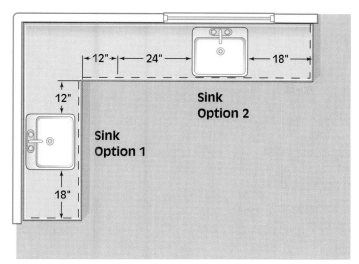

Plan adequate counter space near the main sink. For smaller second sinks, plan on 3- and 18-in. landing spaces.

and chrome it contains. High levels of both are included in good-quality sinks.

Pressed-Steel and Cast-Iron Sinks. Both of these sinks have porcelain-enamel finishes. Cast iron is heavier and less likely to chip than pressed steel. Cast iron is also quieter than both stainless and pressed steel when water is running. These sinks are available in a wide range of colors.

Solid-Surface Sinks. Solid-surface or acrylic sinks can be molded directly into a solid-surface countertop, creating a seamless unit that is especially easy to keep clean. Separate drop-in models are also available. Sinks of this material are even quieter than cast iron, but costly.

Besides the common kitchen varieties, there are sinks for virtually every practical and aesthetic need—perfect circles, sinks that turn corners, deep farm-style kitchen sinks, and so on.

Two- and three-bowl configurations are gaining

Under-mount sinks are attached to the underside of the counter. They work with stone or solid-surface counters.

popularity. This arrangement allows you to separate clean dishes from dirty ones as well as from waste materials. Some sinks come with a colander and cutting board that fits over one of the bowls. Typically, a waste-disposal unit is installed with one of the bowls, usually the larger one.

Like every other kitchen product, there are numerous options open to you. In terms of durability, any one of the materials mentioned above will hold up for years, if not decades, with the right care. Enameled cast-iron sinks tend to discolor but can be cleaned easily with a nonabrasive cleanser recommended by the manufacturer. Stainless steel and stone should be cleaned the same way. However, solid-surface sinks can take a lot of abuse. Minor scratches can be sanded out without harming the finish. You can use an abrasive agent on them. Expect a quality sink to last as long as 30 years.

As with all kitchen fixtures, be sure there is enough counter space on both sides of the sink. Experts recommend 18 and 24 inches of counter space.

Stainless-steel sinks come in a variety of sizes and configurations. Quality sinks are made of 18-gauge steel.

Sink Installations. In terms of installation, there are five types of kitchen sinks to consider:

• *Under-mounted.* If you want a smooth look, an under-mounted sink may be for you. The bowl is attached underneath the countertop.

• *Integral.* As the word "integral" implies, the sink and countertop are fabricated from the same material—stone, faux stone, or solid-surfacing. There are no visible seams or joints in which food or debris can accumulate.

• *Self-Rimming or Flush-Mounted.* A self-rimmed sink has a rolled edge that is mounted over the countertop.

• *Rimmed.* Unlike a self-rimming sink, a rimmed sink requires a flat metal strip to seal the sink to the countertop.

• *Tile-In.* Used with a tiled countertop, the sink rim is flush with the tiled surface. Grout seals the sink to the surrounding countertop area.

Second Sinks. Many homeowners find that adding a second, small sink to their kitchen greatly improves the kitchen's efficiency. The primary sink is usually a full-size model that anchors the main food-preparation and cleanup areas, while the secondary sink serves outside of the major work zone. A second sink is a must when two or more people cook together routinely, but it is also handy if you practice crafts in the kitchen or entertain often and would use it as a wet bar. You can also use a secondary sink as an extra place for washing hands and the like when someone is using the main sink for preparing a meal.

Many manufacturers offer second sinks and faucets that match their full-size models. You have the same options regarding finishes, colors, styles, and the like. If you do install a second sink, you must route water, drain, and vent lines to it. Allow at least 3 inches of counter space on one side and 18 inches on the other.

HOW-TO

See "Installing a Sink," page 226

Integral sinks are made from the same material as the countertop (top). Apron-front or farmhouse sinks (middle) have exposed fronts and are gaining in popularity. Two-sink kitchens (bottom) can make cooking more efficient.

Faucets

State-of-the-art technology in faucets gives you not only much more control over water use, but better performance and a wider selection of faucet finishes as well. Features to look for include pullout faucet heads, retractable sprayers, hot- and cold-water dispensing, single-lever control, antiscald and flow-control devices, a lowered lead content in brass components, and built-in water purifiers to enhance taste.

For a quality faucet, inquire about its parts when you shop. The best are those made of solid brass or a brass-base material. Both are corrosion-resistant. Avoid plastic components—they won't hold up. Ask about the faucet's valving, too. Buy a model that has a washerless cartridge; it will cost more, but it will last longer and be less prone to leaks. This will save you money in the long run.

Besides selecting a spout type (standard, arched, gooseneck, or pullout), you may choose between single or double levers. Pullout faucets come with a built-in sprayer. Others require installing a separate sprayer. Until recently, a pressure-balanced faucet (one equipped with a device that equalizes the hot and cold water coming out of a faucet to prevent scalding), came only with single-lever models. Now this safety feature is available with faucets that have separate hot- and cold-water valves. You may mix your spout with one of many types of handle styles: wrist blades, levers, scrolls, numerous geometric shapes, and cross handles. If your fingers or hands get stiff, choose wrist blades, which are the easiest to manipulate.

Chrome, brass, enamel-coated or baked-on colors, pewter, and nickel are typical faucet finishes. Some finishes, such as chrome, are easier to care for than others; brass, for example, may require polishing. Technologically advanced coatings can make even delicate finishes, like the enameled colors, more durable unless you use abrasive cleaners on them, which will scratch the finish. You may expect a good-quality faucet to last approximately 15 years; top-of-the-line products will hold up even longer.

Pot fillers save you steps to the sink while cooking. Choose one that can reach most of the burners on your cooktop.

The basic types of faucets include

- **High Gooseneck.** Gooseneck spouts facilitate filling tall pitchers and vases and make pot cleaning easier when the sink bowl is shallow. This faucet type is great at a bar sink or auxiliary food preparation sink for cleaning vegetables.
- **Single Lever.** One lever turns on and mixes hot and cold water. Styles range from functional to sleek.
- **Double-Handle Faucet.** Temperature may be easier to adjust with separate hot and cold controls. Most contain washers and seals that must occasionally be replaced.
- **Single-Handle Faucet with Pullout Sprayer.** A pullout faucet allows single-handed on, off, temperature control, and spraying.
- **Pot Fillers.** Pot fillers are mounted to the wall over the cooktop. Some versions have a pullout spout. Others feature a double- or triple-jointed arm that can be bent to reach up and down or swiveled back and forth, allowing the cook to pull the faucet all the way over to a pot on the farthest burner of a wide commercial range.

Don't be sidetracked by how good today's sinks and faucets look, the products you pick must function well in your new kitchen. As a practical matter, compare the size of your biggest pots and racks to see whether the sink and faucet you are considering will accommodate them. You may be able to compensate for a shallow sink by pairing it with a pullout or gooseneck faucet. But a faucet that is too tall for a sink will splash water; one that is too short won't allow water to reach to the sink's corners. If you plan a double- or triple-bowl sink, the faucet you select should be able to reach all of the bowls.

Near-the-Sink Appliances

In many homes the kitchen sink is not only the center of the food-preparation and cleanup areas, it is also the location of a number of additional appliances and products. Some, such as dishwashers and waste-disposal units, have been popular for years and are routinely part of any kitchen remodeling. Others, such as water filters, are only now gaining in popularity.

Dishwashers. Dishwashers have become a standard item in new and remodeled kitchens. Even though it consumes energy in the form of hot water and electricity, a unit that is used properly may require less energy than washing dishes by hand.

Gooseneck faucets are great for filling and cleaning tall pots. Used on a second sink, they are ideal for cleaning produce.

Typically, dishwashers are 24 inches wide and are installed below the counter right next to or very near the sink. If space is scant, consider an under-sink dishwasher, which can be installed under the shallow bowl of a special sink designed for this purpose.

If you wish to locate a dishwasher next to a sink in a corner, be sure to put a cabinet at least 12 inches wide between the sink base and the dishwasher. This cabinet will serve as a spacer when the dishwasher door is open, so you'll have room to stand at the sink while loading the dishes.

Dishwashers are priced according to the number of cycles and other features they offer. Most have rinse-and-hold, soak-and-scrub, and no-dry options. More costly machines feature additional cycles: preheating, which lets you turn down the setting on your water heater, soft-food disposers, delayed-start mechanisms, and solid-state control panels.

SMART TIP

Star Power. Appliances that carry the Energy Star label—a program of the Department of Energy—are significantly more energy efficient than most other appliances. Dishwashers, for example, must be 25 percent more energy efficient than models that meet minimum federal energy requirements. Energy Star refrigerators must be 10 percent more efficient than the newest standards.

Modern dishwashers feature a variety of cleaning settings, electronic controls, and water-saving features.

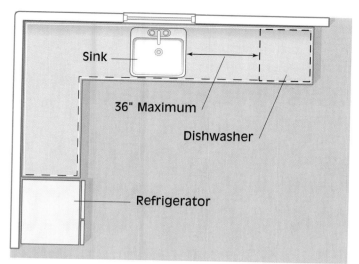

Place dishwashers within 36 in. of the main sink. The appliance will be more functional and easier to hook up.

Waste-Disposal Units. Disposal units conveniently grind up organic wastes and send them down the drain. Some communities require waste-disposal units; others ban them—so check with your local building authorities before deciding whether you want the convenience of one.

A continuous-feed disposal unit allows you to feed waste into it as it operates. A batch-feed disposal unit grinds up 1½ to 2 quarts at a time. Continuous-feed units are controlled by a wall switch, batch-feed models by a built-in switch activated by replacing the drain lid. Local codes often have much to say about which type you can use.

Trash Compactors. Compactors are available in slide-out or drop-front models in sizes ranging from 12 to 18 inches wide. Some models stand on their own, but a well-planned kitchen can incorporate a model that is designed to fit under a countertop like a dishwasher.

Compactors do not use much electricity, but most require special heavy-duty bags. Inside a trash compactor, a screw-driven ram compresses inorganic debris such as cans, boxes, and bottles to about one-fourth of the original volume. Many compactors have a device that sprays deodorizer each time the compactor is operated. Recycling programs may restrict what can be compacted, so check with local authorities.

Water Filters. Whether it's a countertop model, mounted to the faucet, or installed under the sink, point of use (POU) water-filtration systems are becoming more and more popular. No one type of filter system can remove all of the possible contaminants

Hot-water dispensers provide 190° water instantly. You must provide electrical power under the sink for a dispenser.

that can harm your water. So before buying a system, have your water tested by a reputable laboratory.

Hot-Water Dispensers. These handy units heat ⅓ or ½ gallon of water and hold it at a bubbling 190 degrees F, an ideal temperature for making tea, drip coffee, and instant coffee or soup. Some units are said to be more energy efficient than boiling water on an electric range.

The main components of a hot-water dispenser fit under the sink. The dispenser tap may attach to the hole in the sink intended for a spray hose or through a hole in the countertop with lines running through cabinet walls. The dispenser heating element requires access to an electrical line under the counter. A vent and an expansion chamber are safety features.

HOW-TO

See "Installing a Faucet," page 232

See "Installing a Waste-Disposal Unit," page 234

See "Installing a Dishwasher," page 236

See "Installing a Water Filter," page 242

See "Installing a Hot-Water Dispenser," page 244

1 Design Elements

Surfacing Materials

The surfaces of your kitchen help define how it looks and determine how well it cleans up and withstands wear and tear. Choose countertops, wallcoverings, and flooring to suit your style and lifestyle.

Countertop Materials

The market offers lots of countertop materials, all of which are worth consideration for your kitchen. Pick the materials and designs that best suit your needs and the look of the room. You can also enhance a basic design by combining it with an eye-catching edge treatment. Another option is to combine different materials on the same surface.

Plastic Laminate. This thin, durable surface comes in hundreds of colors, textures, and patterns. The material is relatively easy to install; its smooth surface washes easily; and it is heat-resistant, although very hot pots can discolor or even burn it. Laminate stands up well to everyday wear and tear, but it can be easily scorched by hot pots and pans or scratched with knives and other sharp utensils, and surface damage is difficult to repair.

Laminate countertops are available in three ways. You can buy sheets of laminate and adhere them to a plywood base yourself. Home centers and kitchen supply dealers sell post-formed counters. These are the types that come in 8- or 10-foot lengths that you trim yourself. Both the laminate sheets and the post-form counters are available in a limited number of colors and patterns. Another option is to order a laminate counter from a counter fabricator—some home centers and kitchen dealers offer this service as well. The counter will be built to your measurements, and you will get a wide variety of colors and patterns to choose from. Most fabricators also offer a variety of edge treatments.

Ceramic Tile. Glazed tile can be magnificently decorative for counters, backsplashes, and walls, or as a display inset in another material. Tile is smooth and easy to wipe off, and it can't be burned by hot pots. In addition to the standard square tiles, ceramic tiles are available in a number of specialty shapes and sizes, allowing you to create a truly custom look. Ceramic tile costs more than laminate,

Granite, marble, and other natural stones make truly elegant and functional countertops.

but you can save money by doing the installation yourself.

When shopping, you should also consider the finish. There are two kinds: unglazed and glazed. Unglazed tiles are not sealed and always come in a matte look. They are not practical for use near water unless you apply a sealant. On the other hand, glazed tiles are coated with a material that makes them impervious to water—or spills and stains from other liquids, too. This glaze on the tile can be matte or highly polished, depending on your taste.

The upkeep of tile is fairly easy, but you must re-grout and reseal periodically. White grout shows dirt easily, but a dark-color mix can camouflage stains. Still, unless it is sealed, grout will harbor bacteria. So clean the countertop regularly with a nonabrasive antibacterial cleanser. Tile that is well-maintained will last a lifetime, but beware: your glassware and china may not. If you drop them on this hard surface, they'll break.

Solid-Surfacing Material. Made of acrylics and composite materials, solid surfacing comes in ½ inch and ¾ inch thicknesses. This is a premium material that resists moisture, heat, stains, and cracks.

There is almost no limit to the colors and patterns of solid surfacing. It can be fabricated to resemble marble and granite, or it can be a block of solid color. Either way, the material can be carved or beveled for decorative effects just like wood. Manufacturers recommend professional installation.

The surface becomes scratched fairly easily, but the scratches are not readily apparent. Because the material is a solid color, serious blemishes can be removed by sanding or buffing.

Natural Stone. Marble, slate, and granite can be formed into beautiful but expensive counters. Of the three, granite is probably the most popular because it cannot be hurt by moisture or heat, nor does it stain if finished properly. Installers polish granite to produce a high-gloss finish.

HOW-TO

See "Installing Prefabricated Countertops," page 220

See "Installing Tile Countertops," page 224

Laminate counter materials are available in hundreds of colors and designs. Customize the job with a colorful backsplash.

1 Design Elements

Ceramic-tile countertops (left) should be sealed. Solid surfacing and granite (below) make a good combination.

Make use of counter inserts to help with the cooking chores. For example, ceramic tiles inlaid in a laminate counter create a heat-proof landing zone near the range. A marble or granite insert is tailor-made for pastry chefs. And a butcher-block inlay is a great addition to the food prep area.

Granite tiles are a good way to get the look of natural stone at a fraction of the cost.

Marble scratches, cracks, and stains easily, even if waxed. Slate can be easily scratched and cracked and cannot take a high polish.

These are heavy materials that should be installed by a professional. However, you can get the look of granite and marble by installing granite or marble tiles. Cut from the natural stones, these products are available in 12 × 12-inch tiles and are installed and cut in much the same way as ceramic tiles.

Wood. Butcher block consists of hardwood laminated under pressure and sealed with oil or a polymer finish. Because it's thicker than other materials, butcher block will raise the counter level about ¾ inch above standard height. Also, wood is subject to damage by standing water or hot pans. Butcher-block tops are moderately expensive but can be installed by amateurs.

Other kinds of wood counters may be used, especially in serving areas. Any wood used near water must be resistant to moisture or well sealed to prevent water from penetrating below the surface.

Concrete. There aren't a great number of concrete counters, but the material is catching on with some in the kitchen design community. If your goal is to install a cutting edge material in your kitchen, concrete is it. Thanks to new staining techniques, concrete can be saturated with color all the way through, and it can be preformed to any shape and finished to any texture. Set stone or ceramic tile chips into the surface for a decorative effect. Form it to drain off water at the sink. Be cautious, however, as a concrete countertop must be sealed, and it may crack. Installation is best left to a professional.

Stainless Steel. Stainless steel used for a countertop, whether it is for the entire counter or just a section of it, can look quite sophisticated, especially with a wood trim. What's practical about it is its capacity to take high heat without scorching, which makes it suitable as a landing strip for pots and pans

Wood may be unusual for counters, but when done properly it makes a striking addition to the kitchen.

straight from the cooktop. It is also impervious to water, so it's practical at the sink. On the negative side, stainless steel can be noisy to work on, and it will show smudges. Depending on the grade of the material, it may also be vulnerable to scrapes, stains, and corrosion. The higher the chromium and nickel content (and therefore the grade), the better. Also, look for a thick-gauge stainless steel that won't dent easily.

Wall Treatments

It's hard to beat the ease of a coat of paint for adding a fresh face to a kitchen. But there are other ways to finish off the walls, too, such as vinyl wallcovering and paneling. You can go with one, two, or all three of these options in several combinations.

Paint. Basically, there are two kinds of paint: latex, which is a water-based formulation, and oil-based products. You can buy latex and oil paint in at least four finishes: flat, eggshell, semigloss, and gloss. In general, stay away from flat paint in the kitchen because it is difficult to keep clean. The other finishes, or sheens, resist dirt better than flat paint and are easier to clean.

Latex is a term used to describe a variety of water-based paints. They are recommended for most interior surfaces, including walls, woodwork, and cabinets. Latex paints come in a huge assortment of colors, clean up with soap and water, and dry quickly.

Oil-based paint refers to products that use alkyd resins as the solvent. Manufacturers once used linseed or some other type of oil as the solvent and the name stuck. They provide tough, long-lasting finishes. However, the convenience of latex products, along with government regulations limiting the amount of volatile organic compounds oil-based products produce, has forced their use to decline.

This kind of paint is especially good for use over bare wood and surfaces that have been previously painted. If you plan to use it (or latex, for that matter) on new wallboard, you'll have to apply a primer first.

Wallcoverings. Vinyl wallcoverings and coordinated borders offer an easy, low-cost way to put style into your new kitchen. Practical because they are nonporous, stain resistant, and washable, vinyl coatings are available in a great variety of colors, textures, and patterns. Prepasted, pretrimmed rolls are the easiest for a novice to install. Just remember to remove any old wallpaper before applying new covering to walls.

Paneling. If you're looking for a simple way to camouflage a wall's imperfections, paneling is it. Today's paneling options include prefinished softwood- or hardwood-veneered plywood, simulated wood grain on plywood or hardboard, prehung wallpaper on plywood, simulated wood grain or decorative finish panel board, tile board, or other decorative hardboard paneling, and solid pine or cedar plank paneling. For a versatile look, apply wainscoting, which is paneling that goes halfway or three-quarters of the way up the wall. Top it off with chair rail molding; paint or wallpaper the rest of the wall. Depending on how you install it, you can create horizontal, diagonal, or herringbone patterns.

1 Design Elements

Vinyl wallcoverings are easy to install and keep clean. Strippable papers will make future remodeling easier.

Flooring

Floor coverings fall into two broad categories: resilient flooring, which has some resiliency, or bounce, and hard flooring, with no flex whatsoever. Resilient floors are less tiring to stand on than hard-surface floors and less likely to produce instant disaster for dropped glasses or chinaware. But the flooring you select plays more than a practical role in your kitchen.

Before replacing an old surface, make sure the subfloor is in good condition. Subflooring that is in need of repair will eventually ruin any new flooring material that you install.

Resilient Vinyl Tile and Sheet Flooring. Vinyl flooring wears fairly well to very well, needs only occasional waxing or polishing (in some cases none at all), and is easy to clean. It comes in a wide variety of colors and patterns, and is an economical alternative among flooring choices.

These products are available in individual tiles or in large sheets. (The sheets can look like individual tiles as well as a wide range of designs.) Installing vinyl tile is a popular do-it-yourself project. Installing sheet goods is a bit more complex but well within the skills of an experienced do-it-yourselfer.

Vinyl does have disadvantages, however. It dents easily when subjected to pressures such as high-heel shoes or furniture legs. Vinyl surfaces may also scratch or tear easily, and high-traffic areas are likely to show wear. You can control some degree of wear by the type of vinyl flooring you choose. Look for a minimum 10-mil thick up to the most expensive 25-mil-thick flooring. Inlaid vinyl flooring is solid vinyl with color and pattern all the way

An individual tile look, complete with grout lines, is only one of the designs possible with vinyl sheet flooring.

through to the backing. This most expensive vinyl flooring is designed to last 20 to 30 years.

Laminate. This type of flooring consists of laminate material, a tougher version of the material used on counters, bonded to fiberboard core. The decorative top layer of material can be made to look like just about anything. Currently, wood-grain patterns are the most popular, but laminates are available in many colors and patterns, including tile and natural stone designs.

Available in both plank and tile form, they are

Vinyl sheet flooring comes in a variety of styles, designs, and colors. Some manufacturers offer textured surfaces.

Real linoleum fell out of favor during the 1970s. New manufacturing techniques are making it popular again.

easy to install, hold up well to normal traffic, and are easy to clean. Most laminates can be installed directly over any other floor finish with the exception of carpeting.

Wood. Thanks largely to polyurethane coatings that are impervious to water, wood flooring has made a comeback in kitchens. You already may have a wood floor buried under another floor covering. If this is the case, consider exposing it, repairing any damaged boards, and refinishing it. Or install an all-new wood floor. Wood can be finished any way you like, though much of the wood flooring available today comes prefinished in an assortment of shades.

Hardwoods like oak and maple are popular and stand up to a lot of abuse. Softwoods like pine give a more distressed, countrified look. Flooring comes in 2¼-inch strips as well as variable-width planks. Parquet flooring, another good option for the kitchen, consists of wood pieces glued together into a geometric pattern. These prefinished squares can be installed in a way similar to that used for vinyl tiles.

Hard-Surface Flooring. Ceramic tile, stone, and slate floors are hard, durable, and easy to clean, especially when you use grout sealers. Because these floors are so inflexible, anything fragile dropped on them is likely to break. Also, they are tiring to stand on and noisy, and they conduct extremes of temperature. For those who love the look of this kind of flooring, however, the drawbacks can be mitigated with accent and area rugs that add a cushion.

Ceramic tile makes an excellent kitchen floor when installed with proper grout and sealants. The tiles range from the earth tones of unglazed, solid-color quarry tile to the great array of colors, patterns, and finishes in surface-glazed tiles. Grout comes color-keyed, so it can be either inconspicuous or a design element. Ceramic and quarry tiles are best suited to a concrete subfloor, though you can lay them over any firm base. Cost ranges from moderate to expensive. Installation is hard work, but straightforward if the subfloor is sound. This is a great project for do-it-yourself remodelers who want to create special designs with the tiles.

Stone and slate are cut into small slabs and can be laid in a regular or random pattern. Materials are inexpensive or costly, depending on quality and local availability. Even if you find these materials more expensive than other floor coverings, don't dismiss them because of price. They will never need to be replaced, making your initial investment your final one. Because stone and slate are laid in mortar and are themselves weighty materials, a concrete slab makes the ideal subfloor. In other situations, the subfloor must be able to carry a significantly heavy load. Installation is a complex do-it-yourself job.

HOW-TO

See "Installing a Vinyl Sheet Floor," page 184

See "Installing a Ceramic Tile Floor," page 190

See "Installing a Laminate Floor," page 192

See "Installing a Wood Floor," page 194

1 Design Elements

Laminate flooring is available in both tiles and plank configurations. The finish is designed to last for years.

Wood-look designs are the most popular laminate floors. For kitchens, choose glued-edge products.

Lighting

Good lighting plays a key role in efficient kitchen design—and goes a long way toward defining the personality of the room. With the proper fixtures and in the proper places, lighting can help you avoid working in shadows. Install several different lighting circuits, controlled by different switches, and you can change your kitchen's atmosphere easily. Lighting falls into three broad categories:

General, or ambient, lighting illuminates the room as a whole and helps to create a mood.

Task lighting focuses on work surfaces like sinks, countertops, ranges, eating areas, and other places where you need to get a really good look at what you're doing.

Accent lighting brings drama and architectural flavor to a kitchen. Accent lighting controlled with a dimmer switch can also serve as general lighting.

For an effective lighting scheme, plan a mix of these three types, in the amounts specified in "How Much Light Do You Need?" page 43. Bear in mind, though, that several factors affect how much general and task lighting a given kitchen needs. Dark surfaces absorb more light than lighter ones. Glossy surfaces reflect more light (and glare) than matte finishes. And different fixture types do different lighting jobs.

A good lighting plan includes general illumination, task lighting over work areas, and accent lighting.

Fixture Types

Suspended Globes, chandeliers, and other suspended fixtures can light a room or a table. Hang them 12 to 20 inches below an 8-foot ceiling or 30 to 36 inches above table height.

Surface-Mount Attached directly to the ceiling, it distributes very even, shadowless general lighting. To minimize glare, surface-mount fixtures should be shielded. Fixtures with sockets for several smaller bulbs distribute more even lighting than those with just one or two large bulbs.

Recessed Recessed fixtures, which mount flush with the ceiling or soffit, include fixed and aimable downlights, shielded fluorescent tubes, and totally luminous ceilings. Recessed fixtures require more wattage—up to twice as much as surface-mount and suspended types.

Track Use a track system for general, task, or accent lighting—or any combination of the three. You can select from a broad array of modular fixtures, clip them anywhere along a track, and revise your lighting scheme any time you like. Locate tracks 12 to 24 inches out from the edges of wall cabinets to minimize shadows on countertops.

Undercabinet Fluorescent or incandescent fixtures (with showcase bulbs) mounted to the undersides of wall cabinets bathe counters with efficient, inexpensive task lighting. Shield undercabinet lights with valances and illuminate at least two-thirds of the counter's length.

Cove Cove lights reflect upward to the ceiling, creating smooth, even general lighting or dramatic architectural effects. Consider locating custom cove lights on top of wall cabinets, in the space normally occupied by soffits.

Types of Bulbs

Most homes include a combination of warm and cool tones, so selecting bulbs—called lamps by professionals—that provide balanced lighting close to what appears normal to the eye is usually the most attractive choice. Experiment with balancing various combinations of bulbs to create the desired effect. To help you achieve the balance you want, here is a brief description of the different bulbs.

Incandescent. Like sunlight, incandescent bulbs emit continuous-spectrum light, or light that contains every color. Illumination from these bulbs, in fact, is even warmer than sunlight, making its effect very appealing. It makes skin tones look good and enhances the feeling of well-being. Also, they come in a variety of shapes, sizes, and applications. One type even features a waterproof lens cover that makes it suitable for use near a sink or above the cooktop where steam can gather. Incandescent bulbs may be clear, frosted, tinted, or colored, and they may have a reflective coating inside. The drawback is that incandescents use a lot of electricity and produce a lot of heat. Therefore, they cost more to run than other types.

Fluorescent. These energy-efficient bulbs cast a diffused, shadowless light that makes them great for general illumination. They are economical, but the old standard fluorescents produce an unflattering light, making everything and everyone appear bluish and bland. Newer fluorescent bulbs, called triphosphor fluorescent lamps, are warmer and render color that more closely resembles sunlight. Fluorescents are available both in the familiar tube versions and in newer, compact styles. Mixing these bulbs with incandescent lamps, plus adding as much natural light to the kitchen plan as possible, can make fluorescents more appealing. Be aware, though, that in some parts of the country local codes require fluorescent lights be the first type turned on when entering a room to conform to energy conservation mandates.

Halogen. This is actually a type of incandescent lamp that produces a brighter, whiter light at a lower wattage, with greater energy efficiency. The disadvantages are a higher price tag and higher heat output that requires special shielding. However, although halogens cost more up front, they last longer than conventional incandescents. A subcategory of halogen is the low-voltage version. It produces an intense bright light, but is more energy efficient than standard halogen. Compact in size, low-voltage halogens are typically used for creative accent lighting.

Fiber Optics. One of countless innovations gradually finding their way into the home, a fiber-optic system consists of one extremely bright lamp to transport light to one or more destinations through fiber-optic conduits. Used to accent spaces, fiber-optic lighting has the advantage of not generating excessive heat. This makes it ideal as an alternative to decorative neon lights, which get very hot and consume a great deal of energy.

Hanging fixtures (above) can provide either general or task lighting. The tops of the wall cabinets (below) glow from low-voltage accent lights.

When used correctly, lighting becomes an important design element in the kitchen.

How Much Light Do You Need?

Type	Incandescent	Fluorescent	Location
General (ambient) lighting	2–4 watts per square foot of area. Double this if counters, cabinets, or flooring are dark.	1–1½ watts per square foot of floor area	90 inches above the floor
Task lighting			
Cleanup centers	150 watts	30–40 watts	25 inches above the sink
Countertops	75–100 watts for each 3 running feet of work surface	20 watts for each 3 running feet of work surface	14–22 inches above the work surface
Cooking centers	150 watts	30–40 watts	18–25 inches above burners. Most range hoods have lights.
Dining tables	100–120 watts	Not applicable	25–30 inches above the table
Accent lighting	Plan flexibility into accent lighting so that you can vary the mood with a flick of a switch or the twist of a dimmer. Suspended, recessed, track, and cove fixtures all work well.		

HOW-TO

See "Installing Recessed Lighting," page 168

See "Installing Track Lighting," page 172

See "Installing Undercabinet Lighting," page 174

See "Installing a Hanging Fixture," page 175

Windows & Doors

Sunlight brings cheer and sparkle to any kitchen. All you have to do is welcome it inside with windows, glass doors, or a skylight. When you shop for window and door units, make energy conservation a prime consideration. Double glazing is now standard, but most manufacturers offer windows with low-emissivity (low-e) glazing. These windows have films that reflect heat but let in light. The film also blocks ultraviolet light that can fade fabrics. Look for energy ratings that reflect the entire window unit, not just the glazing. You can also add exterior awnings to shade the windows from unwanted heat gain. Because a house loses more heat at night than during the day, drapes can provide privacy and minimize nighttime heat losses from windows.

Selecting Energy-Efficient Windows and Doors

Choose windows, doors, and skylights based on your local climate. Products that meet the following requirements earn the Department of Energy's Energy Star Label. Look for windows, doors, and skylights tested by the National Fenestration Rating Council, an independent testing group.

Northern States
Windows and doors must have a U-factor* of 0.35 or below.
Skylights must have a U-factor* of 0.45 or below.

Middle States
Windows and doors must have a U-factor* of 0.40 or below and an SHGC** rating of 0.55 or below.
Skylights must have a U-factor* of 0.45 or below and an SHGC** of 0.55 or below.

Southern States
Windows, doors, and skylights must have a U-factor* rating of 0.75 or below and an SHGC** of 0.40 or below.

* U-factor is a measurement of heat loss. The lower the number, the less heat lost.
** SHGC stands for Solar Heat Gain Coefficient and is a measurement of how well a product blocks heat caused by sunlight. It is a number between 0 and 1. The lower the number the more heat the product blocks.

Window Types
Before you decide that your kitchen needs more or bigger windows, take down the curtains from your existing windows—the change in light levels may amaze you. If that's not the answer, consider adding or enlarging the windows. Place them wherever

If you want a window to provide natural task lighting for a kitchen sink or work surface, its sill should be 3 to 6 inches above the countertop. For safety reasons, most building codes don't permit windows over ranges or cooktops.

Don't overlook style when selecting a window. If your house is a colonial, for example, stick with a traditional double-hung window instead of the contemporary casement type that may not blend with your home's overall architecture. Also check for other desirable features. A tilt-in unit, for instance, makes cleaning easier. Optional grilles simply pop in and let you create a divided-light window.

For purists, manufacturers fabricate true divided-light windows in standard sizes. There are five common types of windows. They can be used individually, or combined in various ways.

Counter-to-ceiling windows (left) will maximize natural light if you don't need the space for cabinets. Speciality windows (below) add a dramatic touch to the kitchen.

they work best. Sometimes an above-cabinet soffit space provides an excellent site for awning-type windows. Or you may install traditional-style windows. These needn't be the same width as the old ones, but they usually look better if the top edges line up with other windows in the room.

Fixed Windows. Fixed windows are the simplest type of window because they do not open. A fixed window is simply glass installed in a frame that is attached to the house. Fixed windows are the least expensive, admit the most light, and come in the greatest variety of shapes and sizes. But, of course, they can't be used to provide ventilation.

Double-Hung Windows. Perhaps the most common kind used in houses, double-hung windows consist of two framed glass panels, called sash, that slide vertically on a metal, wood, or plastic track. The glass can be a single pane of glazing or divided into smaller panes called lites. One variation, called a single-hung window, is made using an upper panel that cannot slide and a lower, sliding panel.

Casement Windows. Casements are hinged at the side and swing outward from the window opening as you turn a small crank. Better casement windows can be opened to a 90-degree angle, providing maximum ventilation.

Sliding Windows. Sliders are similar to double-hung windows turned on their side. The glass panels slide horizontally and are often used where there is need for a window opening that is wider than it is tall.

Awning Windows. Awning windows swing outward like a casement window but are hinged at the top. Awning windows can be left opened slightly for air even when it rains.

Windows let in light, but they can also make the view part of the design.

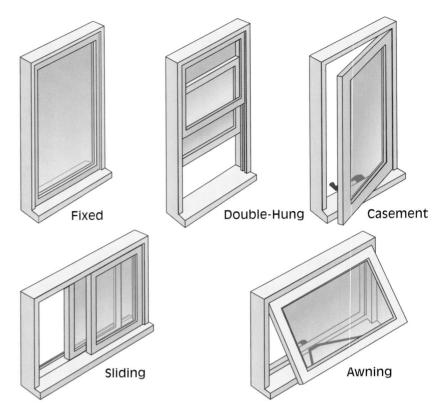

Fixed   Double-Hung   Casement

Sliding   Awning

Choose a window type based on the style of your house. You can duplicate the existing window types or see what houses similar to yours use.

Which Way Should Windows and Skylights Face?

Orient a door, window, or skylight to take best advantage of breezes and seasonal sunlight. Also take into account trees, neighboring structures, and the potential view.

• South light will pour into windows with a southern exposure in winter because the sun's path is low in the sky. But in the summer, when it rides high in the sky, the sun will beat down on the southern roof instead. Southern exposure is an ideal placement for a window because it gains heat through the window in winter, but not in summer, especially if it's shielded by a deep overhang. A skylight on a southern or western exposure will capture solar heat during the winter—and the summer, too. Be careful about this placement.

• East light brightens the morning yet rarely heats up the room. Skylights on north- and east-facing roofs lessen heat gain in the summer.

• West light subjects a kitchen to the hot, direct rays of late-afternoon sun, which can make a room uncomfortable until far into the night. If a west-facing window is your only option, shade it with overhangs, awnings, sun-stopping blinds, or broad-leaf plantings.

• North light has an almost consistent brightness throughout the day. Because it's from an open sky, without direct sun, the light doesn't create glaring hot spots or deep shadows in work areas. North light lacks the drama of other exposures, but kitchen design and colors can compensate for that.

Summer Sun

Winter Sun

W N
S E

1 Design Elements

HOW-TO

See "Installing a New Window," page 126

See "Installing a Skylight," page 128

Replacement Windows

When buying new windows you'll have two important concerns: the type of window to install and the type of installation.

Replacement Installations. You can install your own windows, of course, or buy the units and hire someone to install them. Or you can shop at one of the increasing number of retailers who offer package deals including installation. If you don't do the job, watch out for the common problem of downsizing, or installing windows that are much smaller than your originals. Downsizing windows by excessively packing out the old frame can change the scale of the facade and create clumsy-looking trim details inside and out.

There are a few installation methods available. For double-hung windows, you can remove and replace the sash while leaving the window frame in place. It's a good option for replacing damaged or inefficient sash if the overall frame is still in good condition.

Complete replacement is much like installing windows in new construction. But you have the extra work of removing the old units to start with, and after the windows are in, you need to piece-in siding and drywall, and reinstall trim.

Skylights. In a single-story house or one with a vaulted ceiling, a properly planned and located skylight can provide five times more natural light than a window of equal size located in a wall. It's important to plan for the seasonal angle and path of the sun to avoid unwelcome heat gains and losses from skylights. It's usually better to locate a skylight on a north- or east-facing surface, for example, to prevent overheating and provide diffuse light. Venting models, placed near the roof ridge, can also greatly improve natural ventilation. Seek advice from an architect or designer if you're not sure how a skylight will affect your kitchen's climate.

Door Types

Interior and exterior doors are offered in dozens of shapes, sizes, and materials. Most units are made of wood or wood by-products, but many are made of metal and stamped or embossed to look like wood. Exterior doors often incorporate glass panels. French and sliding patio doors are almost all glass. Most interior wood-based doors are fabricated in one of three ways: as individual panels set in a frame, as a hardboard facing molded to look like a panel door and secured to a frame, or as a thin sheet of plywood secured to each side of a wood framework.

Panel and Panel-Look Doors. Panel door styles offer a variety of choices. They can be constructed with as few as three to as many as ten or more solid panels, in all sorts of shapes and size combinations. Sometimes the bottom is made of wood and the top panels are glass.

Flush Doors. Generally less expensive, flush doors come in a more limited range of variations. You can enhance their simple looks with wood molding for a traditional appeal.

Sliders. Sliding doors consist of a large panel of glass framed with wood or metal. Usually one of the doors is stationary while the other slides. Replacing an existing wood door with one that's all or mostly glass can double its natural lighting potential. For safety and security, be sure that the new door has tempered glass. Enlarge an existing door or window opening, or cut a new one, to gain access to a deck

Skylights allow in five times more light than windows. Used over a sink (top) they provide task lighting. Set near the ridge of a roof (left), they provide general lighting to the room.

Doors with lots of glazing provide natural light, and they help connect the kitchen to the outdoors.

Sunrooms, Greenhouses, and Bays

If a full-scale kitchen addition just does not make sense for your house, you might wish to enhance your existing kitchen, at less cost, with a "mini-addition," in the form of a sunroom or greenhouse-like bump out.

Prefabricated Sunrooms. Prefabs usually have double- or triple-glazed glass panels and come in prefit pieces that can be assembled by amateur carpenters, although this isn't a simple project by any means. For a sunroom you'll need a foundation, usually a concrete slab with an insulated perimeter that goes below the frostline.

A sunroom should face within 20 degrees of due south to take greatest advantage of solar heating in colder climates.

Window Greenhouses. Also called box windows, these units provide a site for year-round kitchen gardening. All you need to do is remove a window and hang a prefabricated unit or a home-built greenhouse outside. Fill it with flowering plants or greenery, grow herbs or vegetables, or use it to give your outdoor garden a jump on spring. This window treatment is also an excellent way to replace a poor outside view with your indoor garden, while keeping the window open to light.

As with sunrooms, window greenhouses work best with southern exposures. You might also have sufficient light from an eastern or western exposure if no trees, buildings, or other obstructions cast shadows. You might as well rule out a northern exposure; a north-facing greenhouse loses great amounts of heat in winter, and many plants don't grow well in northern light.

Bay Windows. Bay units allow you to add a foot or two of sunny space without having to construct a foundation. In this case, you would cantilever the bay window from your home's floor joists. Most window manufacturers sell bays in a variety of widths and configurations, ranging from simple boxes to gentle bows. Installing one is a job best left to a skilled carpenter.

or patio outside. The frame may be wood, aluminum, or wood covered with aluminum or vinyl.

French Doors. Traditional French doors are framed glass panels with either true divided lights or pop-in dividers. Usually both doors open. Manufacturers also offer units that look like traditional hinged doors but operate like sliders. If space is limited, consider outswing patio doors. These units open outward rather than inward like other doors. So you can open them without taking up valuable floor space.

Dutch Doors. Made in two parts, Dutch doors have independently operating sections, top and bottom. Locked together, the two halves open and close as a unit. Or you can open just the top section for ventilation.

1 Design Elements

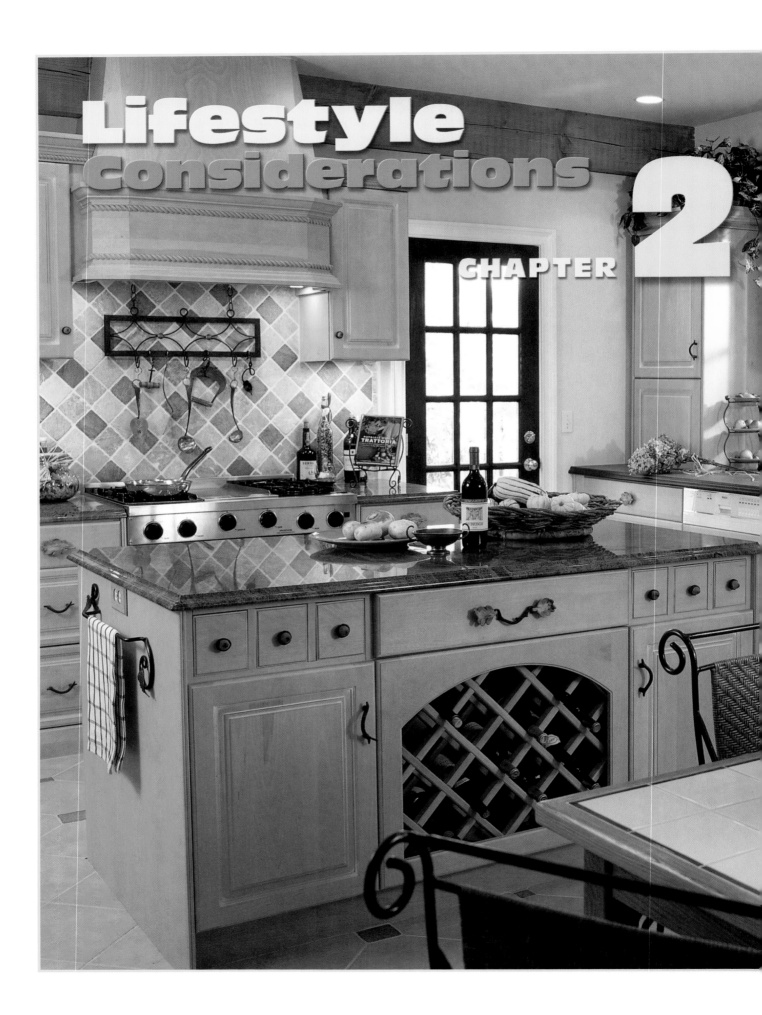

Lifestyle Considerations

CHAPTER 2

Today's kitchen is often the gathering place for family and friends, the spot where the kids do their homework, and your place to pay the bills, plan the family vacation, design a craft project, or have a heart-to-heart talk with a friend over a cup of coffee. All of that is in addition to the kitchen's traditional function as a place to prepare food. This one room has become so important, in fact, that prospective buyers consider it a primary factor in selecting a home. If you're thinking about remodeling the kitchen for resale purposes, you'll be happy to know you may get as much back as you invest—maybe more, depending on where you live. If you're like most people, however, your motivations are much more personal.

Most homeowners undertake a kitchen remodeling project because their old kitchen does not suit the way they live. In this chapter, you will learn how to incorporate such homey touches as eating areas, snack bars, and a variety of special activity centers in the kitchen.

Kitchen Options

The kitchen is a hot-ticket item in the real estate market today, and no wonder: more and more, family life is centered around this room. It's not unusual to find most of the family in the kitchen, even when they're not eating. It's the place to do homework, pay the bills, play games, and even entertain company.

The goal is to create a plan, using the latest design trends, that integrates the way you and your family actually live. A thoughtful look at your lifestyle will help you discover whether you want the open design of a great room, which integrates areas for cooking, dining, and relaxing. If your approach is more formal, you may prefer the traditional arrangement that keeps the kitchen and its cooking clutter off-limits to dining and living areas. In this case, a small table or eating bar for casual family meals and snacks may suit you better.

Whether or not you go for the open-plan kitchen, you may still want to include activity centers in the remodeled kitchen's design. If you love to bake, sew, or create crafts, or you need a space to organize a home office, think of making a secondary

Open floor plans allow cooking and living areas to merge, creating an informal atmosphere.

Connected spaces allow someone working in the kitchen to remain in contact with family or guests in the living area.

work center part of the kitchen to accommodate one or more of these activities.

Whatever the scope of your new kitchen, be sure to incorporate barrier-free design elements. This simply means taking measures to make the space comfortably accessible to all who will need to use it, including those who walk, reach, and lean, or sit and wheel. Barrier-free design follows the same tenets as all good design: form follows function.

Great Rooms

Kitchens to live in have become popular in home design. The large rooms combine separate but open-to-one-another spaces for cooking, dining, relaxing, and entertaining. Such spaces are often called great rooms. Families with young children, for example, will love a kitchen that is part of an open-room plan. This open design allows cooking parents to keep an eye on kids who may be watching TV.

Dinner guests tend to congregate here, too, because they like to stay in touch with the cook. This informal great-room arrangement suits casual contemporary lifestyles, as well as changing attitudes about food. For many families, cooking has evolved from a necessary chore to a creative event where everyone gets involved—guests as well as family.

Room additions give you the chance to expand the kitchen work area and add extras, such as an eating area, to your design.

Getting Space

You can create a great room by building an addition to your home or by combining space from adjacent rooms. (See page 100.) If you choose the latter, make sure that you compensate for load-bearing walls you will remove, and be mindful of any other structural elements that may interfere with your design.

One benefit of combining two or more smaller spaces into one is that the sum of the parts is often greater than the whole. Not only is total floor space combined, so is light and ventilation. Traffic options and floor plans are opened up, too, and focal points such as worktables or counters can do multiple duty for different tasks.

When considering the floor plan, remember that the kitchen is the key element. Traffic must be diverted away from the work areas. One way to manage traffic is to incorporate an island or penin-

sula into the layout. An island will keep the kitchen open to other areas while closing off the cooking zone to anyone who doesn't have to be there. A large island or peninsula with an eating bar also offers a handy place to set up a buffet, serve a snack, or let the kids do homework. An island also provides a convenient spot for guests to gather while dinner is in the works.

SMART TIP

If a peninsula or island separates the kitchen work area from the eating or living area in a great room, consider installing a 48-inch-high snack bar along the dividing line and standard height counters everywhere else. The high counter will help keep dirty dishes, pots, and pans out of sight while you are dining.

Unifying Space

Because a great room is an open plan, you'll want a cohesive decor to flow throughout the spaces. Coordinated fabrics and wallcoverings will help you do this, as will installing the same flooring material throughout. Also, some manufacturers produce furniture quality cabinet designs, as well as matching units to house media equipment, bookcases, desks, and the like, which can dress up the space with a custom-built appearance.

Even appliance manufacturers are great-room conscious. When shopping for a typically noisy appliance, such as a dishwasher, range hood, or waste disposal, ask about low-noise or noise-free models.

Lastly, take advantage of any scenic views you may have by installing lots of windows. If you have an adjacent deck or patio, consider large patio doors.

Peninsulas and islands (right) help separate cooking centers from living areas. Unify separate spaces (below) by installing common flooring materials and wall finishes.

2 Lifestyle Considerations

Eating Areas

Most of us want a table or eating counter in the kitchen that's within easy reach of food-preparation and cleanup areas. If you live in a house that's more than 50 years old or in a newer "traditional" house, chances are you have a formal dining room you rarely use. You may already have ideas about combining underused spaces like this to create one large room for cooking as well as enjoying meals.

Family Kitchen

The concept of the "heart of the home" or "family kitchen" recalls an earlier time when cooking was done over an open hearth and the entire family could gather to savor a good meal together. These days, removing the wall that separates a kitchen and dining room creates somewhat less than a great room, but much more than a food preparation labo-ratory. Though this kind of arrangement can make everyday meals especially convivial occasions, such togetherness may not be everyone's cup of tea.

If you do a lot of formal entertaining, prefer to be left alone while you cook, or just don't relish a meal served within sight of the pots and pans, consider pocket doors, sliding panels, or accordion-fold doors to close off the food-preparation area.

Table Talk

Your kitchen will need minimum clearances to accommodate a table and chairs. In general, a family larger than five or six should look for sit-down space elsewhere. Still, you may want to provide an in-the-kitchen eating spot where you can serve snacks and off-hour meals to just a few people. In terms of dimensions, page 58 shows how to allocate the floor space you'll need for the furniture and for the people who sit around it.

Formal dining areas are possible in great rooms. The area rug and chandelier create a defined area within the larger space.

Informal dining areas can consist of a table in the center of a room or a built-in table (left) placed near dish and silverware storage. Breakfast areas (below) require nothing more than a table and lots of natural light.

2 Lifestyle Considerations

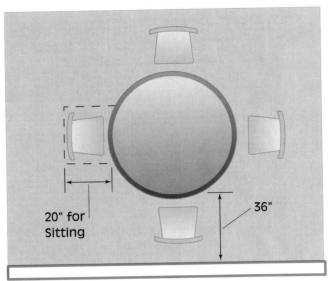

Allow space for diners to rise and sit down comfortably. Typical seating and push-back space is 36 in.

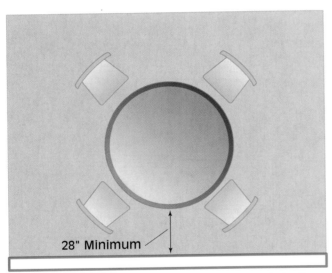

Gain a few inches by arranging chairs at an angle to the wall. Here, seating and push-back space is only 28 in.

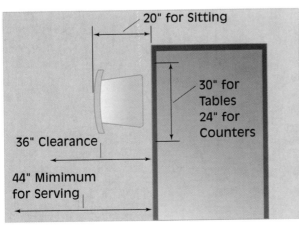

Required table space varies. Plan on 30 in. for a formal dining table and 24 in. at a counter.

Seating Allowances. Because you must have room to sit down and get up, tables, chairs, and access room require a surprising amount of space. Figure on 12 to 15 square feet per person. A family of four will need at least 48 square feet of space for in-the-kitchen dining. To size a round table, figure that a 36-inch diameter table can seat four adults and a 48-incher will seat six. For a square or rectangular table, calculate 24 to 30 inches of table space for each person.

When planning space, you must pay attention to the distance between the table and any nearby walls and cabinets. A seated adult occupies a depth of about 20 inches from the edge of the table, but requires 12 to 16 inches more to pull back the chair and rise. This means you'll need about 36 inches of clearance between the wall and the edge of the table. You can get away with a minimum 28-inch clearance if you place chairs at angles to the wall. On any serving side, plan a 44-inch clearance to allow room to pass.

Also, as you plan a spot for your table, make sure that it doesn't intrude into the kitchen's work areas or interfere with traffic routes. Don't put the eating area too far away, however. The closer you are to cooking and cleanup centers, the easier serving and clearing will be.

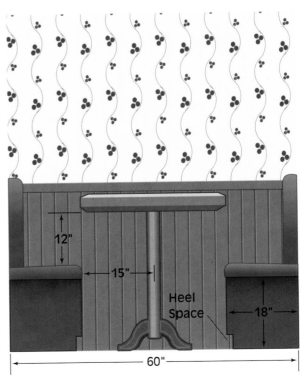

Booths save space. Be sure to leave a minimum of 12 in. between the bench and table for sliding room.

Booths

Not enough room for a table and chairs? Take a tip from diners and restaurants, and plan a booth with bench or banquette seating. Booths conserve floor space because you don't need to slide chairs back. And if you box in the benches, provide heel space, and attach flip-up seats, you gain valuable storage for linens and other table items.

A kitchen alcove or bay window is a natural place for a booth, or you can back one up to an island, peninsula, or wall. Also, you can construct seating units with backs that are high enough to serve as walls of their own.

Plan 24 inches of table space for each person, with at least 15 inches of knee space underneath. This means that a family of four needs a table that's 48 inches long and 30 inches across. Because you slide into and out of a booth, the table can overhang the benches by 3 or 4 inches. Total floor space required for a four-person booth, then, would measure only 5 feet across, compared with a minimum of about 9 feet for a round or square table with chairs. (See the illustration on page 58.)

Gain storage space by installing booth seating with flip-up seats. Use the space to store table linens.

Counters

If you're planning to incorporate a peninsula or island in your new kitchen, you're probably already eyeing its potential as a counter for serving quick meals or snacks. What dimensions do you need for a good fit?

First, how many people do you hope to seat? Remember, each adult requires 24 inches of table space. This means a counter that's 72 inches long can accommodate three stools at most.

How high the top of the counter should be depends on the kind of seating you prefer. A 28- to 30-inch-high counter requires 18-inch-high chairs with 20 inches of knee space. If you make the counter the same height as any others in the kitchen (standard 36 inches), you'll need 24-inch-high stools and 14 inches of knee space. Go up to bar height—42 to 45 inches—and you'll need 30-inch-high stools with footrests.

One problem with snack bars is that everyone faces in the same direction. Dining at a counter may be fine for breakfast or a quick lunch on the run, but you'll want a table for more sociable meals like dinner. Another problem is orientation. A counter that faces a blank wall is undesirable as an eating place, so try to orient yours facing into the kitchen or out a window.

Place eating counters outside of the main work area of the kitchen but close enough to retain contact with the cook.

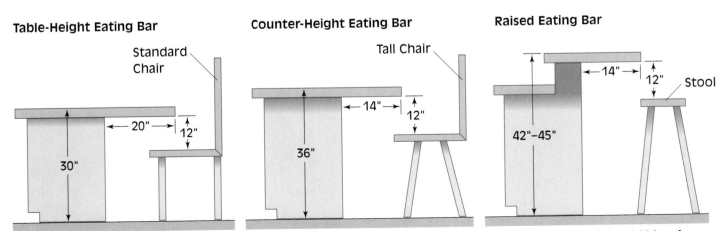

Create knee space based on the height of the eating surface. People sitting at standard-height tables need about 20 in. of space; those at higher counters require 14 in. Chair and stool heights range from 18 in. to about 30 in.

Secondary Work Centers

If your new kitchen will be the hub of the household, it's going to be more than a place to cook and eat a meal. Depending on your family's needs, habits, and hobbies, you may want to incorporate a home office, gardening center, laundry, baking center, sewing and craft area, or entertainment bar into your design. Sometimes a corner or spare countertop will suffice.

Home Office

A desk-height surface with knee space provides a place in the kitchen to draw up lists, make phone calls, pay bills, leave messages for family members, look up recipes, and organize home management in dozens of other ways. This kind of planning center easily expands into a home office that can be used to do homework or run a cottage industry when you add a computer, printer, fax, and answering machine.

Kitchen offices need not be large. The small work area above provides adequate space for making lists. The larger space at left is big enough for a homework area or a convenient spot to pay bills.

2 Lifestyle Considerations

Drawer units, bookcases, and the like that match kitchen cabinets are available from a number of manufacturers.

Whether the space is as modest as a small countertop and a shelf for cookbooks or a complete work station with a full-size desk, file cabinets, and electronic equipment, decide on a spot early in the planning stage so that you can run any electric, telephone, and intercom wiring you need. Situate the area outside the kitchen's main work area, and provide adequate lighting for the kinds of activities you'll be doing there.

You may want to locate other electronic components in the office space, too. Your home's "command central" can be as sophisticated as you can afford: it may include an intercom; a security system with separate controls for window, door, and smoke alarms; a programmable thermostat; timers; TV, DVD, and stereo equipment; and perhaps a closed-circuit-TV system for monitoring children's play areas.

Baking Center

Serious cooks, especially those who enjoy baking, will appreciate a well-appointed baking/mixing center. Allocate at least 36 inches of counter space near the oven or refrigerator—ideally between the two. To make mixing and kneading less tiring, drop the counter height 6 or 7 inches by using 30- or 32-inch-high base cabinets. Plan a countertop that is extra deep, too—30 inches or more—to provide plenty of room for rolling out dough. The surface should be heat- and moisture-proof.

A countertop made of smooth stone will provide a cool surface that keeps rolled-out dough from sticking, but a smooth laminate will work, too. You'll also want counter space for setting up a mixer or blender, laying out ingredients, and loading cookie sheets or baking pans and a cooling rack. Include good fluorescent undercabinet lighting, so you're not working in your own shadow.

Give special thought to where you want the mixer. Some manufacturers offer mixer platforms that rise up out of a base cabinet, eliminating the need for awkward tugging and lifting to reach or replace the appliance before and after use. In addition, you'll want to keep small tools within hand's reach. Provide enough places to store the rolling pin, mixing bowls, and flour sifter, as well as cake, pie, muffin, and bread tins. Extra-deep cabinet drawers are handy for this use, as are carousel or slide-out trays. Items like cookie sheets and rectangular cake tins are best stored on edge in vertical compartments so that you don't have to stack them.

Lastly, consider all of the ingredients you want to keep on hand. Large pullout or tip-out bins are ideal for flour and sugar. Smaller containers can hold baking powder, nuts, raisins, vanilla, chocolate, and other spices and decorations.

Table-height surfaces are more convenient for kneading and rolling out dough than standard counters.

Gardening centers require a waterproof surface for cutting and arranging flowers, and potting plants.

Gardening Center

If you're an avid gardener, what better place to nurture new or ailing plants than a sunny kitchen window or greenhouse window unit? A full-scale kitchen gardening center might include an easy-to-clean counter for cutting and arranging flowers, starting seeds, and potting plants; a separate deep utility sink; a faucet attachment for watering; grow lights; and storage for pots, soil, plant food, and other supplies. Your center could also be as simple as a deep window sill surfaced with ceramic tile to stand up to water.

Laundry

If your current laundry facilities are in the basement, finding a place for a washer and dryer near your remodeled kitchen will save a lot of steps. There are a number of design criteria to keep in mind for a laundry center. A side-by-side pair of full-size appliances measures 48 to 58 inches wide. To conserve floor space you might consider stackable laundry machines, which are about half as wide as conventional machines but usually have smaller tubs. Full-size units are also 42 or 43 inches high, which is 6 to 7 inches taller than standard kitchen counter height, so you can't run a countertop over them. And because standard-size washers are usually top-loading, you can't put a dryer or cabinet above them.

If you want to fit laundry appliances under a counter, consider installing a set of front-loading stackable units side by side. The convenience of being able to do laundry while cooking dinner may more than compensate for their smaller capacities. If you

SMART TIP

Plan for a built-in ironing board near the laundry area. Ironing board kits come in cabinets that are surface mounted to the wall or fit between studs. Most include a built-in electrical outlet.

Laundry areas placed near the kitchen can share some of the same finishes used in the main cooking area. A well-equipped laundry includes a counter for folding and sorting clothes, a sink, hanging rack, and cabinets for storage.

have a two-bowl sink, you can reserve one side for laundry when necessary. Don't forget a cabinet for storing detergent, fabric softener, and any other laundry supplies.

Sewing and Crafts

A few cupboards and drawers positioned well outside the work triangle near a peninsula, island, or table make an excellent station for sewing or crafting. A roll-top counter appliance garage with an electrical outlet might be just the thing to store a portable sewing machine so that you don't have to lift it onto a counter. Depending on the overall feeling in your kitchen, you might even keep some materials, such as dried flowers, raffia bows, or spools of thread, on open shelves or pegs so that they are available for a quick mend or a moment of inspiration.

Entertainment Bar

People who entertain a lot, especially in a great-room kitchen, will appreciate an area well stocked with glassware and equipped with trays and plates suitable for serving hors d'oeuvres and desserts. An area such as this can be quite simple: a short length of counter and cabinets, for example. However, a bar sink, a second dishwasher, an auxiliary refrigerator, and a warming drawer are helpful in this setting to keep pre- and post-meal clutter away from the main preparation and cleanup areas of the kitchen.

A place to relax, such as a window seat (above), isn't a work center but it can be an important part of a new kitchen. Site entertainment bars (right) near the living area, but out of the way of anyone working in the kitchen.

Safety Considerations

More building codes govern the kitchen than any other room in the house. That's because so many accidents occur there. With that in mind, safety should reign as a primary factor in any kitchen remodel. The goal should be to lessen the chance of injury while increasing the performance of the room's layout, materials, fixtures, and appliances.

Take the following steps when designing for safety. And remember: you don't have to be very young or very old to suffer an injury in the kitchen. One of the most common Sunday morning hospital emergency room visits is by someone who has sliced open a hand while cutting a bagel.

Use Proper Lighting. Never work in a dim space. Good general lighting, supplemented with proper task lighting clearly focused on a work surface, without glare or shadows, can vastly decrease your chance of injury while preparing a meal. In addi-

tion, good lighting should be adaptable to meet the needs of younger, as well as older, eyes.

Use Slip-Resistant Flooring. Falling with a hot casserole or sharp knife in your hand can have serious consequences. Choose a slip-resistant material for your floor, such as matte-finished wood or laminate, textured vinyl, or a soft-glazed ceramic tile indicated specifically for flooring. If you select tile, it helps to use a throw rug with a nonskid backing—especially around areas that get wet. Remember to inquire about the slip-resistance rating of any flooring material you may be considering for your new kitchen.

Keep a Fire Extinguisher Handy. A grease fire in the kitchen can spread rapidly. That's why it's so important to have a fire extinguisher within arm's reach of the ovens and cooktop. For maximum protection, there should be at least two extinguishers in any kitchen—one located in the cooking area

Good lighting will help prevent accidents. Be sure your new kitchen has adequate general and task lighting.

The word **PASS** is an easy way to remember the proper way to use a fire extinguisher.

Pull the pin at the top of the extinguisher that keeps the handle from being accidentally pressed.

Aim the nozzle of the extinguisher toward the base of the fire.

Squeeze the handle to discharge the extinguisher. Stand approximately 8 feet away from the fire.

Sweep the nozzle back and forth at the base of the fire. After the fire appears to be out, watch it carefully since it may reignite!

Create safe cooking areas. This cooktop has slightly staggered burners and all of the controls are in the front, making for a safe unit.

Well organized storage not only makes the kitchen efficient, it helps make it a safe place to work as well.

and one stored in another part of the room. You want them to be handy; however, you don't want fire extinguishers to fall into the hands of children. Install them high enough so that they are out of reach of curious youngsters.

Install GFCIs. Water and electricity don't mix. Make sure every electrical receptacle is grounded and protected with ground-fault circuit interrupters. These devices cut electrical current if there is a power surge or if moisture is present. Most building codes require them in any room where there is plumbing to protect homeowners against electrical shock.

Consider Lock-Out Options. New smart-home technology allows you to lock your range and ovens so that no one can use them while you are out of the house. The simple lock-out device can prevent burns, fires, or worse. You can choose between lock-out covers or a programmed lock-out system. Or you can install timers on all appliances you don't want in use when you can't supervise the cooking.

You might also consider designating one wall cabinet for storing cleansers and other toxic substances—drain cleaner, for example. Include a lock on the cabinet, and keep the key in a safe place.

Regulate Water Temperature. Install faucets with antiscald devices. These units prevent temperatures from rising above preset limits. Another option is a programmable faucet that "remembers" temperature settings.

Design a Safe Cooktop. How many times have you been scalded reaching over a pot of boiling water or a hot element? Avoid this dangerous situation by selecting staggered burners for your cooktop, or one straight row of burners.

If you can't find single burners, turn modular two-burner units sideways, placing them parallel with the front of the countertop. Never choose a unit with controls at the rear of the cooktop; controls should be along the side or in front.

Use Space Efficiently and Safely. You can have all the space in the world and still put family members in compromising situations. Avoid swinging doors. When placing appliances, think about how the traffic area will be affected when a door is open. Locate ovens and the microwave at a comfortable height that doesn't necessitate reaching in order to retrieve hot food. Make use of cabinet accessories to keep stored items organized and easy to reach.

Avoid sharp corners, especially at the end of a run of cabinetry or on the island or peninsula. If space is tight and you can't rearrange most elements, install a rounded end cabinet and choose a countertop material that will allow a bullnose edge.

Universal Design

Universal design addresses the needs of multigenerational households and people with special needs. As Baby Boomers bring home their aging parents while raising families of their own, it is not uncommon to have young children and grandparents living under one roof. Indeed, as our population ages it benefits everyone to think about ways to make the kitchen functional—and safe—for every member of the family. This section addresses all of these concerns.

Incorporating universal design into your remodeling is always smart, particularly if you plan to stay in your house as you grow older. Analyze your lifestyle and your family's needs now—and what you anticipate them to be in the future. Do you have young children? Do you expect to have an elderly parent living with you? Will you remain in the house after you retire? Planning to include some universal-design features in your new kitchen now will save you money later on, because it's more expensive to make changes to an existing plan.

According to the National Kitchen and Bath Association (NKBA), one of the most practical universal-design elements you can include is the installation of counters at varying heights, which allows you to perform some tasks (slicing vegetables, for example) while seated and others (such as rolling out dough) while standing straight, not bending. Another idea that makes sense for any kitchen is a pullout counter near the cooktop and another at the oven. They provide handy landing places for hot pots, pans, and dishes.

Designs For Everyone

Some items to incorporate in your design include appliances with digital displays, which are easier to read and fairly standard on today's appliances; placing wall-mounted outlets and switches at the universal reach range of 15 and 42 inches from the floor; reserving a base cabinet for storing dishes, making dinnerware easier to reach; installing wrist-blade-style faucets that don't require grabbing or twisting; and buying a side-by-side style refrigerator, which places most foods at accessible heights. Compact work areas eliminate wasted steps.

It might also be worthwhile to investigate some of the smart-home technology available. This includes devices that allow you to call home from any phone to turn on the lights, heat the oven, raise the thermostat, or program dinner to start cooking. Of course, this sophisticated technology is expensive and may be more practical for new construction; some things are too complicated to retrofit into an existing home.

It seems that new technological advances are brought to the marketplace almost every week. The key is to look at universally designed features and match them to your home and situation. Don't forget: The goal is to make your life easier—and safer. If adding any of these features will destroy your budget or drastically change your concept of the room, don't use them, but be sure to retain any features that can save your family pain or injury.

Counter heights should suit those who work in the kitchen. This raised dishwasher makes loading and unloading easy.

Accessible Design

Accessible design normally means that a home—or in this case a kitchen—is barrier free. It also indicates that the room complies with design guidelines for disabled people found in government regulations such as the American National Standards Institute's A117.1 (ANSI A117.1-1986). There are a number of guidelines governing accessible design. Their goal is to provide design criteria for someone who uses a wheelchair to get around.

If a disabled person in your family will use the new kitchen, design appropriate clearances. A standard wheelchair occupies 10 square feet and has a turning diameter of 5 feet. Doorways must be at least 32 inches wide, and aisles must be a minimum of 42 inches wide, according to the NKBA.

A lowered cooktop with an angled nonfogging mirror installed above the surface lets someone seated see what's cooking. If you don't like the look of an open space below the cooktop, install retractable doors that open to accommodate the wheelchair and close for a finished look. Induction cooktops feature automatic shutoffs, cool-to-the-touch cooking surfaces, and are easy to keep clean.

Low, shallow base cabinets outfitted with pull-out and slide-out bins and trays, carousel shelves, and lazy Susans maximize accessibility, as do lower counter heights—30 to 31½ inches as opposed to the standard 36 inches. Light-colored countertops with a contrasting edge treatment that clearly defines where the surface ends are recommended for people with impaired vision.

Many American cabinet manufacturers have introduced a line of specially designed cabinets and accessories that accommodate everyone in the family, including those with special needs.

You might also want to consider having a second microwave near the kitchen table. The cabinet you choose to house it should have a drop-down door strong enough to hold hot dishes.

Provide leg room for those in who work at counters while seated. Note the opening next to the small sink.

Design Criteria

Here are some guidelines for making your kitchen efficient and functional under any circumstances:

- Design a floor plan that incorporates wide aisles (at least 42 inches) around the work area. Also, plan 60-inch-diameter turning circles at strategic places.
- Make doorways a minimum of 32 inches wide to accommodate wheelchairs and walkers. Avoid swinging doors and specify pocket or sliding types whenever possible. If you must use swinging doors, levers are easier to use than doorknobs.
- Plan lots of counter space near the food-preparation and cleanup areas. This space will allow the quick release of hands from heavy pots and objects.
- Install a variety of counter heights in addition to the standard 36 inches to serve different needs. A 32-inch-high counter with leg room below provides

Contrasting colors along the edges of counters and tables help make these areas visible to those who have poor eyesight.

Pullout cutting boards provide more work surface, and they are at a convenient height for someone in a wheelchair.

workspace for someone in a wheelchair and can serve double duty as a baking center, which calls for the same height. A 42-inch-high eating bar can provide a place for a person with back pain to work without bending over. An alternative to fixed-height counters is adjustable counters. Another flexible counter option is a slide-out surface, similar to a breadboard, with reinforced tracks capable of bearing extra weight.

- Install wall cabinets lower on the wall and with shallow shelves so that they can be reached easily by most people.
- Equip base cabinets with convenient pullout bins and swivel trays. Mixer platforms that rise up out of a base cabinet can be used for any heavy item, eliminating the need for awkward tugging and lifting while cooking.
- Make sure that electrical outlets and TV and phone jacks are no less than 15 inches from the floor. Light switches should be 42 inches from the floor—6 inches lower on the wall than standard installations.

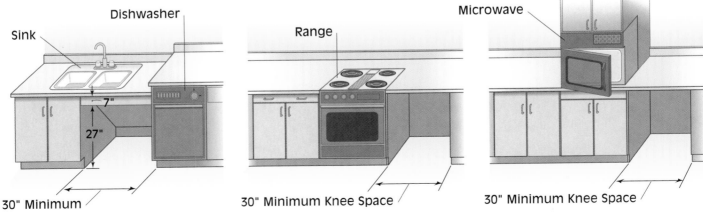

Adequate knee space is a basic criterion for universal design. If providing leg room under a sink, be sure to cover pipes to protect users from burns. Openings next to ranges, dishwashers, and microwaves make these appliances accessible to everyone.

All of these should be easily reached by someone in a wheelchair or walker.

- Try out the controls and knobs when shopping for appliances to ensure easy manipulation. Labels should be easy to read.
- If possible, buy cooking units with front-mounted knobs, which are easier to reach. However, they may be unsafe for use where there are young children.
- Be sure the cooktop has staggered burners, which allow the cook access to the back without reaching over hot pots in the front.
- Install wall ovens and cooktops at heights geared to the specific needs of the cooks in your kitchen. Also, there are special 30-inch-high slide-in ranges that are designed for use by someone in a wheelchair but are convenient for anyone to use.
- As for a refrigerator, choose a side-by-side model for universal access, or use a modular unit that allows custom placement of individual units at locations most suited to specific workers and their tasks.
- Install a single-lever faucet with a programmed temperature-control valve. These faucets are easy to use and protect against scalding.
- Use nonslip cushioned flooring.
- Attach brass rails below the edge of the countertop to serve as grab bars. Grab bars should be 1½ inches in diameter.
- Install a chair rail to save walls from wheelchair gouges and to add interest as well.
- Try to find room for a half bath adjacent to the kitchen area.

Wheelchair users need adequate space to turn around, lower-than-normal counters, and leg room under fixtures and appliances.

Drawer storage makes retrieving pots and pans easy for someone in a wheelchair. Storing items where you use them is the most efficient type of storage.

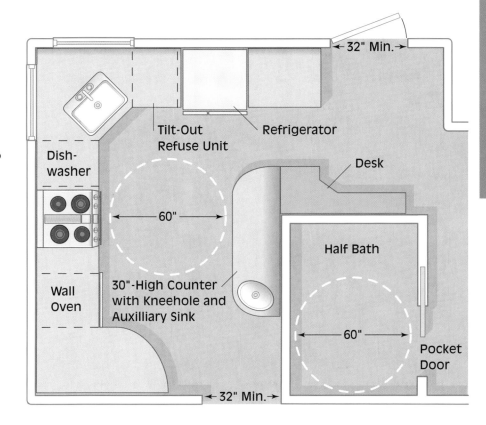

Tilt-Out Refuse Unit

Refrigerator

Desk

Dishwasher

Wall Oven

30"-High Counter with Kneehole and Auxilliary Sink

60"

32" Min.

Half Bath

60"

Pocket Door

32" Min.

Creating a Design

CHAPTER 3

Cookbook spot is nice

Your kitchen's style is influenced by the cabinets, the layout, the appliances, the countertop material, the color of the walls, the texture of the floor, and the shape of the windows. After you have considered all of these elements, you must blend them into a cohesive whole that serves your purpose and shows off your personality through design.

Your renovation plans might include adding on square footage or incorporating space from an adjacent room or closet. Regardless of the kitchen's ultimate size, the work flow should fall into the classic work triangle, which divides the kitchen into three main task areas. The layout will likely fall into one of several basic kitchen shapes.

You may decide to stay with the layout you have and simply replace all or some of the elements in it. If traffic flow and the arrangement of appliances or doorways make work inefficient, however, you can play with alternative ideas provided in the section on do-it-yourself floor plans.

Developing a Style

No matter what your taste—country, traditional, contemporary, or eclectic—as you work on your basic layout you should think about the details that will make your new kitchen suit your way of life.

Architectural Style

A kitchen's design is distinguished more than anything by the style of the cabinets. Assisted by decorative details like the wall and floor treatments, window style, and accessories, the door fronts of the cabinets will put a face on the kitchen's architecture. There are many variations on the following three themes, but most of the differences are in the details.

Traditional. Today's traditional style incorporates elements of English and American eighteenth- and early-nineteenth-century design. Marked by symmetry and balance and enhanced by the look of fine-crafted details, it is dignified, rich, and formal.

Choose wood cabinetry finished with a cherry or mahogany stain or painted white, with details like fluted panels, beaded trim, bull's-eye corner blocks, and dentil and crown molding. For the door style, a raised cathedral panel (top slightly arched) is typical. An elegant countertop fabricated from marble or a plastic laminate faux version fits well into this setting, as do hand-painted tiles. Polished-brass hardware and fittings will add a distinctive touch.

Colors to consider include classic Wedgewood blue or deep jewel tones. Windows and French doors with true divided lights or double-hung units with pop-in muntins have great traditional style appeal. Use formal curtain panels or swags as window treatments.

Furnish this kitchen with an antique or reproduction hutch, where you can display formal china, and a table and chairs in traditional Windsor or Queen Anne style.

SMART TIP You may not need to replace your kitchen cabinetry to get fine-furniture quality details. Try adding crown molding to the top of existing cabinets and replacing the hardware with reproduction polished-brass door and drawer pulls to achieve a traditional look.

Cherry-stained cabinets and crown molding place this kitchen squarely in the traditional category. Note the upholstered stools and the traditional light fixtures.

Traditional-style cabinets (above) usually have panel doors and decorative molding. Contemporary cabinets (right) rely on sleek, unadorned door and drawer styles.

Contemporary. Sleek and unadorned, contemporary style cabinets consist of plain panel doors and hardware that's hidden or unobtrusive. Contemporary kitchens make extensive use of materials like chrome, glass, and stone. Indeed, its roots are at the turn of the last century, when architects and designers rejected the exaggerated artificial embellishments of the Victorians by turning to natural products and pared-down designs.

Today, contemporary style is taking a softer turn, even in the kitchen, a place where hard edges, cool reflective surfaces, and cutting-edge technology abound. It's not unusual to see updated versions of traditional fixtures and fittings or new uses for natural materials in a contemporary kitchen, especially as improved finishes make these products more durable and easier to maintain. And although black and white are classic mainstays in a contemporary room, many people prefer warmer shades of white.

When selecting cabinets for your contemporary kitchen, pair a frameless door with a wood finish. Laminate cabinetry is still compatible with this style, but for an updated look, wood is a better choice. Although a contemporary room is often monochromatic or neutral, don't be afraid to use

color or mix several materials or finishes, such as wood and metal. Combinations of wood and various metals—stainless steel, chrome, copper, brass, and pewter on surfaces like cabinet doors, countertops, and floors—make strong statements, as do stone and glass. Creative combinations like these keep the overall appearance of the room sleek but not sterile. For more visual interest, apply a glazed or textured finish to neutral-colored walls. And bring as much of the outdoors into this room as possible. Install casement style windows, skylights, or roof windows to blend with contemporary architecture. Easy access to adjoining outdoor living spaces, such as decks, patios, or open-air kitchens, is highly desirable. For window treatments, Roman shades or vertical blinds offer a crisp, tailored look.

Stay with metals for lighting fixtures and hardware. Chrome, pewter, or nickel would work well. Keep your eye on function, not frills. The contemporary kitchen tends to be pared down to the essentials of the room.

Stainless-steel appliances, here matched to a stainless-steel table, are a mainstay of contemporary design.

Furnishings for a contemporary kitchen tend to have a sleek architectural look, too. In fact, much of what is considered classic contemporary furniture has been designed by well-known twentieth-century architects. Chair and table legs are typically straight, with no turnings or ornamentation. For a sophisticated look, mix complementary materials; for example, pair a glass table with upholstered chairs or a metal table with wood chairs. Display contemporary pottery on a shelf or inside a glass cabinet.

Country. A simple door style, a light stain or distressed-color finish, and unpretentious wooden or ceramic knobs and handles on drawers and doors pull the country look together.

Whether you call it American, French, English, Italian, or Scandinavian, this style is always a favorite because of its basic, casual, relaxed feeling. In fact, every country has its own version. "Country" implies a deeper connection to the outdoors and the simple life than other styles and uses an abundance of natural elements. Start off with plain wood cabinetry stained a light maple, or add a distressed, crackled, or pickled finish. This is the perfect kitchen for mixing different finishes because unmatched pieces underpin the informal feel of a country room. Cabinet door styles are typically framed, sometimes with a raised panel. Bead-board cabinets are a typical American country choice. Or leave the doors off, allowing colorful dishes and canned and boxed goods to become part of the decor. For the counter-top, install butcher block or hand-painted or silk-screened tiles. Another option is a colorful or patterned countertop fabricated from inlaid solid-surfacing material. A working fireplace will definitely add charm to your country kitchen, but a simple potted herb garden on the windowsill will do so, too.

Wood floors are a natural choice in a country setting, although terra cotta tiles are an attractive accent to a European-inspired setting. Be sure to add throw rugs, preferably braided or woven rag, in front of the sink and range for added comfort underfoot.

For a custom touch, add a stenciled backsplash or wall border. If you want a truly individual look, try a faux finish like sponging, ragging, combing, or rubbed-back plaster. These techniques are easy and add texture to your walls, providing a richer, warmer feeling. Use the space in the soffit area or above a window to hang herbs for drying.

Install double-hung windows. (Standard casement windows look too contemporary in this setting.) Finish them with full trim, and top them with simple cotton curtains, or just install valances. Don't overdress them.

Other Styles. The styles discussed here are really only the tip of the iceberg of styles and looks possible for your kitchen. Others you have probably heard of include Art Deco, Arts and Crafts, and Shaker style. You can also combine styles. Find common elements in different styles that will make them work together. Good examples of compatible looks include country and traditional or Shaker.

Elements of country design include such items as the farmhouse table and color scheme (above) to beadboard wall and ceiling treatments and a connection to the outdoors (below).

Color Basics

Of all the ways to personalize a kitchen, color is the most versatile. In fact, the dominant color of a room can actually affect the mood of those within. Red is stimulating, and in its vibrant forms is usually reserved for accents. Yellow and orange are welcoming and happy, but when used over large areas these colors can promote subtle feelings of unrest; pastel creams, peaches, and corals are good alternatives for large expanses. Blues and greens are restful and calming. Warm up blue with a touch of yellow or coral, and mix almost any color with green, the background color of nature. The brightness of your kitchen colors should be measured against the intensity of light.

SMART TIP The type of light in a room will affect how a color looks. Place large swatches of the colors you are thinking about using throughout your kitchen to see how they react to morning, afternoon, evening, and artificial light.

Color Schemes. Color can be used in many ways. The method of choosing colors to convey a desired overall effect is called creating a color scheme.

Monochromatic color schemes vary a single hue. You might use only shades of blue or a range of greens, for example. Some beautiful kitchens have been done in one shade of one color, with variety supplied by the gleam of stainless steel or copper or the texture of tile or marble.

Related or analogous schemes consist of a range of colors in the same family—all of the tones of autumn leaves, for example, or the various green shades of spring, lightened with touches of yellow. For more on selecting colors, see "Color Wheel Combinations," page 80.

Complementary color schemes use opposites on the color wheel, such as reds and greens or blues and yellows.

Neutral colors such as gray, white, and black mix well with most colors or work well on their own.

Adding white to any color lightens its value, so white added to red pro-

Bright backsplashes add vitality to the simplest color schemes. Consider colorful counter inlays and flooring.

Painted-finish cabinets aren't for everyone, but they do add personality to a kitchen design.

duces pink. Black darkens its value, so black added to red produces a shade of maroon. Remember this point when you devise complementary or mono-chromatic schemes: once you establish your color scheme, different intensities of the same color will serve to vary and fortify the effect.

Color and Space. Color can expand or con-tract the perceived size of a room. A general principle is that dark colors make a room look smaller; light ones do the opposite. Strong con-trasts, such as light cabinets and dark wallpaper, visually take up more space than if these two el-ements were of the same color and intensity.

Color Trends. Keep in mind that the cabi-nets, tiles, countertops, and appliances you se-lect will be with you for a while, and trendy colors can become dated quickly. There are cer-tain limitations, too, on the colors you can choose: most appliances come only in white and a limited range of neutral hues. One way to cope

Strong primary colors tend to work best in a kitchen when they are combined with subtler shades.

Color Wheel Combinations

The color wheel is the designer's most useful tool for pairing colors. Basically, it presents the spectrum of pigment hues as a circle. The primary colors (yellow, blue, and red) are combined in the remaining hues (orange, green, and purple). The following are the most often used configurations for creating color schemes.

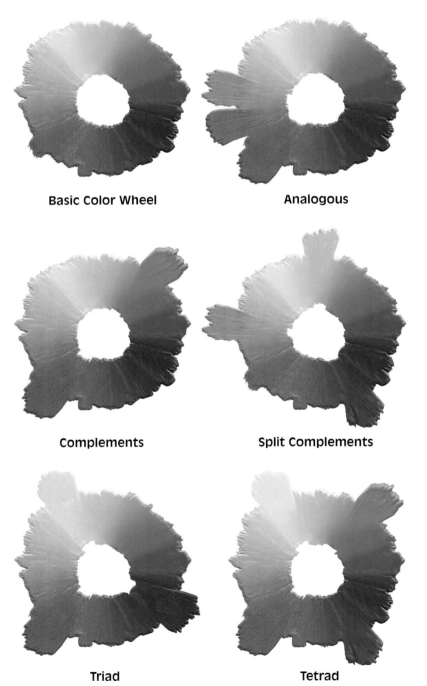

Basic Color Wheel

Analogous

Complements

Split Complements

Triad

Tetrad

Add texture to your design through such elements as a tin ceiling or hand-painted tile.

with both the dating and color-matching problems is to select appliances with changeable front panel inserts. You simply remove a piece of trim from the door, slip in the color panel of your choice, and replace the trim. Another option is to go with appliances that accept external door panels that match your cabinetry. Lastly, a time-honored and economical solution is to stick with neutral, white, or stainless steel finishes for appliances—and introduce color on wall, floor, and countertop surfaces that can be replaced or changed inexpensively whenever you wish.

Texture

Brick, vinyl, slate, wood, stone, tile, fabric, and other materials add texture to your kitchen. A glossy plastic laminate countertop, for example, has a shine quite different from the gleam of a satiny stainless-steel sink. By varying textures you can enhance your color scheme.

Details make a difference. The window seat and desk (above) form a separate area for relaxing. The distinctive eating area (left) enhances the design of this room.

Details

You might want to express your individual style using design elements like tile backsplashes with scenes of nature, refrigerator panels of punched tin, burnished-copper range hoods, brick-faced cooking alcoves, exposed ceiling beams, or crown moldings. Maybe you have a treasured plate collection you want to mount in a soffit or display on wall-hung shelves. Perhaps you'll create an interesting vignette with a hand-painted motif or spice up the room with a wallpaper border or stenciled design. The shape and color of your kitchen gains depth and distinction from the details that reflect your individual tastes and interests.

Creating a Layout

What if your existing kitchen is critically cramped, and no amount of rearranging is going to make it much better? Should you dig deep into your finances, call in an architect or remodeling contractor, and plan a kitchen addition? The answer is a qualified "maybe."

Adding Space

Full-scale additions almost always cost more per square foot than new construction, so you should realistically expect to recover only part of your remodeling investment— say 75 to 90 percent—when you sell your home. Also, lot-line restrictions may limit the amount of new space you can add, especially on the sides or front of your home. Before you add square footage with new construction, consider some alternatives to gain space:

Conversion. One option is to convert a covered porch or entryway into kitchen space. If it's constructed on good footings and has a roof that's in good shape, you may be able to enclose, wire, and insulate the space for considerably less than the cost of a full addition.

Annexation. Also, look to adjacent ~~square feet you might annex. Often relocating a closet or removing a n~~

Transposition. If your kitchen ~~small but also inconveniently loca~~

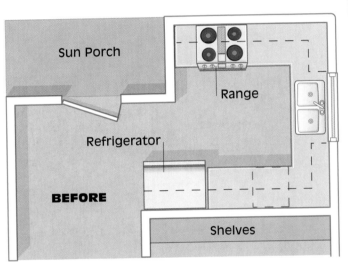

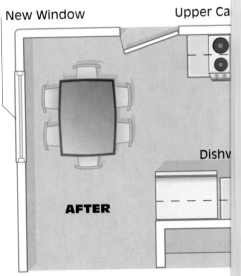

Conversion. Since sunrooms and porches often have foundations already in place, it is usually a good idea to try to incorporate these areas into a new kitchen design.

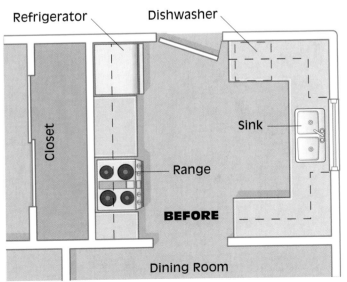

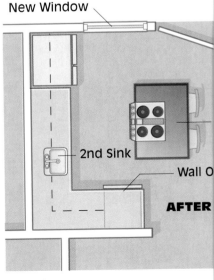

Annexation. An existing closet, part of a hallway, and even a seldom-used room are good candidates for providing extra space for your kitchen.

able to switch it with another room, such as a bedroom or dining room, as long as plumbing changes are not too extreme.

Addition. If none of the mini-addition ideas will solve the space problem, there are good reasons to go ahead with an addition:

- Besides providing the larger kitchen you want, an addition can provide you with a family room, expanded dining facilities, a sunroom, deck, or other desirable living space.
- If your kitchen is not only too small but also inconveniently located, an addition may enable you to move it and convert the existing space to some other use, such as a new bedroom.

- A skillfully designed addition may also improve your home's exterior appearance, as well as its views and outdoor living areas. The new space may provide you with the opportunity to add a new deck or patio as well.

Planning a kitchen addition starts the same way as any remodeling plan—with graph paper, appliance and cabinet templates, and so forth. But before you break ground, check out your ideas with a knowledgeable contractor, architect, or designer. He or she can tell you whether your scheme is feasible and what building permits you may need, and might suggest refinements that will save money, add value, or do both.

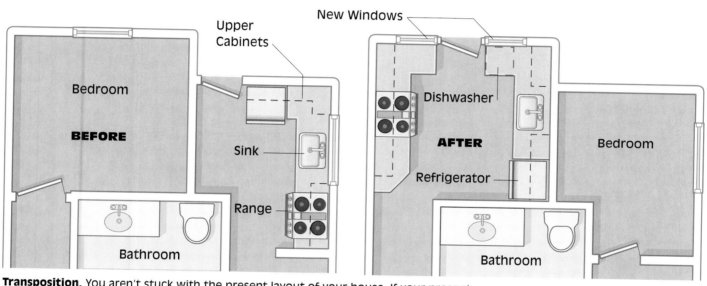

Transposition. You aren't stuck with the present layout of your house. If your present kitchen is in a bad location, consider switching spaces with another room.

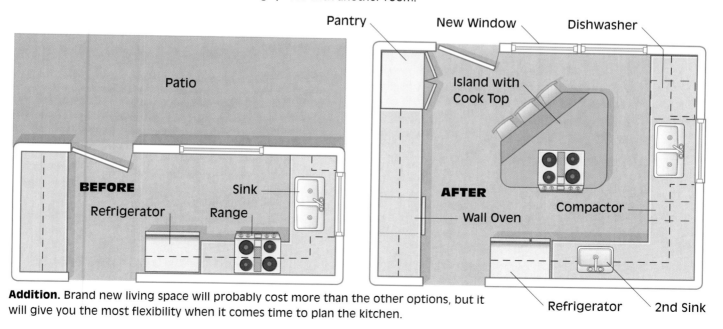

Addition. Brand new living space will probably cost more than the other options, but it will give you the most flexibility when it comes time to plan the kitchen.

Work Triangle

The so-called work triangle seems to be a mantra chanted over and over by anyone talking, writing, or thinking about a kitchen's function. There's a good reason for this. Kitchen efficiency experts have determined that the kitchen's three necessities—sink, range, and refrigerator—should be arranged in a triangular pattern whose three sides total 12 to 26 feet. The minimum and maximum distances conserve walking distance from point to point without sacrificing adequate counter space between work stations. These dimensions are to some degree arbitrary, and the sides of the triangle needn't be exactly equal. You'll discover that many efficient work triangles have unequal sides, yet each pattern can be the basis of an excellent kitchen.

Traffic Patterns

Pay special attention to the through and in your existing kit layout you may be considering. to move easily from one place kitchen and from the kitchen to house, as well as outdoors.

It's also important that thro interfere with the work triangle. ing a hot pot from the range to you on a collision course with y for the back door.

Often, you can cure a faulty ply by moving a door or removin wall. Another way to improve functions is to experiment with b

The work triangle connects the range, refrigerator, and sink. It is designed to save steps while cooking.

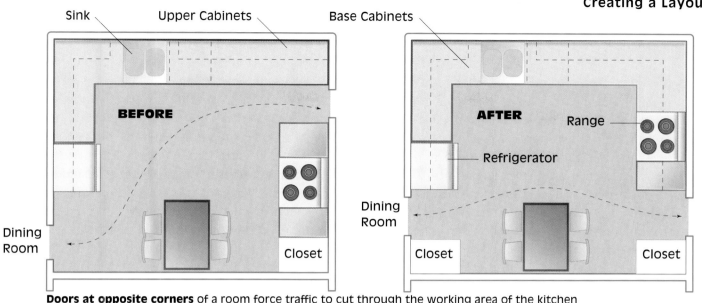

Sink   Upper Cabinets   Base Cabinets

BEFORE

Dining
Room

AFTER   Range

Refrigerator

Dining
Room

Closet   Closet   Closet

Doors at opposite corners of a room force traffic to cut through the working area of the kitchen (left). Moving the doorways (right) allows traffic to bypass the work triangle.

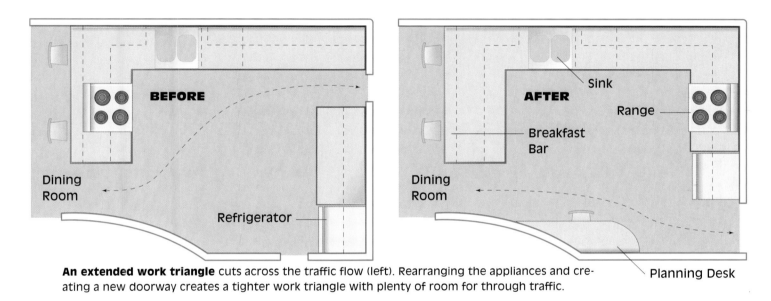

BEFORE

Dining
Room

Refrigerator

AFTER

Sink

Range

Breakfast
Bar

Dining
Room

Planning Desk

An extended work triangle cuts across the traffic flow (left). Rearranging the appliances and creating a new doorway creates a tighter work triangle with plenty of room for through traffic.

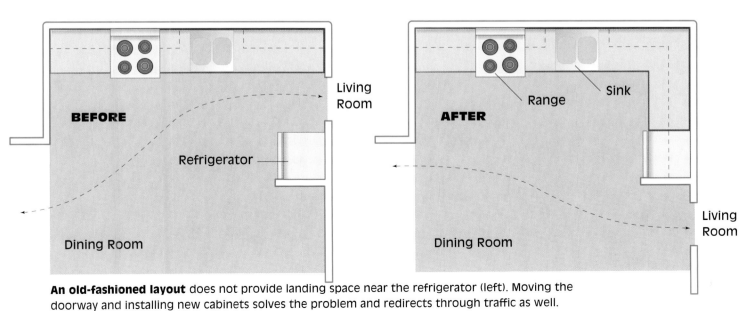

BEFORE

Living
Room

Refrigerator

Dining Room

AFTER

Range   Sink

Dining Room

Living
Room

An old-fashioned layout does not provide landing space near the refrigerator (left). Moving the doorway and installing new cabinets solves the problem and redirects through traffic as well.

Basic Layouts

This section will help you think about the layout of your new kitchen. We've taken what designers and kitchen professionals consider the basic kitchen shapes—one-wall, galley (corridor), L-shaped, U-shaped—and with the help of the National Kitchen and Bath Association, we have picked layouts that show how more-complex designs evolve from these simple layouts.

Professionals rely on the basic shapes because the layouts lend themselves to efficient interpretations of the work triangle. Real-life designs become more complex because each kitchen should address the unique needs of the individual homeowners. As you will see, the basic shapes are starting points for creating the layout that best suits your needs.

One-Wall Kitchen

A one-wall kitchen lines up all its cabinets, counter space, and equipment along one wall. This arrangement flattens the work triangle to a straight line. Try to locate the sink between the range and refrigerator for maximum accessibility.

One-wall kitchens make the most sense in tiny single-room apartments or in a narrow space. They are sometimes used in a larger multifunctional area to minimize the kitchen's importance and maximize the room's open space. In this context, the kitchen wall could be closed off from the rest of the room with sliding doors, screens, or shutters when it is not in use.

If you are starting with a one-wall kitchen and are able to acquire even a small amount of additional space, there are many options open to you.

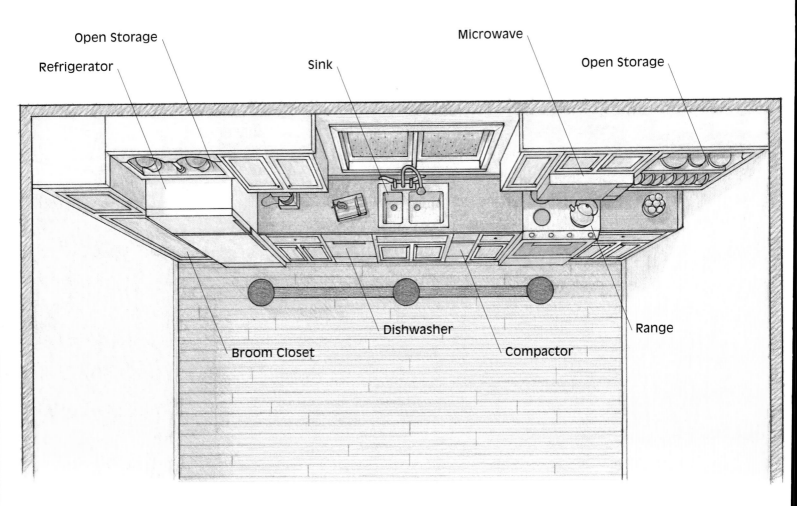

Open Storage · Refrigerator · Sink · Microwave · Open Storage · Broom Closet · Dishwasher · Compactor · Range

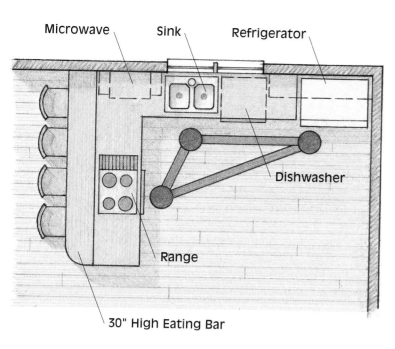

Microwave   Sink   Refrigerator

Dishwasher

Range

30" High Eating Bar

◄ **Variation One.** Adding a peninsula to a straight run of cabinets will allow you to open up the work triangle and create what is really an L-shaped room. The peninsula need not be as large as this one, but if you do add a range as shown here, be sure to allow adequate clearances on each side. The NKBA recommends 15 in. on one side and at least 9 in. on the other.

► **Variation Two.** Start with the L-shape, add an island, and you've created a well-organized work center. This version adds a full-height wall, but you could leave the eating counter peninsula as shown above as well. This design assumes the kitchen is open to a larger room; the angles on the edge of the island create interest.

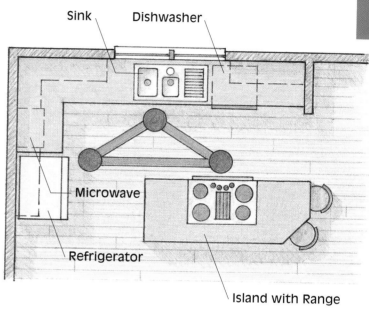

Sink   Dishwasher

Microwave

Refrigerator

Island with Range

Start with one wall and add a distinctive island, and you've not only created an eye-catching design, you've increased the usable work area as well.

Galley Kitchen

A galley, or corridor, kitchen places appliances, cabinets, and counters along opposite walls. This scheme enables you to establish a good work triangle, but it usually does not leave enough room for multiple cooks. The simple layout works best as a one-cook kitchen.

Try to allow a 48-inch-wide aisle between the facing base cabinets. This makes it possible to open cabinet and appliance doors easily, with space left over for an adult to maneuver around them. Base cabinets are 24 inches deep, so you need a minimum width of 8 feet for a galley kitchen. If space is really tight, you can cut down the aisle to a bare minimum of 36 inches—but watch that appliance doors don't collide with each other when they're opened. Think twice, too, about a corridor arrangement that has doorways at both ends. This promotes traffic from outside passing through the work triangle.

To ease as many traffic problems as possible, place the refrigerator near the end of a galley kitchen. This will keep people who want something from the refrigerator from interfering with the cook. Another option is to install the primary refrigerator in the food-preparation area and a small model for soft drinks or snacks close to the doorway.

Storage is a real challenge in this compact layout. One solution is to install tall cabinets that extend to the ceiling. You'll have to keep a stepladder handy for gaining access to what's on top, so reserve that space for items that you don't use as often. Another solution, the one chosen in the kitchen below, is to fill the room with cabinets and place seldom-used items elsewhere.

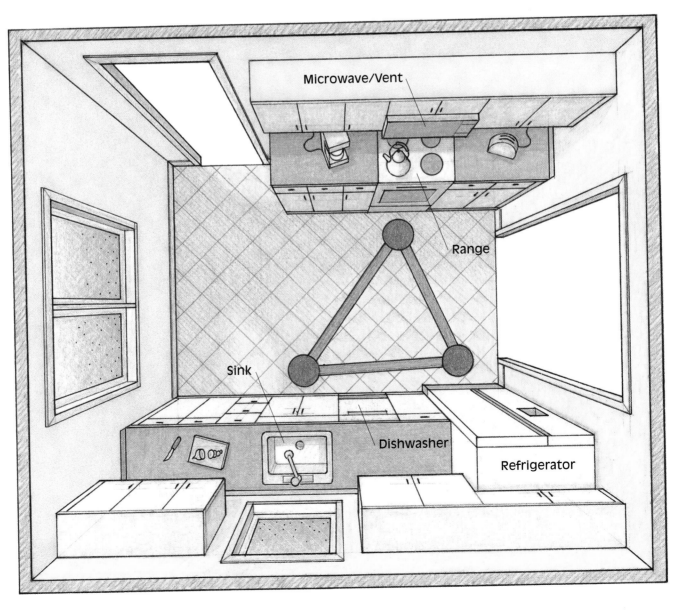

Microwave/Vent

Range

Sink

Dishwasher

Refrigerator

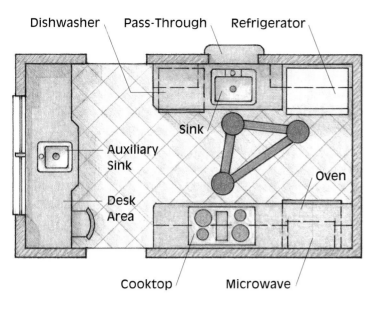

Dishwasher Pass-Through Refrigerator

Sink

Auxiliary Sink

Desk Area

Oven

Cooktop Microwave

◄ **Variation One.** Although slightly larger than the basic layout shown on the opposite page, this design shows what moving doors can accomplish. Through traffic does not need to intrude on the main work space, and the new layout provides room for a small desk and a second sink as well.

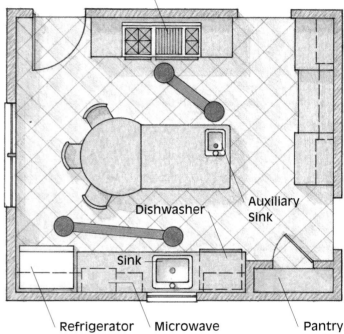

Cooktop/Oven

Dishwasher

Auxiliary Sink

Sink

Refrigerator Microwave Pantry

► **Variation Two.** Sometimes a design element that is important to you will interfere with a basic rule. In this case, the eating area cuts off the straight line between the cooktop and the refrigerator. The small detour is acceptable.

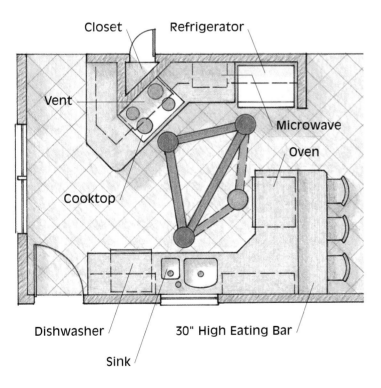

Closet Refrigerator

Vent

Microwave

Oven

Cooktop

Dishwasher

Sink

30" High Eating Bar

◄ **Variation Three.** Two cooks can function efficiently in this layout. The angle that holds the cooktop creates visual interest, and it provides more counter space than does a straight run.

The classic galley is small, but it can be appealing. To solve the storage problem, try running available wall cabinets all the way to the ceiling.

L-Shaped Kitchen

An L-shaped kitchen lays out the work centers along two adjacent walls. L-shaped layouts typically have one long and one short leg, creating large amounts of continuous counter space. Although L-shapes require more space than galleys, they permit an efficient work triangle that discourages through traffic. Try to place the sink at the center of the work triangle, ideally under a window.

One advantage of an L-shaped layout is that you can often fit a kitchen table or booth into the corner diagonally opposite the L. Planned with care, an L-shaped kitchen can accommodate two cooks with ease. One can prepare food on counters adjacent to the sink while the other works at the range.

L-shaped kitchens are also natural candidates for incorporating a snack counter into the design. If the short leg of the L opens up to a family room or living room, a counter is a good transition to an open floor plan. This arrangement will, however, deprive you of wall space for cabinets. So be sure to plan out your storage needs carefully before deciding on the counter.

Another advantage to this layout is the opportunity for incorporating an island into the floor plan, if space allows. (Attach a peninsula to one leg of the design, and you've created a U-shaped space.) If you do include an island or peninsula in an L-shaped kitchen, plan the clearances carefully. Walkways should be at least 36 inches wide. If the walkway is also a work aisle, increase the clearance to 42 inches. A 36-inch clearance is fine for counter seating, unless traffic goes behind it. In that case, clearance should be 65 inches.

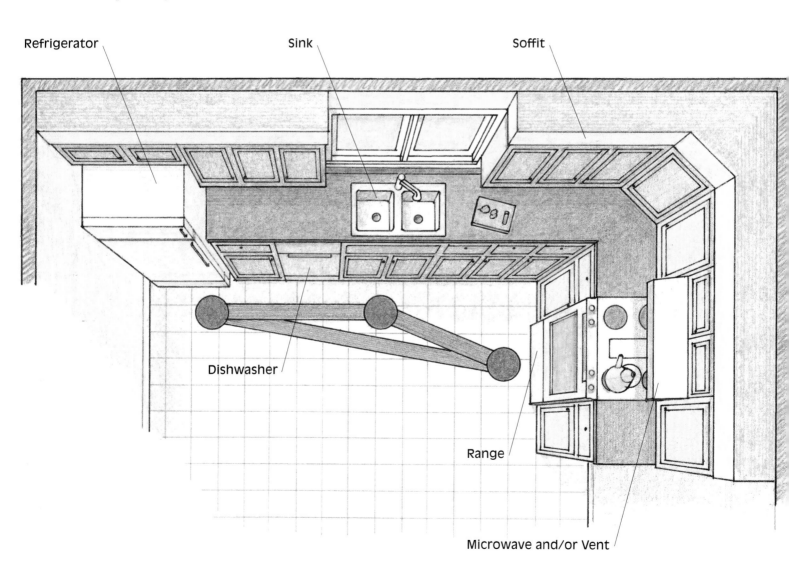

Refrigerator   Sink   Soffit

Dishwasher

Range

Microwave and/or Vent

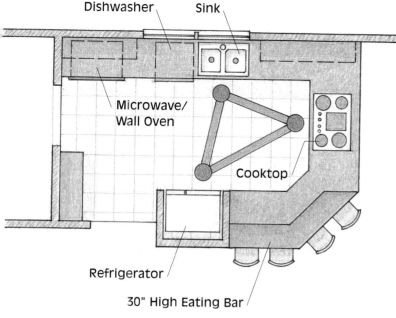

Dishwasher   Sink

Microwave/
Wall Oven

Cooktop

Refrigerator

30" High Eating Bar

◄ **Variation One.** Adding a peninsula to the basic L-shaped kitchen creates a U-shaped layout. From a cook's viewpoint, this is an extremely efficient shape because of the compact work area. The U-shape is actually considered one of the basic kitchen shapes and is covered more thoroughly on the next page.

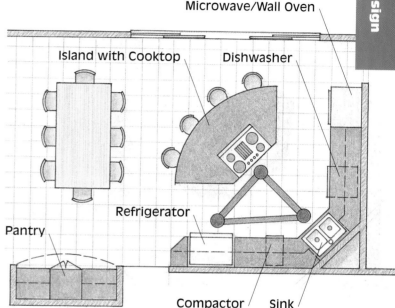

Microwave/Wall Oven

Island with Cooktop   Dishwasher

Refrigerator

Pantry

Compactor   Sink

► **Variation Two.** A new island allows you to move one of the major appliances off the L. This design is for a large kitchen, but even in half the space, the L plus island creates an efficient layout. Counter seating on the island is a bonus.

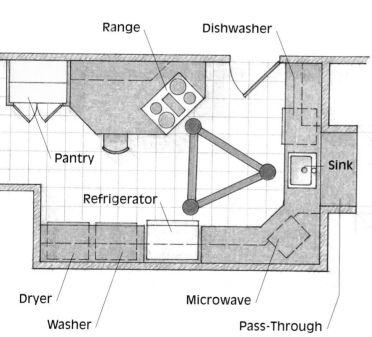

Range   Dishwasher

Pantry

Sink

Refrigerator

Dryer

Washer   Microwave   Pass-Through

◄ **Variation Three.** This kitchen is a little less than 10 ft. wide, but it shows how good design can make even a small space efficient. The doorway into the work area is not the most ideal situation, but sometimes it can't be avoided.

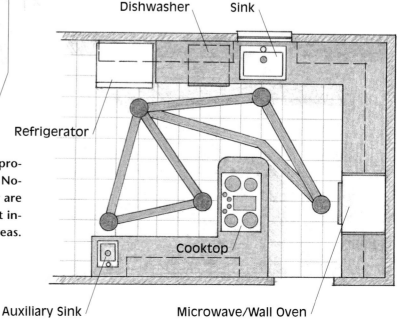

Dishwasher   Sink

Refrigerator

Cooktop

Auxiliary Sink   Microwave/Wall Oven

► **Variation Four.** A double L-shaped layout provides plenty of work space for a second cook. Notice how the second sink and the refrigerator are placed so that noncooks can use them without interfering in the work areas.

U-Shaped Kitchen

A U-shaped kitchen arranges cabinets, counters, and appliances along three walls, making it highly effective. Some plans open up one or more walls to an adjacent area like a family room or informal dining space. An extra dividend is freedom from through-traffic.

A U-shaped plan incorporates a logical sequence of work centers with minimal distances between them. The sink often goes at the base of the U, with the refrigerator and range on the side walls opposite each other. The U-shape takes up lots of space, at least 8 feet along both the length and width of the kitchen. Corners are a problem, too, because access to storage can be a challenge. Lazy Susan shelving helps make use of this otherwise dead space.

As with the other basic shapes, U-shaped layouts need not be absolute. Extending one of the walls with a peninsula creates a G-shaped kitchen. This layout is so common that many designers think of the G-shape as one of the basic kitchen designs.

A G-shaped plan is ideal for providing room for two cooks to operate independently or in concert without interfering with each other. The plan defines two separate work triangles that usually, but not always, share the refrigerator.

Often there's a second sink and separate cooktop and oven areas. With this arrangement, one cook moves between the refrigerator, sink, and cooktop while the other moves between the refrigerator, second sink, and oven. Sometimes both work triangles can share two points, like the sink and refrigerator, and diverge at the cooktop and ovens.

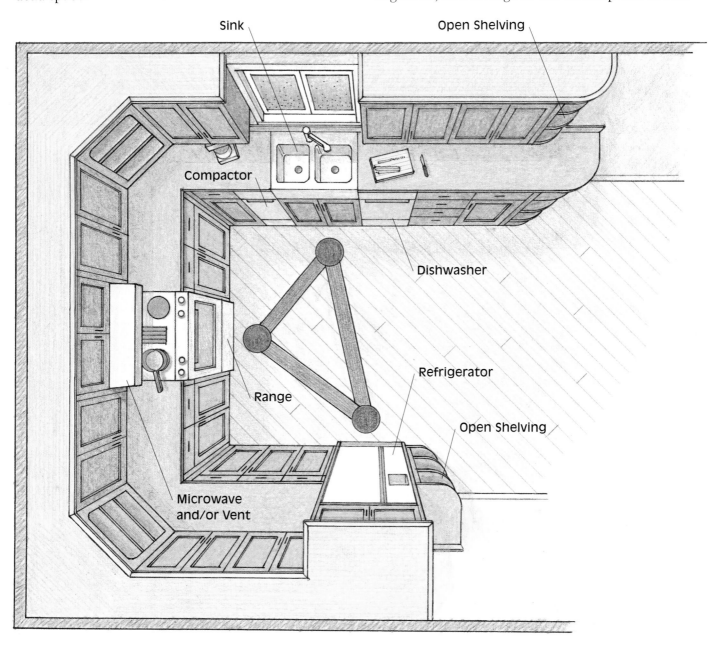

Sink

Open Shelving

Compactor

Dishwasher

Range

Refrigerator

Open Shelving

Microwave and/or Vent

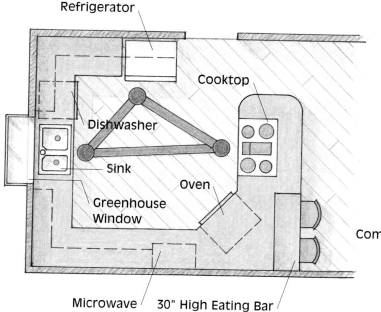

Refrigerator

Cooktop

Dishwasher

Sink

Oven

Greenhouse Window

Microwave 30" High Eating Bar

◄ **Variation One.** Many designers consider the G-shaped layout a basic kitchen shape. It is formed by adding a peninsula to the end of the basic U-shape. This layout makes it easy for multiple cooks to work together. Adding a second sink and modular refrigeration to this design would make it even more efficient.

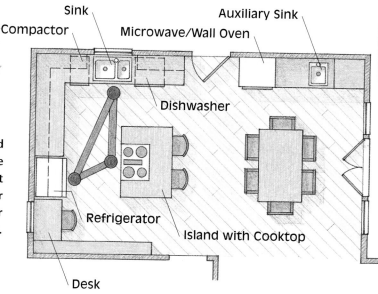

Sink

Compactor

Microwave/Wall Oven

Auxiliary Sink

Dishwasher

Refrigerator

Island with Cooktop

Desk

► **Variation Two.** Adding an island to a U-shaped kitchen makes the space more functional. In large spaces, it allows you to create two areas without sacrificing a compact work area. The area near the table is a good location for a microwave for reheating leftovers.

◄ **Variation Three.** Having a large space with which to work allows for layouts that truly fit the way you work in the kitchen. The turn in the snack counter permits diners to face one another, making that area more appealing.

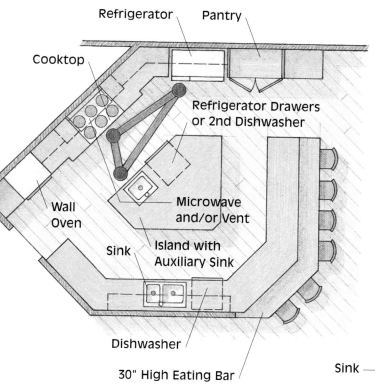

Refrigerator   Pantry

Cooktop

Refrigerator Drawers or 2nd Dishwasher

Wall Oven

Microwave and/or Vent

Sink

Island with Auxiliary Sink

Dishwasher

30" High Eating Bar

► **Variation Four.** One of the strong points of the U-shape is the way through traffic need not interfere with the work areas. This kitchen has three doorways, yet most of the work areas are located out of the flow of traffic.

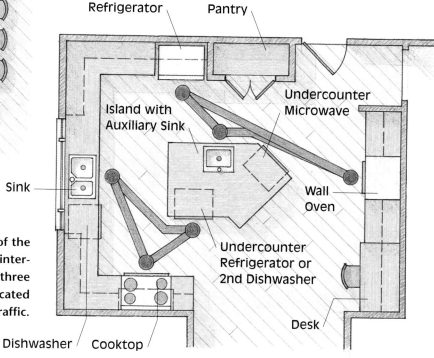

Refrigerator   Pantry

Island with Auxiliary Sink

Undercounter Microwave

Sink

Wall Oven

Undercounter Refrigerator or 2nd Dishwasher

Desk

Dishwasher Cooktop

Off-the-Wall Space

If you've run out of wall space but have floor space to spare, consider improving your kitchen's efficiency with a peninsula or island.

Peninsulas. Properly sized and properly placed, peninsulas cut down on steps and increase counter space. Peninsulas also offer flexible storage because you can design them for access from either side. The peninsula base and ceiling-hung cabinets become convenient places to keep tableware and other dining-area supplies.

To prevent doors from colliding, allow a minimum of 48 inches of floor space between a peninsula and the counter opposite it. If plumbing and ventilation hookups permit, you might choose to place the range or sink in the kitchen side of a peninsula. On the other side you might choose to install an elevated eating counter.

Islands. In a big L- or U-shaped kitchen, you can shorten the distance between the sink, range, and refrigerator with a center island. This arrangement works especially well in the large kitchen of an older home, visually breaking up open floor space, increasing efficiency, and sometimes providing eating space.

Some homeowners choose to install a range or cooktop in the island; others use it for the sink and dishwasher. Either way, allow for adequate counter space on either side of the sink or cooking unit. As with a peninsula, make sure you'll have at least 48 inches of space between an island and any other counter. Consider using a different surface here, too, such as butcher block for chopping or marble for rolling pastry dough.

A built-in table added to a run of counter and cabinets forms a peninsula that becomes a sunny breakfast nook.

Island fixtures help create multiple work areas (above) and provide locations for additional storage. Fitted with a cooktop or range (right), they become ideal locations for eating bars.

Measurements for Planning

With a pencil, graph paper, measuring tape, ruler, eraser, and scissors, you can draw an outline of the space you have and try out different arrangements of appliances, counters, and cabinets. You can also buy commercial planning kits that have a floor-plan grid and cutouts of standard-size cabinets, appliances, tables, and the like.

Careful Measuring

Start by making a rough floor plan of your existing kitchen. Include doors and windows, obstructions, breaks in the wall, outlets and switches, and any other pertinent information.

Measure accurately, all in inches, so you don't confuse 5'3" with 53"—a significant difference. Write measurements on the rough sketch as you go. Start at any corner of the room, and measure to the first break or obstruction—a window or range, for instance. Note this measurement on your sketch. Measure from that point to the next break or obstruction, and so on around the room. Also measure the height of doorways and windows from the floor up and from the ceiling down.

Measure the vertical and horizontal location of electrical outlets, light switches, and lighting fixtures. Show the rough locations of gas and plumbing lines, as well as ducts and vents.

Measure around the room at two or three heights: floor level above the baseboard, counter height (36 inches), and with arms stretched high (6 or 7 feet). Add up the measurements recorded along the walls for overall measurements. Now measure the overall length and width of your kitchen at the floor, and note this on your sketch. These should equal the corresponding overall measurements. If there's a significant difference in the measurements at different heights, your room is out of square, and it may be tricky to get a snug fit for your cabinets, which are square.

Great results begin with careful planning and measuring. Cabinets are available in a variety of sizes to fit just about any space.

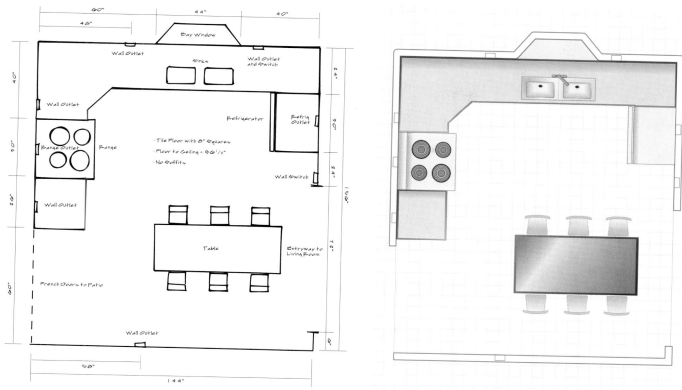

Begin planning by carefully measuring your existing kitchen (left). Record all dimensions in inches to avoid confusion. Transfer the drawing to graph paper (right), and use cutouts to create new layouts.

If the difference is too great to be masked by molding and caulk, say ½ to ¾ inch, you may need the help of a professional.

Scale Drawings

You can use each square of ¼-inch graph paper to represent 6 inches of actual floor space. Lay out the room's four walls to scale, referring to your rough sketch. Draw all irregularities on your scaled plan, being sure to account for the thickness of any walls that project into the room. Draw the existing doors and windows to exact scale, even if you expect to change them when you remodel. Also indicate existing utility lines and electrical connections.

Don't bother with appliances, cabinets, counters, or any other elements you plan to rearrange. These are best dealt with by cutting scaled templates from graph paper. Then you can move the templates around to experiment with any layout that occurs to you.

Cabinets. Assembling a run of kitchen cabinets and appliances requires fitting a series of standard-size components into a space that's probably not an exact multiple of any dimension. The job isn't difficult, however, because custom and stock cabinet widths progress in increments of 3 inches. By jug-

gling sizes you can usually put together a series of cabinets that ends up just shy of the total distance from one wall to another. You'll make up the difference with filler strips at one or both ends.

The drawings on page 98 depict typical cabinet dimensions, but if you're taller or shorter than average, you may want to alter the heights at which your cabinets will be installed. You also may mix and match installation heights to create specialized work sites. Most base cabinets are 30½ inches high. Toe space and the base on which they rest bring them up to 34½ inches. Add another 1½ inches for the countertop, and the total counter height comes to 36 inches.

Adjusting Heights. Some studies indicate that the standard 36-inch counter height is too low for most people and that 37½ inches is better. If you want to elevate your counters an inch or so, increase the height of the toe space.

The distance between the countertop and the bottom of the wall cabinets typically measures 15 to 18 inches. The 18-inch height allows room for tall appliances on the counter or for a microwave oven installed under the wall cabinets. The 15-inch height makes upper shelves in the wall cabinets more accessible to shorter people.

Preparing Your Plan. Use the dimensions for cabinets, appliances, and sinks in the tables at right when you draw and cut out templates for your scaled kitchen plan. There's not much you can do about appliance dimensions, of course, but most manufacturers can modify stock or semi-custom cabinets to your order for special equipment or space needs.

Corners. One of the trickiest parts of planning a run of cabinets and appliances comes when you arrive at a corner. Storage here tends to be inefficient, especially in the deeper recesses of base cabinets, where things sneak out of sight, out of reach, and soon out of mind as well. There are a variety of alternatives, however, thanks to specialty cabinets.

The two most popular ways to turn a corner are with blind bases, straight units that have a door on only one side and overlap the beginning of the next run, and corner bases, which integrate two cabinets into a single L-shaped unit. With blind bases you usually need a filler so that doors will clear each other. Wall cabinets also come in blind and corner units. When ordering blind cabinets, you must specify whether you want a left- or right-hand version.

Another way to negotiate a turn is to situate a sink, refrigerator, or range there. Corner sinks may arrange basins at right angles to each other and fit into a standard corner base. Be sure to allow adequate counter space on either side of a sink or appliance. Use the small triangle of counter space in the corner to hold useful or decorative items, or make it a raised platform for plants.

A peninsula offers an excellent opportunity to take advantage of dead corner space inside cabinets. Items that can't be easily reached from the kitchen side can be stowed on the opposite side. Like blind bases, peninsula corner cabinets come in left- and right-hand configurations.

Alter these typical dimensions to suit your needs. For example, tall people are more comfortable working at a higher-than-standard counter.

Sink Base Cabinet. A dummy drawer covers the bowl. Wide doors provide access to plumbing below the sink.

Drawer Base Cabinet. Storage drawers come in a variety of sizes. Plan storage needs carefully before ordering.

Base Cabinet. Widths are available up to 48 in. Combine base cabinets with efficient add-on storage options.

Cabinet Dimensions (in inches; ranges in 3-in. increments)

Cabinet	Width	Height	Depth
Base unit	9–48	34½	24
Drawer base	15–21	34½	24
Sink base	30, 36, 48	34½	24
Blind corner base	24 (not usable)	34½	24
Corner base	36–48	34½	24
Corner carousel	33, 36, 39 (diameter)	X	X
Drop-in range base	30, 36	12–15	24
Wall unit	9–48	12–18, 24, 30	12, 13
Tall cabinet (oven, pantry, broom)	18–36	84, 90, 96	12–24

Appliance Dimensions (in inches)

Appliance	Width	Depth	Height
Cooktop	15, 30, 36, 42, 46 (with grill)	22	X
Wall oven	24, 27, 30	24	24–52
Range	24, 30, 36	24, 27	36, 72 (oven above)
Professional range	36–68	30–36	35–37
Vent hood	30, 36	18–20	7–9
Refrigerator	28–36	28–32, 24 (built-in)	58–72
Modular refrig./freezer	27	24	34½, 80
Upright freezer	28–36	28–32	58–72
Chest freezer	40–45	28–32	35–36
Dishwasher	18, 24	24	34½
Compactor	15, 18	24	34½
Washer and dryer	27–30	27–30	36, 72 (stacked)
Grill	18–36	21–22	X
Microwave oven	18–30	12–16	10–18

Corner appliances make efficient use of this normally wasted space. Be sure to allow for landing space on the counter.

SMART TIP Draw up your kitchen plan in this order: sink, range, refrigerator. Once you have the basic triangle located, add the other appliances, such as wall ovens and a dishwasher, and then the cabinets, counters, and eating areas.

Sink Dimensions (in inches)

Sink Type	Width	Front to Rear	Basin Depth
Single-bowl	25	21–22	8–9
Double-bowl	33, 36	21–22	8–9
Side-disposal	33	21–22	8–9, 7
Triple-bowl	43	21–22	8, 6, 10
Corner	17–18 (each way)	21–11	8–9
Bar	15–25	15	5½–6

Do-It-Yourself Floor Plans

There are many ways to revise the floor plan of an existing kitchen. The room's peculiarities, combined with the special desires of the homeowners, lead to solutions that other remodelers might never consider.

So why bother to study how others might do things? With a little inspiration from one project here, a clever idea from another there, you'll be attuned to the possibilities that exist in your own remodeling project. To acquaint you with some possibilities, we've prepared floor plans for four existing kitchens, then redesigned them to better suit the families that live there.

Annexing a Pantry

Our first remake comes from a turn-of-the-century home. Back then, few components were built-in. Instead, cabinets and appliances were treated like furniture that could be moved about.

The original kitchen supplemented meager counter and storage space with an adjacent walled-off "butler's pantry," not a bad feature if you happen to have a butler or other live-in help. Meals, even breakfast, were prepared in the kitchen and pantry by servants and then carried to a formal dining room to the left.

The typical modern family of four has no servants and would much rather eat light meals in the kitchen, where anything they might have forgotten is just a few steps away. To make space for a table and four chairs, we removed the wall between the kitchen and pantry. Then, to create an efficient work triangle, we also relocated the door to the dining room and arranged cabinets, counters,

and appliances in a more efficient U-shaped layout.

An angled range with an overhead vent hood occupies dead corner space, with a microwave oven and tall storage cabinet to the left. There wouldn't have been enough space for a sink under the original window to the right of the range's new location, so we closed up that window—in the old pantry—moved the sink a couple of feet, and installed a greenhouse bay behind it. Now the refrigerator ends the run of cabinets and counters.

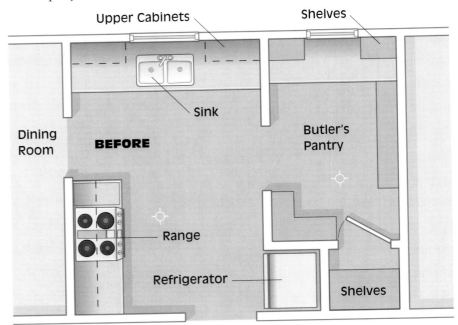

An inefficient layout was only one of this kitchen's problems. There was no counter space and most of the available storage was in another room.

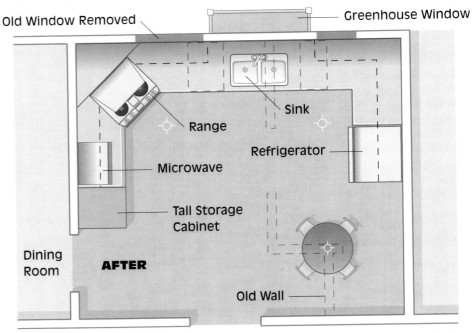

Removing a wall and moving a doorway opens up the space to allow for a classic U-shaped layout and a much more efficient work triangle.

Reorganizing Wasted Space

The builder of this family-style kitchen meant well but failed to achieve a layout that worked smoothly. Lack of floor space is no problem here. In fact there seems to be way too much of it. Imagine repeatedly taking a dozen or more steps back and forth from the refrigerator to the sink or carrying hot, heaping plates to a table stranded in the middle of nowhere.

Counter space is also poorly allocated. There's too much next to the refrigerator and none at all to the right of the burner top. Also, every time the wall-oven door is opened it blocks traffic from the adjacent doorway.

Shrinking the Kitchen. The redesign cuts the working and dining areas down to size and adds some new angles. We moved the sink to an angled peninsula, making room for a compactor to the left of the sink. At the end of the peninsula, a custom-made, movable octagonal table is within easy reach of the refrigerator and cleanup center. Pull the table away from the peninsula, and it can seat up to eight.

The angles of a new china closet and the counter space next to the relocated refrigerator parallel those of the table and peninsula. Now the refrigerator has a handy "landing" counter, where groceries can rest on their way from store to storage, either in the refrigerator or the new pantry next to it. Moving the cooktop to the sink's former site provides generous counter space to the left and right of the burners. This also makes it possible to bring the wall oven closer to the other appliances, out of the through-traffic lane.

Wide-open spaces aren't always a good thing. Here, there are too many steps between the major appliances, as well as a critical shortage of counter space.

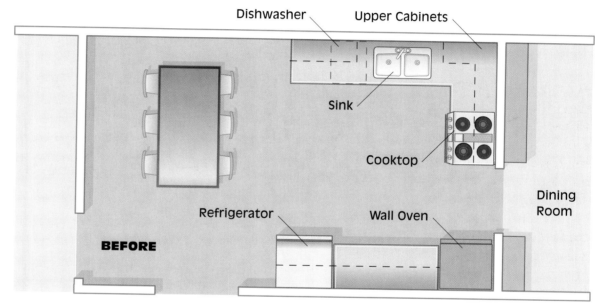

Adding a peninsula and table cuts the kitchen to a manageable size. It also allows for shifting the locations of the sink and cooktop, creating a more efficient work triangle.

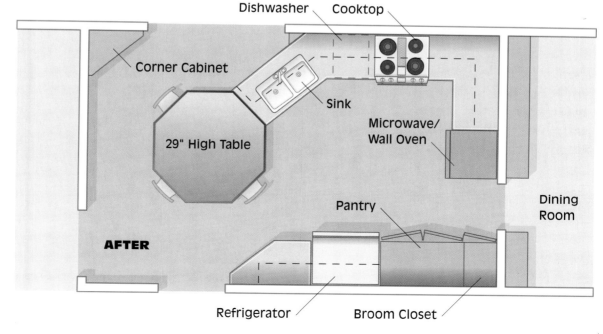

Revamping an Outdated Kitchen

As old kitchens go, this one worked reasonably well. The range was a long hike from the sink, but otherwise the L-shaped layout defined a manageable work triangle and there was space left over for a table, chairs, and extra storage near the dining room.

However, as you'd expect in an older house, the cabinets, countertops, and equipment were almost worn out—providing a splendid opportunity either to remedy the layout's minor flaws or to create a dynamic new layout.

Fine-Tuning. Besides suffering from a somewhat awkward work triangle, this kitchen lacked counter space for today's blenders, food processors, coffee makers, toaster ovens, bread machines, and other countertop appliances.

In the first tune-up redesign, moving the range to the corner helps solve both problems: the triangle's legs are shorter, and the counter space next to the refrigerator is increased by more than a foot. Adding a peninsula next to the sink further increases usable counter and cabinet space. With more storage in the kitchen proper, we decided to replace the extra floor-to-ceiling cabinets at the left with a planning center. Wall-hung cabinets and a built-in desk make a handy new place to conduct family business.

Splurging. Now look what could happen to the ho-hum kitchen if the homeowners spend a bit more. The second redesign moves the sink, not the range. A triangular peninsula accommodates the sink, dishwasher, a planter, and a planning desk.

To further tighten the work triangle, we have angled the refrigerator slightly. This move cramped the space formerly occupied by the table and chairs, so they were replaced by a piano-shaped table jutting out from the wall. Lastly, the space next to the dining room has become a hospitality center, complete with a bar sink.

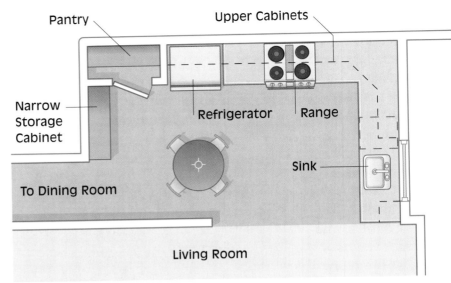

Before. This L-shaped layout put the refrigerator a long way from the sink and lacked an adequate amount of available storage space.

Fine Tuning. Moving the appliances tightens the work triangle. A new peninsula by the sink increases the work and storage space.

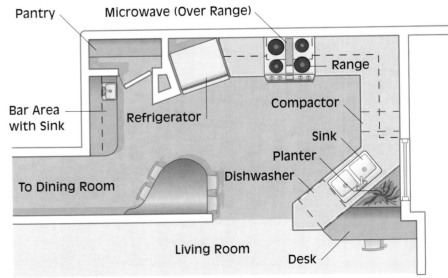

Splurging. Angling the refrigerator and sink, and adding a distinctive table add interest to the design. Moving the desk creates room for a wet bar.

Stretching into a Porch

Older homes often have kitchens that are tiny by today's standards, but many open to a side or back porch that begs to be brought in from the cold. Enclosing a porch is an obvious way to add kitchen space. If your porch has a solid foundation and a sound roof, enclosing it is a feasible project for even a beginning do-it-yourselfer. And because a porch is already part of the house, you needn't worry about setback and lot-line ordinances that affect additions.

Case Study. This small kitchen stranded a range at one end of a compact L and positioned the refrigerator as a roadblock to traffic passing to and from a back porch. Using the porch's existing roof and floor enabled the owners to triple their kitchen space, at a fraction of what an all-new addition would have cost. At first, what to do with all that new-found space posed a problem. The plan on the bottom right shows the homeowners' well-thought-out solution.

A kitchen eating area was one priority, so about half of the old porch now provides a delightful place for family meals, with big windows offering views of the back and side yards. Converting the dining room window into a doorway provides access to the eating area and back door without passing through the kitchen's work zone.

In the kitchen area, elongating the old L more than doubles cabinet and counter space. Baking, cooking, and cleanup centers are well defined but still convenient to each other. A new sink fits into dead corner space, with a planter behind it. Plants thrive in the light streaming in through the windows in both walls.

Now the refrigerator stands against the new back wall, handy to the eating area. In the refrigerator's old location the owners have stacked a washer and dryer, with adjacent counter space for sorting and folding laundry, storage for laundry supplies, and a broom closet for cleaning equipment.

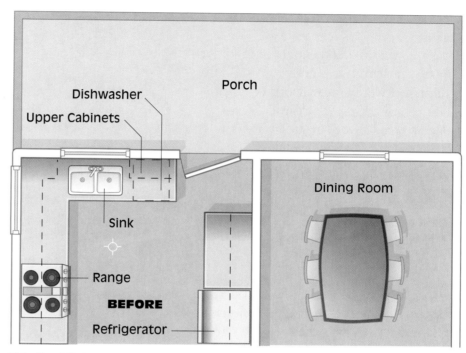

This tiny kitchen has a lot of potential. The existing, little-used porch offers the potential space the owners need to open up the space.

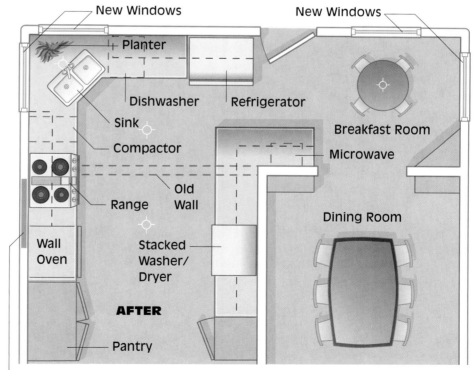

The kitchen doubled in size and now has a much more efficient design. It also has a sunny, informal eating area that the family can enjoy all year round.

Finances & Contracting

CHAPTER 4

The dreams you have for your new kitchen can quickly disappear when it comes time to sit down and add up the price of new cabinets, appliances, fixtures, and other materials like countertops, flooring, and wall-covering. So unless your source of funds is unlimited, you'll have to develop a budget carefully before making any major purchases.

For a large project such as a kitchen remodeling, there are a number of financing options available. Sometimes, financing a new kitchen is simply a matter of compromise, knowing what you need and choosing to wait for what you'd like.

Believe it or not, professional advice from an architect or certified kitchen designer can help trim the fat from the tab, too. These trained professionals know more than one way to solve a problem. The contractor can also help you save money by suggesting economical shortcuts or alternatives in building techniques and materials.

Lastly, decide on the scope of your participation in the job. Obviously, any work you can do yourself will save on labor costs.

Creating a Budget

Kitchen remodeling costs can run from a few thousand dollars to a hundred thousand or more. Where your project falls in this broad spectrum depends on the most basic question: how much can you afford?

A major kitchen remodeling is one of the better home improvement investments. At the time of resale, it can return 75 to 90 percent of the amount invested. But you should also consider how much you want to spend in relation to the total value of your home. Budget advisers suggest that this figure should be no more than about 10 to 15 percent.

Allocating Costs

Before you solicit bids from architects or contractors, you should determine a preliminary budget. After you've worked out a rough plan, visit several kitchen showrooms in your area. Choose some cabinet styles you like, and ask the dealer to give you a ballpark figure for what you have in mind. Then go to appliance and plumbing suppliers. Choose two or three models of each piece of equipment you'll need. Jot down the price and list of features each model has. At a building-supply dealer, do the same for flooring and countertop materials, as well as any windows, doors, and skylights you'd like. A visit to an electrical supplier and a lighting showroom will give you an idea of those costs.

Next, make up lists of various possible equipment combinations and the prices. Add up the totals. Double each estimate to account for additional materials and labor if someone will be doing all or part of the work for you, and you'll have an approximation of what the project will cost.

Getting Bids

Once you have a rough estimate that falls within your budget, you're ready to proceed with soliciting bids. This can only be done when you, an architect, or a kitchen designer have prepared final building plans.

Request bids from at least two but preferably three contractors to get the best possible price. Provide each bidder with a complete set of plans. You can expect to wait two to four weeks to receive your bids. A contractor needs to assess the project properly, based on plans, to draw up all anticipated costs.

The usual method of bidding on remodeling projects and new construction is fixed-price bidding, rather

Estimating costs for a kitchen make-over can be tricky. Collect estimates from material suppliers before soliciting bids.

Sources of financing for a kitchen remodel like this include personal savings, loans, and the equity you have in the house.

th n cost-plus estimates. With a fixed-price bid, the c ntractor studies your construction plans, estim tes the costs to do the work, adds in his overhead ar l profit, and comes up with a price for the job. O ce the contract is signed, the contractor is obliga d to perform the work specified in the contract f the agreed-on sum. If, however, you decide to m ke changes after you have signed the contract, th n the contractor is given a chance to adjust the fi al price. Stay away from cost-plus estimates, w ere you agree to pay the contractor any costs he in urs plus a profit margin. That kind of estimate is t open-ended for a large project.

You may receive widely varying bids. The most e pensive does not guarantee the best work. That c ntractor may have high overhead, or the job may c me at a busy time, which may involve hiring extra w rkers or paying overtime. Conversely, a low bid c uld be submitted by someone who needs the work a the moment or who will do some of the work pers nally. If you feel that a bid is out of line, ask the c ntractor for a reason. Often, relatively small anges in your design or requirements can produce gnificant savings.

Financing Your Project

Many families can't afford to pay cash for a major remodeling. If you've lived in your home for a number of years, the money for a new kitchen could come from the equity you've built up as a result of appreciation and mortgage amortization. Refinancing an old mortgage spreads the cost over 15 to 30 years—and the interest on a home mortgage is tax deductible.

Personal and home equity loans are two other sources of cash. Shop carefully for interest rates. With personal loans, you may have to pledge an asset as security and pay the principle and interest back in three to five years.

Home equity loans are generally based on the equity you've built in your house. They typically have lower interest rates and longer terms than personal loans. There are two types: home equity lines of credit and lump sum loans. With a line of credit, you receive—and pay interest on— the money you use. The advantage of a line of credit is that you can draw money gradually and pay for the project as it proceeds. As its name implies, a lump sum loan is disbursed in its entirety at one time, so you start paying interest on the whole principal from day one.

Working With Professionals

There are many options for implementing your design ideas. You could hire designers and contractors to do all of the work for you. Or you could do all or part of the work yourself. But even if you plan on doing much of the work, you may still need the services of professionals. Some communities insist that registered architects draw up the plans for major renovations or additions.

Architects

An architect's job is to prepare floor plans and specifications for the construction phase. You can also hire an architect to supervise the entire job, from planning through construction. When hiring an architect, you'll sign a contract that sets forth the services to be performed and the fees to be paid. If you've hired your architect to work on your project from start to finish, expect to pay somewhere between 10 and 20 percent of the total construction cost. Architects charge a flat fee for preparing floor plans and working drawings.

Kitchen Designers

Kitchen designers plan out the functional details of a kitchen and often work in conjunction with cabinet dealers or design-and-build firms. If you plan to purchase your cabinets from one of these sources, the design fee will be included in the price of the cabinetry package. If you plan to buy the cabinets from another source, you can negotiate a flat fee with a designer for just the design work.

When choosing a kitchen designer, look for the initials CKD after his or her name. These letters indicate that the designer has been tested and certified by the National Kitchen and Bath Association (NKBA).

Contractors

When it comes time to start construction, you'll have to decide who's going to do the work. You can hire a general contractor, who will take the entire job from start to finish. Or you can hire individual contractors, such as a plumber, an electrician, a carpenter, and the like, to do separate parts of the job until the kitchen is done.

General Contractors. A general contractor takes responsibility for all construction phases of your job.

Planning and organization lead to a well-run pro. produces the kind of results you want.

He or she will supply the labor and materia ule and coordinate the various trades, con and pay subcontractors, obtain any necess ing permits, arrange for required inspectic ferent stages of the work, and generally see plan is brought to fruition.

Ask for bids from several contractors. a good number.) Be sure you give them all information to work with if you want to their quotes legitimately.

Be certain that the contractor you cho established member of the business comm your area. Ask for references. Find out whe were satisfied with the contractor's perforr terms of both quality and schedule. You'll a to know that your contractor is in good f shape, because any default on materials or tractor payments may end up as a lien on you Talk to local building trade suppliers (lumt concrete companies) to find out whether yo tractor has a good reputation within the indu can also check with the local Better Busines or Chamber of Commerce to see whether ti customer complaints on file.

Subcontractors. If you hire a general contractor, he or she will hire and manage the subcontractors, who are members of individual trades. If you act as your own contractor, you must hire, schedule, and supervise the subs.

Doing It Yourself

If you decide to do some of the work yourself, plan on working at the beginning or end of the construction process. This way you can move at your own pace without holding up the subcontractors you've hired, which could increase the expense. For instance, do some of the demolition work, such as removing old cabinets and appliances, or some of the preparatory work, such as installing and taping drywall. Finishing work you should consider might include painting and wallpapering, staining, or laying down vinyl tiles. Even some new kinds of hardwood flooring are designed for do-it-yourself installation.

If something is beyond your reach, either due to lack of funds or lack of experience, put it off until you can handle it. Try to remodel the kitchen in stages. The project will take less of a bite out of your pocket this way, and in the end you'll get the results you really want.

What Every Contract Should Contain

You have the right to a specific and binding contract. The more detailed it is, the better. Get specifics on every part of the project and on every product purchased. It is the details that will save you in the long run. Every contract should include basic items, such as:

- The contractor's name and proper company name, as listed on the business license
- The company's address, telephone number, and fax number
- The company's contractor license number if applicable (Some states don't require contractor licensing. If this is the case, find out the company's business license and verify it.)
- Details of what the contractor will and will not do during the project, such as daily cleanup around the site, final cleanup, security measures to be taken during the demolition phase, and so on
- A detailed list of all materials and products to be used, including the size, color, model, and brand name of every specific product (If you have written specifications, you'll need two signatures to change them—yours and the contractor's.)
- The approximate start and completion dates of the project (You might ask for estimated completion dates for various stages; for example, one-third, halfway, and two-thirds through the process.)
- Your signature required on all plans before work begins (This prevents last-minute surprises.)
- Notification of your right of recision
- Procedures for handling changes in the scope of the work during the course of the project (Change orders should require both your signature and the contractor's.)
- A listing and full description of warranties that cover materials and workmanship for the entire project
- A binding arbitration clause in case of a disagreement (Arbitration enables both parties to resolve disputes quickly and effectively without litigation.)
- A provision for the contractor's statements and waivers of liens to be provided to you prior to final payment

Include anything else that needs to be spelled out clearly. Remember: if it isn't in writing, it does not exist legally.

Construction Basics

Basics

In This Chapter

Your plans are set. Appliances, cabinets, and other components are on order. Now it's time to tear out your old kitchen and prepare for a new one.

If the kitchen is the heart of a home, remodeling might be compared to open-heart surgery. Prepare to live with dust, noise, and disorder for some time. Your normal kitchen routine will be disrupted. You can eat out every night, but rather than go hungry or go broke on restaurants, try setting up a temporary kitchen—in the dining room, for example. Move the refrigerator there, and set up a cooking station with a microwave and toaster oven. Use a nearby bathroom as a water supply. Adjust your menu accordingly.

The makeshift kitchen won't exactly be homey, but remember the inconvenience you experience now will turn into a distant memory once you finish your new kitchen.

Taking Your Old Kitchen Apart

Demolition involves more than attacking your outdated kitchen with sledgehammers and pry bars. It is much safer and more efficient to dismantle the room in an organized manner. Begin by emptying the cabinets and refrigerator and removing any small appliances.

Removing the Sink

With all of the small items stored in some other part of the house, it's time to get serious about demolition. Shut off the water supply to the sink, and open the faucets to drain residual water in the supply lines. Disconnect the supply lines using a basin wrench. **1** Place a bucket under the drain trap, and use a wrench to disconnect the trap from the sink tailpiece. If the drain line is made of plastic, you may be able to loosen the nut by hand. Reach under the sink, unscrew the sink-mounting lugs (if there are any), and lift up the sink, faucets and all. **2**

Appliances, Countertops, and Cabinets

Disconnect the refrigerator, range, and any other plug-in appliances. Turn off the water supply and the electrical power (at the circuit breaker or fuse box) to the dishwasher. If you have a gas range or cooktop, close the shutoff valve on the gas line.

Taking Your Kitchen Apart

Difficulty Level:

Tools & Materials: ❖ Screwdriver ❖ Basin wrench ❖ Putty knife ❖ Groove-joint pliers ❖ Drill with screw-driving attachment (optional) ❖ Reciprocating saw for tile counters ❖ Carpet scrap ❖ Hand truck (optional)

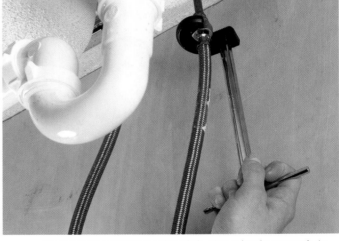

1 Shut off the water to the sink. Use a basin wrench to disconnect the water supply lines from the faucet. Disconnect the drain line.

4 Pull dishwasher from under the counter and remove. Work with a helper when moving large appliances. To protect flooring, place appliance on scrap carpeting.

5 Unscrew the bottom of the counter from mounting blocks. Some older laminate countertops may be nailed directly to the tops of the cabinets.

Remove the access panel on the bottom of the dishwasher. Use a wrench to unhook the water supply line. Disconnect electrical lines to the dishwasher. Most dishwashers are attached to the underside of the countertop through a metal clip. Open the dishwasher door to locate the clip. **3** Once you have separated the dishwasher from the counter, you can pull the appliance out into the middle of the floor for removal. **4** When removing large appliances, be sure to get help and use a hand truck to avoid injury.

You'll be surprised at how easily counters and cabinets come out once they're empty. In most cases, you simply unscrew laminate countertops from underneath and lift them off. **5** Very old lam- inate countertops may be nailed or screwed to the tops of the cabinets. Solid surfacing material is usually attached to the tops of the cabinets with an adhesive caulk. Wedge a putty knife between the counter and cabinet to pry it loose. **6** For ceramic tile counters, cut through the tile and substrate with a reciprocating saw or a handheld grinder fitted with a dry-cutting diamond blade. Make a series of cuts in the countertop, and lift out large sections. Be sure to wear safety glasses and heavy work gloves.

Remove cabinet doors and drawers, and then remove screws that attach the cabinets to one another, usually at the stiles. Unscrew the base cabinets from the wall and remove them; remove the wall cabinets. **7**

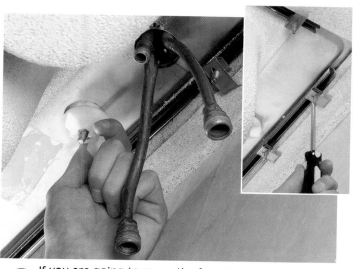

2 If you are going to reuse the faucet, unscrew the nuts that hold the faucet to the sink deck. Unscrew the mounting clips if your sink has them (inset).

3 Shut off electric power and water supply to the dishwasher. Disconnect plumbing and electric service. Unscrew clip that holds dishwasher to counter.

6 Working with a helper, lift off the countertop and remove it from kitchen. For tile counters, use a reciprocating saw to cut the counter into sections.

7 Disconnect cabinets from one another at their face frames. Unscrew and remove base cabinets from their mounting cleats. Unscrew and remove wall cabinets.

5 Construction Basics

Removing Walls

There are two basic types of walls in every house, and it is essential that you can identify each before attempting to remove one. If you skip this step, you risk injury to yourself and serious damage to your house.

Bearing Walls. A wall that supports structural loads and transmits those loads to the foundation of the house is a bearing wall. Except for gable walls, most exterior walls are bearing walls. Usually, a wall that runs lengthwise through the center of a house is a bearing wall. In the attic, bearing walls hold up the ends of joists (particularly where two sets of joist ends overlap). You may also be able to identify bearing walls from the basement. Look for walls that rest atop a beam or a basement wall. If you are not sure about the kind of wall you are dealing with, the safest thing to do is assume that it is a bearing wall. In order to remove bearing walls safely, you have to identify all the loads involved and provide alternative support for them. Seek professional advice from a builder or an engineer when a bearing wall must be removed.

Wiring and Plumbing. Before removing a wall, check the area immediately above and beneath it from the attic and basement, if possible. Look for wires, pipes, or ducts that lead into the wall. There is no way to tell for sure how big the job is until you've pulled the drywall or plaster from at least one side of the wall. Wiring is easy to relocate, but moving plumbing supply lines (hot- and cold-water pipes) is more difficult. Changing plumbing vent pipes is trickier still because of code requirements that restrict their placement. Heating ducts and drainpipes

CAUTION Walls and ceilings may contain pipes, wiring or ducts, so check these areas carefully before working on them. Also, cover heating registers and exposed drains to keep them free of debris during demolition.

are the toughest to relocate. Consult a professional if you are unsure of what to do. With luck, the wall you open up will contain nothing but dust.

Before you begin, take measures to protect yourself and the house from the debris that you will generate during construction.

Gutting a Wall

Turn off the circuit breakers that control the room's power. If you will be relocating plumbing fixtures or working on walls containing pipes, make sure the water and gas valves have been shut off before proceeding. Take down any pictures, mirrors, plants, switch plates, outlet cover plates, and heating grilles. Remove any cabinets mounted in or on the wall. Pull off door and window trim and baseboards using a pry bar. Tap the short end of the bar under the trim with a hammer, and then push the bar to lever the trim away from the wall. **1**

Remove plaster by knocking a hole in the wall with a hammer. **2** Pry out lath and plaster in one operation. For drywall, use a reciprocating saw to cut through panels. **3** Pry off sections with a pry bar. **4** Remove nails and screws from studs. **5**

Dealing with Dust

You probably can't stop the dust generated during demolition from penetrating into other areas of your home, but you can keep the mess to a minimum. Before you begin any demolition, close off the kitchen from other rooms by hanging plastic sheeting over doorways and pass-throughs and covering heating and cooling registers. Seal the edges of the sheet with heavy duct tape. Overlap two sheets to create a flap in the door you will use to get into and out of the room. You may find it helpful to place a small fan blowing out in a kitchen window. This will help keep any dust generated from migrating to the rest of the house.

Cutting a Wall

Difficulty Level: 🦇🦇

Tools & Materials: ❖ Basic carpentry tools ❖ Reciprocating saw ❖ Pry bar ❖ Masonry chisel (for plaster) ❖ Goggles and dust mask

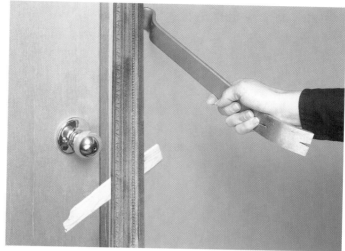

1 Pull off trim and molding using a pry bar. Tap the short end of the bar under the trim with a hammer; then push the bar to lever the trim away from the wall.

2 If you are sure that the interior of plaster walls is free of piping and wiring, cut through the old plaster with a hammer and pry out the plaster and lath.

3 For drywall, shut down any utilities located within the wall. Use a reciprocating saw to cut through the drywall. Cut along the wall studs.

4 Use a pry bar to pull the panel sections from the wall. If you did a good job cutting along the studs, it should be easy to remove large sections of panel.

5 With the drywall cleared away, remove any protruding nails from the studs. If you are going to resurface the wall, check and repair damaged framing.

5 Construction Basics

Removing Non-Bearing Walls.

Non-bearing walls, also called partition walls, support only the wall covering attached to them. Usually a non-bearing wall can be removed without affecting the structural integrity of the house. If a wall does not support joist ends and does not lie directly beneath a post, it may be a non-bearing wall. Walls that run parallel to ceiling joists usually are non-bearing walls. Again, if you are not sure of the type of wall, seek the advice of a professional.

If you are sure you are dealing with a non-bearing wall, you can remove it to enlarge a room or change the layout of the space.

Begin by exploring the interior of the wall to make sure it does not contain wiring, pipes, or heating or cooling ducts. If you cannot tell what is inside the wall from looking at its exterior, carefully cut sections of the wall away to see what is inside. Most partitions do not contain insulation, so it should be easy to search the interior.

Remove the surface finish by following the directions on "Gutting a Wall," page 114. Use a sledge hammer to begin loosening the studs. **1** Give each stud a sharp wack if you will not be reusing them. If you plan on reusing the studs, treat them carefully. Once they are loose, twist and pry them away from the top and bottom plates. **2** Go over each stud to remove nails. When the studs are gone, pry away the top plate from the ceiling and the bottom plate from the floor. **3**

Removing a Non-Bearing Wall

Difficulty Level: 🔧🔧

Tools & Materials: ❖ Basic carpentry tools ❖ Sledgehammer ❖ Reciprocating saw ❖ Pry bar

1 Use a sledgehammer to loosen one stud at a time. Use light force; you will not be able to reuse the lumber if it becomes damaged.

2 Twist each stud away from the wall top plate. Be careful not to step on nails that protrude through the bottom plate.

3 Use a wrecking bar to remove the top plate and lever up the bottom plate. Remove all debris promptly to avoid tripping over it.

Building Partition Walls

A partition wall can extend all or part of the way to the ceiling. It does not, however, play a role in the structural integrity of the house. Usually any walls used in a kitchen are not large, so they can be built one at a time on the subfloor and tipped into place. (See page 118.) If space is limited, though, you may have to assemble the wall piece by piece.

Building a Wall in Place

When there is not enough room to assemble a wall using the tip-up method, build the wall in place. Begin by laying out the stud locations on the top and bottom plates as explained on page 118. Siting the wall perpendicular to the ceiling and floor joists will make securing the wall in position easy. You simply nail the plates to the existing framing. If the wall is parallel with the joists, you will need to install blocking between the joists.

Snap a chalk line across the ceiling, and attach the top plate. Use a plumb bob to establish the location of the bottom plate. Nail the bottom plate into position. **1** If the wall turns a corner, such as for a pantry, check to be sure the corner is square. Place the first stud in position, and use a level to make sure it is plumb before securing it to the plates. **2** Toe-nail the studs in position. Add an extra stud at the corners to provide a nailing surface for drywall. **3**

Building a Wall in Place

Difficulty Level: 🦴🦴 to 🦴🦴🦴

Tools & Materials: ❖ Basic carpentry tools ❖ Framing square ❖ Chalk line ❖ Framing lumber ❖ Circular or power miter saw ❖ 10d (3 inch), 12d (3¼ inch), 16d (3½ inch) nails ❖ 4-foot level

1 Establish the location of the top plate, and then hang a plumb bob to the floor to lay out the bottom plate. Attach it to the subfloor with 16d (3½ in.) nails.

2 Begin attaching the studs to the plates. Make sure the first stud is level and then nail it into position with 12d (3¼ in.) nails.

3 Build up corners to provide nailing surface for drywall. This method uses three studs and scrap blocking at the corner.

5 construction Basics

Using the Tip-Up Method

Most partition walls are built with 2×4 lumber and have a single top and bottom plate. If a wall will contain the drain line for plumbing fixtures, however, you might want to use 2×6s to frame it.

Mark the location of the partition on the floor using a chalk line. If the wall will turn a corner, use a framing square to ensure square corners. **1** Mark the stud locations on the plates by measuring in 15¼ inches from the end of the plate for the location of the second stud and drawing a line with a combination square. **2** Make an X just to the right of the line. From that line, draw a line every 16 inches along the plates. This technique ensures that the edges of 4×8 drywall or paneling have at least one-half of a stud as

a nailing base. The second stud measurement is shorter than the rest because the drywall will be pushed into the corner during installation.

Cut all the studs to length by measuring from floor to ceiling and subtracting the thickness of the plates and ¼ inch for tip-up room. Build the frame by driving a pair of 16d (3½ inch) nails through each plate into the ends of each stud. **3** Raise the wall into position by aligning the bottom with the layout lines, and shim the top plate. **4** Nail a pair of 16d (3½ inch) nails every 24 inches or so through the bottom plate into the subfloor (into joists wherever possible). Make sure the wall is plumb. **5** Nail up through the top plate, and shim into the ceiling framing or into blocking.

Building A Tip-Up Wall Partition

Difficulty Level: 🔨🔨🔨 to 🔨🔨🔨

Tools & Materials: ❖ Basic carpentry tools ❖ Framing square ❖ Chalk line ❖ Framing lumber ❖ Circular or power miter saw ❖ 16d (3½ in.) nails ❖ 4-foot level

1 Mark the location of the new wall on the floor. If possible site the wall so that it runs perpendicular to floor and ceiling joists.

2 Cut the top and bottom plates to length. Measure 15¼ in. from the edge, and draw a line. Measure 16 in. from the line for each additional stud.

3 Cut the studs to length by measuring from the floor to the ceiling and subtracting 3¼ in. (that equals the thickness of the plates and ¼ in. tip-up room).

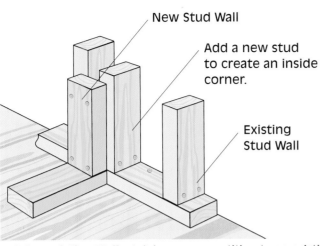

New Stud Wall

Add a new stud to create an inside corner.

Existing Stud Wall

Joining Existing Walls. Joining a new partition to an existing wall will require some work on the old wall. Open up the wall, and install additional studs as shown.

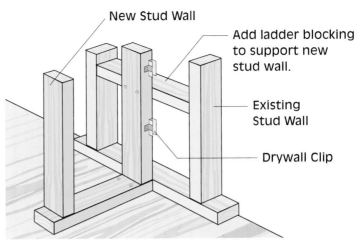

New Stud Wall

Add ladder blocking to support new stud wall.

Existing Stud Wall

Drywall Clip

Other options include installing a 2x6 nailer in the adjoining wall cavity or nailing up ladder blocking between existing studs as shown above.

4 Slide the frame into position, tip it upright, and shim between the top plate and the ceiling. Nail through the bottom plate into the subfloor.

5 Use a spirit level to make sure the wall is plumb. Be sure to check in a few places along the wall. Nail through the top plate and shims.

5 Construction Basics

Removing a wall not only opens up the room, it also allows you to install a distinctive architectural feature, such as an arch (above). If extra floor space is impossible to find, consider removing part of the wall (left) to visually open the room to the adjoining space.

DESIGN IDEAS

See "Great Rooms," page 53

See "Eating Areas," page 56

See "Counter Heights," page 60

Great rooms can consist of the kitchen and an eating area (above) or a kitchen and a family room (right). They are often created by removing the wall between the two rooms. Half walls (below) provide both a boundary and a connection between the two spaces.

Installing Drywall

Drywall, also called wallboard, has a core of gypsum plaster that is sandwiched between two layers of paper. Drywall comes in sheets that are 48 inches wide. Sheets are available in lengths from 8 to 16 feet in 24-inch increments and in thicknesses of ¼, ⅜, ½, and ⅝ inch. For studs spaced 16 inches apart or less, use ½-inch drywall. Use ⅝-inch thickness if the studs are spaced every 24 inches. In some old houses, stud spacing can be irregular. In that case, support the drywall by using 1×3 or 2×4 furring strips nailed horizontally across the studs at 16- or 24-inch spacing.

Before you begin, make sure the framing is straight and rigid. You can attach wood shims to concave sections of studs to bring their edges out to the desired line. Studs that can't be corrected with shims should be pulled out and replaced. Mark stud locations on the floor, so you will know where to sink nails or screws.

Planning the Job

You can install drywall vertically or horizontally. Vertical installation may be easier to install if you are working alone. The goal is to install the sheets so that you end up with the least amount of seam area to tape. Keep in mind that the edges of drywall sheets along their long dimension are tapered, making it easier to get a smooth taping job. Those along

Installing Drywall

Difficulty Level: 🔨🔨

Tools & Materials: ❖ Basic carpentry tools ❖ Drywall panels ❖ Drywall saw ❖ 48-inch aluminum drywall T-square (or straightedge) ❖ Utility knife ❖ Power drill with drywall screw clutch ❖ Drywall hammer ❖ Drywall nails or galvanized drywall screws long enough to penetrate at least one inch into the framing ❖ Panel lifter

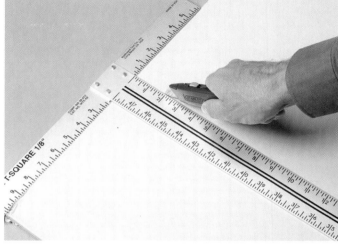

1 To cut drywall, score the face paper with a sharp utility knife. Use a straightedge, such as a drywall T-square, as a guide.

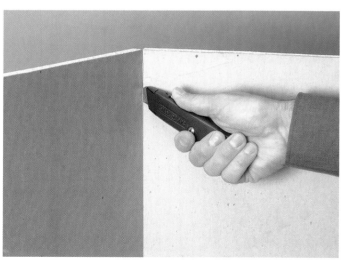

3 After you have snapped the panel, stand it on edge, bend the panel slightly at the break, and cut through the paper backing using a utility knife.

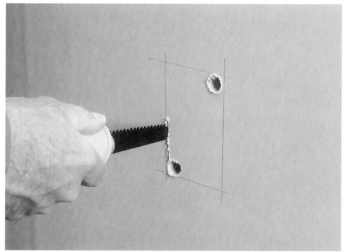

4 To make a cutout for an outlet or switch, draw an outline of the opening on the panel and cut the opening with a drywall or keyhole saw.

the short dimension are not tapered, so they are more difficult to finish. Be sure to stagger edges. To prevent cracks, avoid making joints directly next to doors and windows.

Cutting Drywall

Mark the sheet with a straightedge. Draw a utility knife against the straightedge to score the paper facing. **1** Snap the panel along the cut. **2** At this point only the paper on the other side of the score line will be holding the panel together. Use the utility knife to cut through the paper. **3** Cut openings for plumbing, electrical receptacles, and switches by tracing an outline of the item on the wall and cutting with a keyhole saw. **4**

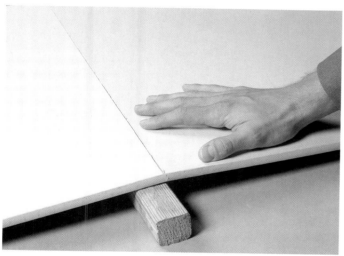

2 You can snap the panel along the line with your knee or lay it over a piece of scrap lumber, snapping it with gentle pressure.

5 When installing panels that fall near the floor, use a drywall lifter or simple lever to move the panel into position, leaving your hands free to guide the panel.

Installing Drywall

For horizontal installations, install the top panel first, butting it against the ceiling. If you're working alone, a pair of nails can support the panel before you nail or screw it in place. Fasten the panels with a drywall hammer—which leaves a small dimple around the nailhead—a drywall drill, or a regular drill fitted with special clutch that disengages once the screw penetrates the surface. Space nails or screws about every 6 inches around the edges of the panel and every 12 inches in the panel field. Sink the fasteners to dimple—but not break—the facing paper.

Use a panel lifter or a simple lever made from scraps of wood to lift the bottom panel (or in vertical installations each panel) in place. **5** Base molding will cover the gap near the floor.

Nails or Screws?

Drywall screws hold better than nails, but for small jobs and patches nails will suffice. Use 1⅜-inch ring-shank drywall nails for ½-inch drywall and 1⅜-inch nails for ⅝-inch drywall. Drywall screws should be at least 1 inch longer than the thickness of the panel you are installing. To drive screws, use a drywall drill or a standard drill fitted with a drywall clutch. The clutch releases the screws before they sink too far into the drywall.

5 construction Basics

Finishing Drywall

Drywall intended as a base for wallcovering or paint should be finished with drywall tape and joint compound. The compound should be sanded smooth because the smallest dents and ridges will show through paint, especially paint with a glossy sheen. For a top-notch job, plan on applying joint compound in three stages, sanding the surface after each application. Drywall meant to receive tile simply needs to be taped with one coat of compound.

Applying Compound and Tape

Begin by filling screw and nail dimples with joint compound. **1** You will find it easier to load a 6-inch knife with compound and make a broad pass over a section of dimples all at once rather than trying to fill each individual dimple. Apply the compound in thin layers.

There are two types of drywall tape: self-adhering fiberglass mesh tape and paper tape. The fiberglass tape is not embedded in joint compound as paper tape is, saving a step. But paper tape prevents cracking better than fiberglass. As a rule of thumb, use fiberglass tape along the tapered seams and paper tape for inside corners and butt seams.

Apply fiberglass tape to the seams. For paper tape, begin by applying compound to a joint with the 6-inch knife. Force the compound down into the joints to fill them level with the wall. At butt joints, where the nontapered ends of two panels

Taping Drywall

Difficulty Level: 🦇🦇

Tools & Materials: ❖ Utility knife ❖ 6-inch-wide drywall knife ❖ 12-inch-wide drywall knife ❖ Sanding block ❖ Tin snips (if you need to cut metal corner bead) ❖ Ready-mix joint compound ❖ Perforated paper tape or fiberglass mesh tape ❖ Metal corner bead (only if outside corners are present) ❖ Pole sander with swivel head and 120-grit sandpaper inserts or sanding screen (optional) ❖ Dust mask

1 Fill nail and screw dimples, and any other small dents in the field of the drywall, with compound. For best results, apply compound in thin layers.

4 For inside corners, apply compound to both sides of the corner. Place a folded section of paper tape over the joint, and embed the tape.

5 For outside corners, attach plastic or metal corner bead. Apply joint compound to both sides of the corner, using the raised bead as a guide for your knife.

join, fill the crack and create a slight hump. This hump will be finished flat later.

Embed the paper tape in the compound. **2** Be sure to center the tape over the joint. Spread a thin layer (⅛ inch thick) of joint compound over the tape, holding the knife at an angle. **3** Remove the excess, and feather the edges.

Corners. For inside corners, start by applying compound to both sides of the inside corner joint. Fold a length of paper tape along its centerline, and embed it in the corner. **4** Spread a thin layer of compound over the tape. Cover outside corners with metal corner bead. Nail the bead in place, and cover the flanges with drywall compound, using the raised corner as a guide for your knife. **5**

Finishing. After 24 hours or when the compound is completely dry, sand all joints and dimples smooth. Fix a sheet of 120-grit sandpaper or a drywall sanding screen into your pole sander if you have one. **6** If you are hand sanding, use a sanding block or a sheet of sandpaper folded into quarters. At this point your goal is to remove large ridges and clumps of drywall from the surface. The job does not need to be perfectly smooth just yet.

Use a wide (12-inch) drywall knife to apply a second coat of compound. **7** Apply this coat more carefully, making sure to feather the edges so that the compound blends with the surface of the drywall. Sand again, and repeat as necessary until you have a completely smooth surface.

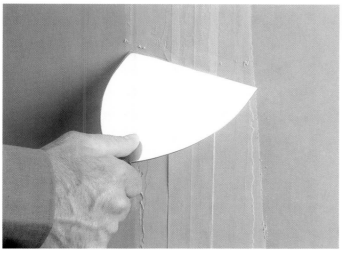

2 Embed the paper tape in compound with a 6-in. knife. Keep the tape straight, and use your knife to smooth out any wrinkles.

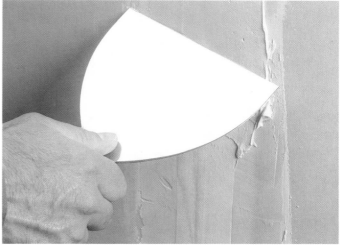

3 Spread a thin layer of compound over the tape. Go over the joint with your knife to remove any excess compound. Feather the edges of the joint.

6 Sand each coat of compound as needed. Smooth the rough spots, and feather the edges. You will find that a pole sander saves time.

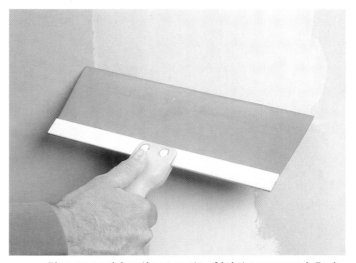

7 Plan on applying three coats of joint compound. Each coat covers a wider area than the previous coats. Use a large 10- or 12-in. taping knife for the final coats.

5 Construction Basics

Enlarging a Window

A major kitchen remodel is often a good time to find ways to bring more natural light into the room by adding a window or enlarging an existing window opening. But before you start cutting away the studs, add temporary supports to carry the building load.

Check with your local building department, but in most cases you can widen an exterior opening to as much as 96 inches without temporary shoring in the following cases:

- The window is below a floor rather than the roof. (The rim, or perimeter, joist can likely carry the load of the floor joists.)

- The window is in a gable end wall.

If the window sits directly below an eave, it carries the weight of the roof. You must install temporary shoring while you replace the header.

You can provide temporary support with jack posts and 2×10 planks as shown at right. Place the planks and post about 24 inches away from the wall while you remove the wall and install the new header. Consult a structural engineer concerning the size of the header necessary.

Installing a New Window

Once the rough opening is complete, remove the supports and install the window. Work from the outside to place the unit in the opening. **1** Tack in a few nails to temporarily hold the window in place. Shim around the sides and bottom until the window is level. Drive galvanized roofing nails through the nailing flange and into the sheathing. **2** Add head flashing per the manufacturer's instructions, and nail on the window casing. **3** Finish up outside by caulking between the trim and the siding of the house with a weather-resistant caulk. **4**

From the inside, stuff insulation in the gap between the window frame and the rough opening. **5** You can also fill these openings with an expanding foam insulation. Choose a low-expanding foam. High-expanding products expand so much that they can apply enough pressure to some window frames to force them out of plumb. Finish the job by patching the vapor barrier, if one exists, and installing the interior trim.

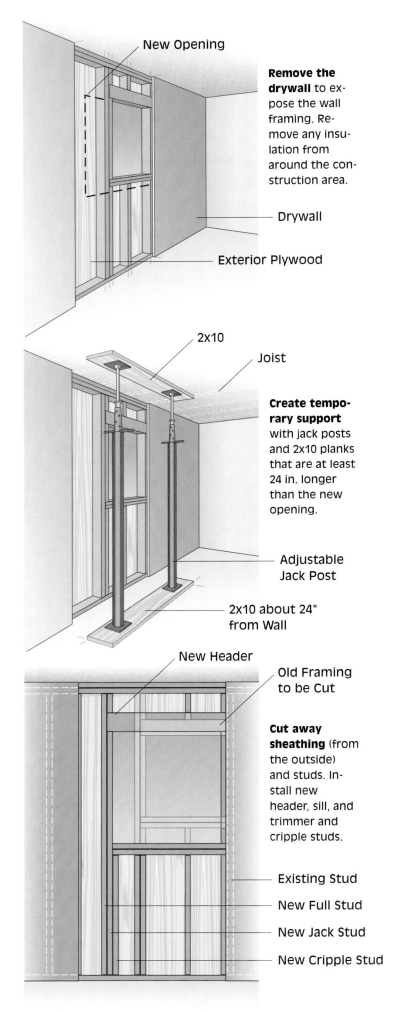

New Opening

Remove the drywall to expose the wall framing. Remove any insulation from around the construction area.

Drywall

Exterior Plywood

2x10

Joist

Create temporary support with jack posts and 2x10 planks that are at least 24 in. longer than the new opening.

Adjustable Jack Post

2x10 about 24" from Wall

New Header

Old Framing to be Cut

Cut away sheathing (from the outside) and studs. Install new header, sill, and trimmer and cripple studs.

Existing Stud

New Full Stud

New Jack Stud

New Cripple Stud

Installing a New Window

Difficulty Level: 🪶🪶🪶

Tools & Materials: ❖ Window unit ❖ Pry bar ❖ Shims ❖ Level ❖ Hammer ❖ Roofing nails ❖ Exterior casing ❖ Casing nails ❖ Caulk ❖ Fiberglass insulation or low-expanding foam insulation ❖ Work gloves ❖ Interior casing

1 Working from outside, put the new window in the opening. Tap in a few temporary nails to hold the window in place.

2 Use pairs of tapered shims (inside) to level the window. Fasten the window in place by nailing through the perforated flange with galvanized ⅞-in. roofing nails.

3 Install head flashing, slipping it under the siding. Rip the exterior casing to the proper width, and nail it with exterior casing nails.

4 Seal out moisture and drafts by applying an exterior-grade caulk around the perimeter of the trim. Clean up any excess caulk before it cures.

5 Inside, stuff insulation or low-expanding foam in the gaps between the window and the framing. Install interior trim.

5 Construction Basics

Installing Roof Windows & Skylights

Installing a roof window or skylight is possible for some do-it-yourselfers, but before deciding to go ahead, be sure you are up to the task.

You'll need to do some of the work inside a cramped attic and part of it crawling around on the roof. If you build a light shaft between the roof and ceiling, you're in for measuring and cutting framing and finishing materials that have tricky angles.

When you have selected your skylight or roof window, read and follow the manufacturer's instructions. The steps below cover some aspects of installation not always included in the instructions.

Planning the Location

First, use a keyhole saw or a saber saw to cut out a piece of the ceiling drywall about 2 feet square, somewhere near the center of where you want the shaft opening to be. Standing on a stepladder and armed with a flashlight, look through the test hole, and inspect the roof and ceiling framing to deter-

The ceiling opening for the skylight can be larger than the skylight itself, flooding the room with light. It will be easier to frame, however, if it has ceiling joists on two sides.

mine the final location for the opening. Although where you want the sunlight to fall is an important factor, you should also locate the ceiling opening to minimize reworking the framing.

Most skylights and roof windows are designed to fit between two rafters (or three rafters with the middle one cut out). You will need to orient the ceiling opening the same as the roof opening, ideally with joists for its sides. You can make the ceiling opening somewhat larger than the roof opening by adding a light shaft with angled walls. The end of the skylight opening nearest the eaves is usually directly underneath the skylight, and the end nearest the roof's ridge flares out to allow in more light; see the drawing at left.

Cutting the Ceiling Opening

When you have decided where the skylight will go, remove the insulation at that spot in the attic, and mark the final opening of the bottom of your light shaft on the ceiling drywall. Cut along the outline with a keyhole saw or saber saw, and remove the ceiling drywall or plaster. (See the photo above.) If there is a joist in the middle of the opening, don't cut it until you're ready to frame the new opening.

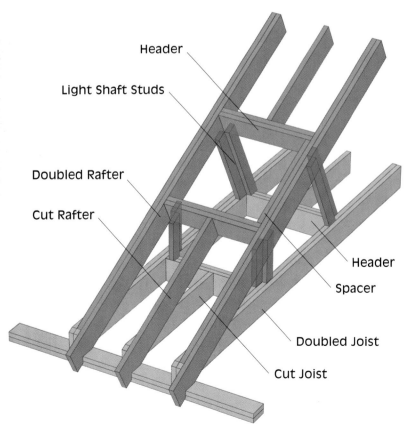

Header

Light Shaft Studs

Doubled Rafter

Cut Rafter

Header

Spacer

Doubled Joist

Cut Joist

A skylight requires that you build two new rough openings—one in the roof rafters and one in the ceiling joists—as well as a light shaft, which will run through the attic.

Marking the Roof Opening

Hang a plumb bob from the underside of the roof above the corners of the ceiling opening nearest the eaves, and mark the positions. **1** Use these marks to measure the rough opening for the skylight (provided by the manufacturer). Trace the outline on the underside of the roof sheathing. Drive a pilot nail through the roof sheathing at each corner of the opening. If you'll be cutting out a rafter for the roof opening, you'll need to reinforce the roof framing before you cut. Reinforce the rafters at the top and bottom of the openings with 2×4s nailed across them. **2** Be sure that the temporary supports span the width of the opening by at least one full rafter bay on each side of it. Then cut through the roof to make the new opening as described on page 131, "Cutting a Roof Opening," and remove the shingles and sheathing.

With a sliding T-bevel, mark where you'll install the new headers for the rough opening—they should be the same dimension lumber as the rafter you're removing. **3**

SMART TIP

Large skylights or those that are not energy efficient can lead to wasted energy or overheating. In cold climates, purchase skylights with low-e glazing. Those with U-values below 0.35 are considered extremely energy efficient. To combat overheating, equip skylights with operable shades or blinds.

Installing a Skylight

Difficulty Level: 🔧🔧🔧

Tools & Materials: ❖ Basic carpentry tools ❖ Electric drill ❖ Goggles ❖ Roofing compound ❖ Chalk-line box ❖ Sliding T-bevel ❖ Framing lumber (as needed) ❖ Framing anchors ❖ 12d (3¼ inch) and 16d (3½ inch) common nails ❖ Roofing cement ❖ Trowel ❖ Circular saw with carbide-tipped blade ❖ Keyhole saw (or reciprocating saw) ❖ Skylight ❖ Aluminum step flashing (usually comes in bundles of 100)

1 Transfer the locations of the outside corners of the planned ceiling opening to the roof sheathing using a plumb line, and mark the roof opening.

2 Reinforce the rafters with 2x4s nailed across the framing. Drive nails up through the corners of the planned opening.

3 After you have peeled away the shingles and cut out the roof sheathing, mark the locations of the headers on the rafters. (See "Cutting a Roof Opening," page 131.)

Continued on next page

5 Construction Basics

4 Cut out the center rafter, if necessary, and install headers of the same dimension in order to pick up the roof load of the missing rafter.

5 Mount the skylight in the opening according to the instructions. Some skylights require a curb, or a supporting frame of 2x4s, to raise them off of the roof.

6 Install aluminum step flashing under each shingle as you replace them. Apply roofing compound over each layer before moving on to the next course.

7 Cut the studs that will form the light shaft. Use one of the studs to mark the location of the inside header on the ceiling joists.

8 The rough opening in the ceiling requires headers and reinforced joists similar to those of the roof opening to make up for the missing ceiling joist.

9 Complete the light shaft by building a frame wall around the opening. Install drywall on the interior of the opening, and insulate the attic side.

Framing the Opening

For a skylight that spans more than two rafters, cut out the rafter in the center of the opening using a reciprocating saw. **4** Then end-nail the headers in place with 12d (3½-inch) nails.

Installing the Unit

Follow the manufacturer's instructions for installing the window. **5** For some skylights you'll need to build a curb, a frame made from 2×4s placed on edge and then installed on top of the roof opening. This curb raises the skylight a few inches above the surface of the roof. Secure the skylight in only one place until you have made sure that the window is properly aligned. If it is not straight, you'll likely notice it when you trim out the inside.

Replace the shingles, installing aluminum step flashing as you go. Aluminum step flashing comes in packages of precut pieces. Interweave one flashing piece to overlap and underlap each successive shingle, as shown. **6** Apply roofing compound under each course of flashing and shingles.

Building the Light Shaft

Follow the same steps for building the rough opening in the ceiling. **7** If you remove joists, provide double joists at the sides to compensate. Install double header joists across the opening at both ends. **8** Use two pieces of lumber of the same width as the ceiling framing.

Next, install trimmer joists to close in the sides of the hole to the final dimensions of your ceiling opening; use 12d nails. To provide a better connection than toenailing, you can use L-shaped framing anchors. (Use 4-inch anchors for 2×4s, 6-inch anchors for 2×6s, and so on.)

Frame the sides of the shaft with 2×4s. Copy the required angles with a sliding T-bevel. Cut the angles accurately: a circular saw or power miter saw makes this easier. Insulate the sides with fiberglass, carefully cut to fit between the framing. After insulating, staple a sheet of 6-mil polyethylene over the inside face of the studs for a vapor barrier. Use polyurethane caulk to seal the sheet to the existing ceiling barrier (or the back side of the ceiling drywall if there is no barrier). Finally, apply drywall as described in "Installing Drywall," pages 122–125. **9** Apply wood trim, if necessary, at the joint between the roof window and drywall.

Cutting a Roof Opening

If you've left the nails that you drove in at the corners of the roof opening, that makes it easier to snap a chalk line on the shingles to mark the opening. Cut asphalt shingles along this line using a utility knife and straightedge to bare the roof sheathing below. Drill a test hole to gauge the depth of your roof sheathing; you want to set your circular saw blade at that depth so that you don't damage the rafters underneath.

Use the circular saw to cut the opening through the roof sheathing. If you need to cut through wood shingles, place a board below the saw. By doing this, you can ease the saw forward without bumping into the bottoms of the shingles. When cutting through the roof sheathing, keep in mind that you will probably hit nails, so use a carbide-tipped blade.

5 Construction Basics

Window & Skylight Options

Frame a corner with windows to create a display area or a sunny spot for growing herbs.

DESIGN IDEAS

See "Windows and Doors," page 44

See "Skylights," page 48

Make natural light part of your design. Skylights (left) bring light deep into the room. A bank of windows (below) lights a work area.

Windows and skylights that face south collect the sun's warmth and warm the room during the cold months.

Specialty windows add a decorative touch to the room. Both the delicate stained glass window (left) and the large divided light window (right) complement the rooms in which they are installed.

Plumbing Basics

Compared with the systems of pipes that carry water to and from a bathroom, a kitchen's plumbing needs are relatively simple: hot and cold water supply lines, a drainpipe, and the necessary venting where you plan to install the sink. If you'll be installing a gas range, the gas line routed to its location is also considered plumbing. All of your kitchen's other water users—waste-disposal unit, dishwasher, water purifier, ice maker—tie into the same lines that serve the sink.

With luck, you already have supply and drain lines at or near the place where you'll put the sink. If not and you plan to move the sink more than a couple of feet, prepare to move supply, drains, and venting. The same holds true if you plan on adding a second sink to your new kitchen.

Explaining all the plumbing materials and skills needed to do your own plumbing work is beyond the

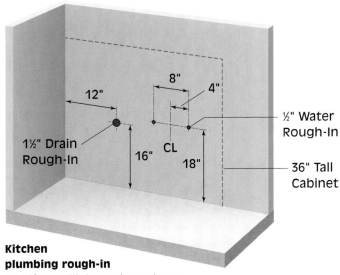

Kitchen plumbing rough-in locations will depend on where you want to place the sink. The standard height for water pipes exiting a wall is 18 in. Kitchen faucets have 8-in. center spreads, so place each pipe (hot and cold water) 4 in. off center. The drain should exit the wall at least 16 in. above the kitchen floor. The drain should be 12 in. in from one or the other side of the cabinet wall.

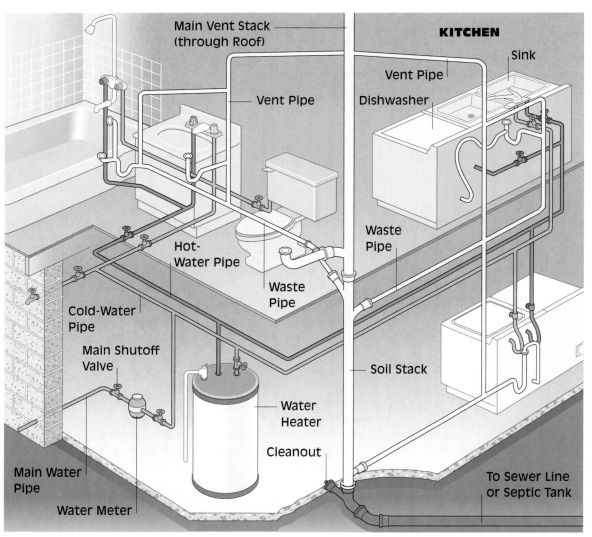

In a typical household plumbing system, water arrives from the municipal system or a private well. The cold-water supply lines branch from this main line; hot-water lines are first routed through the water heater. All fixtures receiving water are also connected to drainpipes and vent pipes. All drain and vent lines converge on soil and vent stacks, which extend through the roof.

scope of this book. However, an understanding of kitchen plumbing basics can help you deal knowledgeably with a plumbing contractor.

Kitchen Plumbing Anatomy

Hot and cold water come to a sink through a pair of supply lines made of copper, brass, plastic, or galvanized steel. If your kitchen was originally plumbed with steel, the pipes should be replaced.

Because supply lines are small in diameter and the water flows under pressure, supply lines are easily rerouted. That's not so with drain lines, which depend on gravity. Water exits the sink through a curved trap, and a small amount retained in the trap forms an airtight seal that prevents sewer gases from leaking into the house.

The trap in turn connects to a drainpipe. Wastewater from the trap typically drops down the drain to a larger pipe called a stack, which probably also serves one or more of your home's bathrooms. An upper extension of the drain, known as a vent, also typically connects to the stack, which rises as a main vent through the roof to expel gases and prevent suction that could siphon water from the trap.

Plumbing codes restrict the distance a sink's trap can be located from its drain/vent line. The distance varies somewhat from one community to another, but don't plan on moving the sink more than about 36 inches without having to break into the wall and extend branch lines or add a new stack.

Bringing Gas to a Range

Gas travels through black iron pipes threaded together with couplers, elbows, and tees. You can hook up a range or cooktop with flexible gas piping, but moving or adding permanent gas pipes is a job for a professional plumber. Even if you routinely handle plumbing chores, working with gas is far more dangerous.

When you make any type of connection in a gas line, remember to always test your work after turning the gas back on by brushing all connections with soapy water; if the solution bubbles, tighten that connection.

Complying with Codes

If you plan extensive plumbing changes, you'll probably have to apply for a building permit. In some communities, a licensed plumber must sign off on any plumbing work. In others, an inspector checks a job twice—once while the walls are still open and again after all fixtures have been hooked up.

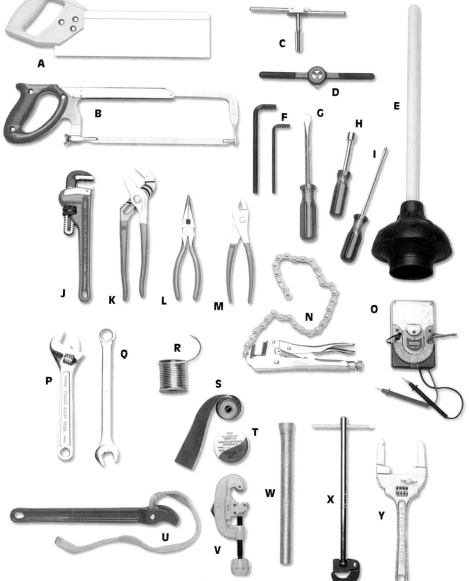

Basic tools for plumbing include (A) backsaw, (B) hacksaw, (C) tap, (D) diestock, (E) plunger, (F) Allen wrenches, (G) flat-blade screwdriver, (H) nut driver, (I) Phillips screwdriver, (J) pipe wrench, (K) groove-joint pliers, (L) needle-nose pliers, (M) pliers, (N) chain wrench, (O) multi-tester, (P) adjustable wrench, (Q) open end wrench, (R) solder, (S) emery cloth, (T) flux, (U) strap wrench, (V) tubing cutter, (W) tubing bender, (X) basin wrench, (Y) spud wrench.

5 Construction Basics

Wiring Basics

All of the intricacies of the home wiring system are beyond the scope of this book, but some basic information, along with working in a safe manner, will allow you to complete simple electrical projects.

If your home's electrical system is up to current standards, the main service cable that enters your house will contain three wires—two "hot," or "live," wires that carry 120 volts of electricity each and one neutral wire. When you open the panel box, you can see that the cable separates into the three wires. The two hot wires feed a main breaker switch, which shuts down or supplies power to the entire house through branch circuits, each with its own circuit breaker. The neutral wire will be connected to a bar on the side or bottom of the box.

Electric cable carries electricity from the panel or fuse box to all the outlets and switches in your home. The path electricity takes is a closed loop. It runs from the panel to the outlets via the "hot" wires and back to the box by way of the neutral wire in the cable. If you try to draw too much power through a circuit, the circuit breaker or fuse will shut down power to that circuit.

Grounding

Electricity always seeks to return to a point of zero voltage (the ground) along the easiest path open to it. Touch an electric fence, and the current goes right through you to the ground. If a short occurs in your electrical system—a hot wire is off its terminal and touching the metal box of a light fixture, which is now charged, for example—the normal circuit is broken. Touch the box, and you become part of the circuit unless the circuit is grounded.

Electrical cable should contain a grounding wire (in metal armor cable the metal is the grounding device). This wire provides a safe path for the electricity back to the panel should a short circuit occur. The third grounding plug on most appliances extends this protection to them. The panel box is grounded by heavy copper wire attached to the cold-water pipes or grounding rods, or both.

Getting Power to the Kitchen

Your kitchen lights and power outlets may be wired to circuits protected by 15- or 20-amp breakers in the panel. If you simply want to replace old lighting fixtures with new ones, you may already have adequate power. It is possible to replace all of the outlets and switches without running new wiring or cutting into the wall. But if you plan on adding new appliances or additional lights or if a breaker trips whenever you operate two appliances at once, you need additional circuits to the kitchen. Discuss your new

Splicing and Capping Wires

To connect wires from different cables, strip ½ inch of insulation from the individual wires. Hold the wires parallel with one another, and twist them together by tightening down on a wire connector (turning clockwise) so that the exposed wires are covered. Tighten the connector by hand; don't use pliers.

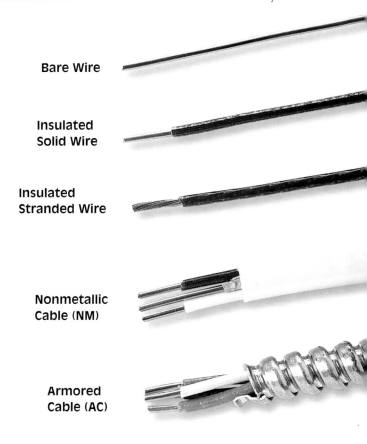

Bare Wire

Insulated Solid Wire

Insulated Stranded Wire

Nonmetallic Cable (NM)

Armored Cable (AC)

power requirements with a licensed electrician.

Working with Wires

Wires are covered with insulation and bundled in cables. To make electrical connections you will need to strip away the protective covering.

Place a cable ripper about 8 inches from the end of the cable, and pull toward the end of the cable. **1** Expose the individual wires in the cable, and cut away the sheathing. **2** Then use a multipurpose tool to strip the insulation from the ends of the wires. **3**

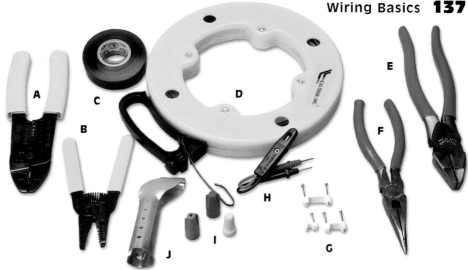

Basic tools for wiring include (A) multipurpose tool, (B) wire stripper, (C) electrical tape, (D) fish tape, (E) lineman's pliers, (F) needle-nose pliers, (G) cable staples, (H) circuit tester, (I) wire connectors, and (J) cable ripper.

Stripping Wires and Cables

Difficulty Level:

Tools & Materials: ❖ Cable ❖ Cable ripper ❖ Multipurpose tool or utility knife

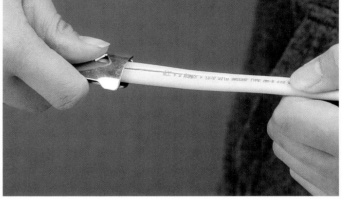

1 You can use a utility knife, but a cable ripper does a better job of removing the outer sheathing. Put the ripper in place and pull toward the end of the cable.

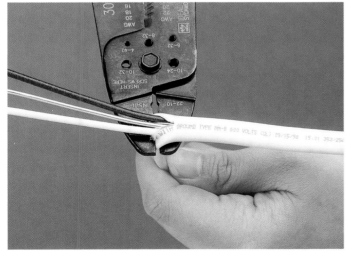

2 Pull the sheathing back to expose the individual wires. Cut away the sheathing with a utility knife or multipurpose tool. Don't nick the insulation on the wires.

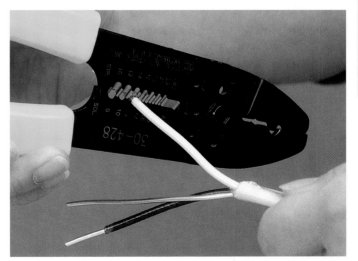

3 A multipurpose tool make stripping the insulation from wires easy. The holes are sized for different wire gauges. Place the wire in the right hole, and pull.

Installing New Wiring

Gutting floors, walls, or ceilings down to the framing gives you the opportunity to replace outdated wiring and to locate electrical fixtures just where you want them. It is also a good time to extend a circuit by running cable from an existing receptacle to a new one, or to run cable for a whole new circuit.

The easiest kind of wiring to snake through the structure is plastic-sheathed, nonmetallic cable called NM cable, or sometimes by the brand name Romex. NM cable contains a black-sheathed (hot) wire, a white (neutral) wire, and a bare (ground) wire. Check with your electrical inspector to see which type and gauge of cable is acceptable for your project. As a rule of thumb, you will probably get by with 12-gauge cable for kitchen lights and outlets. Special equipment, such as disposal units, dishwashers, and microwave ovens, may require 10-gauge or larger. Use the product literature as a guide.

Suiting the Box to the Task

Each switch, outlet, and light fixture must be installed in a metal or plastic box attached to the structure. Ask the local building department which type of box is acceptable. Round or octagonal boxes are usually used for ceiling fixtures or as junction boxes (boxes that are used to contain only wiring). Rectangular boxes usually contain switches or receptacles. You can choose among boxes that come with various types of fasteners, including screws,

CAUTION

Electricity can be dangerous, but if you use common sense, you can work with it quite safely. It's most important to remember always, without fail, to turn off the power at the main service panel before working on a circuit. Use one hand to disconnect or reactivate a fuse or circuit breaker, and keep the other hand in your pocket or behind your back. Before starting work, check the circuit with a neon circuit tester to be sure that it is shut off. If you always follow this rule, you should never suffer an electrical shock.

Running New Cable

Difficulty Level: to

Tools & Materials: ❖ Power drill-driver with ¾-inch bit ❖ Basic electrical tools ❖ Cable staples ❖ 5d (1¾ in.) nails ❖ Junction boxes, switch boxes ❖ Cable ❖ Metal stud plates (if needed) ❖ Hammer

Maximum Number of Wires Permitted per Box

Type of Box	Wire Gauge		
(Size in Inches)	14	12	10
Round or Octagonal			
4 x 1½	7	6	6
4 x 2⅛	10	9	8
Square			
4 x 1½	10	9	8
4 x 2⅛	15	13	12
Rectangular Boxes			
3 x 2 x 2¼	5	4	4
3 x 2 x 2½	6	5	5
3 x 2 x 2¾	7	6	5
3 x 2 x 3½	9	8	7

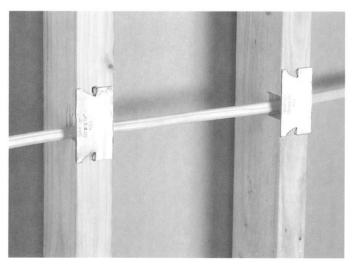

3 If you can't drill through the center of the stud, notch the studs for the cable. Install metal wire shields at least 1/16 in. thick to protect the cable.

nails, brackets, and clips suited for different conditions of new and existing construction.

The National Electrical Code specifies the maximum number of wires per box. Use the chart on page 138 to determine the required box size.

Running Cable

Before reworking any branch circuit, shut off the power to the circuit at the panel or fuse box. Begin your wiring by figuring out where you want the boxes to go and nailing them to the studs. **1** Most plastic boxes come with their own nails; use 5d nails for the flanges of metal boxes. Mount them so that the face of the box will be even with the finished wall surface. Switch boxes are usually mounted 48 to 52 inches above the floor, while outlets are mounted 12 to 18 inches above the floor.

To run the cable, drill holes through the studs at least 1¼ inches back from the facing edge, so nails or screws won't puncture the cable. **2** If you can't drill through the center of the studs, saw out notches of the same depth and cover the edge of the notch with a wire shield to protect the cable. **3**

Starting from your power source (junction box) run the cable to where you need the power. Leave 6 inches or so of cable ends poking out of the box to give you enough wire to connect the devices later. **4** Where cable runs up studs, and about 8 inches above or below each box, attach staples or clips for electrical cable to the studs. **5**

1 Attach the outlet or switch box in the desired location. Boxes for switches and receptacles are made of plastic or galvanized steel.

2 Drill ¾-in. holes at least 1¼ in. back from the stud face as a pathway for the new cable. This will protect the cable should you nail into the wall later.

4 Run the cable from receptacle to receptacle as needed. Leave about 6 in. of cable extending from each box to make your connections.

5 Support cable where it runs up studs and just before and after each receptacle with wiring staples or special plastic clips made for wiring.

5 Construction Basics

Fishing Wiring through Floors and Walls

Snaking new wiring behind finished walls, ceilings, and floors can be difficult, but it's possible to do with metallic fish tape. The tape is stiff enough to guide through holes in walls and floors and flexible enough to make the necessary turns. To use it, you will need to cut openings in the drywall in a few key spots and fish the tape through the openings. Where it emerges, attach the tape to the cable and then pull the cable through the hole.

Pulling Cable from Floor to Floor. To pull cable from a basement to a kitchen on the first floor, make a cutout for the new box in the wall and drive a pilot nail through the floor next to the wall where you want the new receptacle to be. The nails should be long enough to penetrate the flooring material and the subfloor. From the basement or crawl space, have a helper drill a ¾-inch hole through the subfloor and bottom plate of the wall, using the pilot nail as a guide. **1** Fish the tape through the opening in the wall and into the basement. Connect the tape to the cable, after making sure that the cable is not connected to a live circuit. **2** If it is, turn off the circuit's power at the panel box. Wrap the end of the cable around the loop at the end of the fish tape. Secure the cable in place with electrical tape. As you pull the end of the tape up through the hole, the cable will come along with it. **3** From there you can make the necessary connections.

Running Cable between Floors

Difficulty Level: 🐟🐟

Tools & Materials: ❖ Power drill-driver with ¾-inch bit ❖ Fish tape ❖ Basic electrical tools ❖ Keyhole saw ❖ Electrical boxes ❖ Electrical tape ❖ Electrical cable

1 Drive a pilot nail through the floor to mark the location of the new box. Then drill an access hole through the subfloor and the bottom plate of the wall.

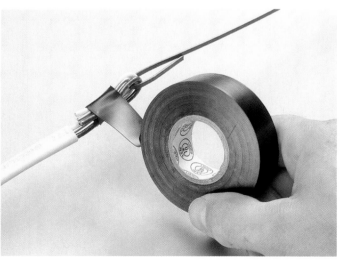

2 Feed fish tape through the wall opening and into the basement. Make a hook at the end of the cable, and attach it to the fish tape with electrician's tape.

3 Pull the tape and cable up through the opening in the floor from the basement. Things will go easier if a helper guides the cable through the first opening.

Pulling Cable Horizontally. If you want to run the cable to another point on the wall, try to make the horizontal run in the open basement ceiling. If you can't, you can run it through the kitchen walls.

To run cable behind baseboards, remove the baseboard carefully (because you will reuse it) and cut out a strip of drywall along the bottom of the wall. **1** Either create notches in the studs or drill ¾-inch holes through the middle of each stud. If you choose to notch each stud, cover the cable with metal wire shields. **2** Cut a drywall patch to cover the opening, and nail it into place. **3** There is no need to apply joint compound, because the patch will be hidden behind the baseboard you will reinstall. Nail the baseboard in place, set the nails, and fill the holes with putty. Paint as needed.

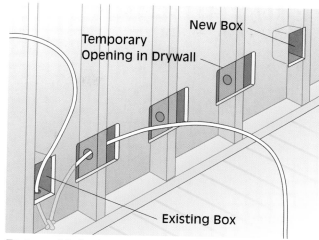

To run cable horizontally behind a finished wall, cut an opening for each stud and drill holes in the studs. Use fish tape to pull the new cable through the wall.

Running Cable through Walls

Difficulty Level: 🔶🔶

Tools & Materials: ❖ Basic carpentry tools ❖ Cable ❖ Wire shields

1 Draw a line along the top of the baseboard. Remove the baseboard and draw a second line ½ in. below the first as a reference for removing the drywall.

2 Notch the bottom of the studs or drill ¾-in. holes through the middle of the studs. Use metal wire shields at least ¹⁄₁₆ in. thick to cover the cable.

3 With the cable in place, replace the drywall and attach nailing into the studs. Nail above or below the metal shields. Replace the baseboard.

5 Construction Basics

Creating New Circuits

Remodeling plans often call for adding new electrical circuits to meet increased demands. In addition, appliances such as dishwashers and waste-disposal units often require a separate circuit to power the appliance. You will need to run wiring from the appliance to the main panel.

Working on a service panel is dangerous, so take all safety measures. If your installation is special in any way or if you are not confident of completing the hookup correctly, have a licensed electrician do the work at the panel after you have done the room wiring. Many local building codes require a licensed electrician make the final hookups at the panel anyway.

Turn off the power to the house at the main breaker switch, which is usually mounted at the top of the service panel. **1** Ideally, each breaker should be labeled. **2** Remove the panel's cover plate, and note the breaker arrangement. Look for breakers that are not in use or spare slots for additional breakers. Use one of these for the new circuit. **3**

Bringing the Cable to the Panel. Use a screwdriver to pry out a perforated knockout from the side or top of the panel box. Attach a cable clamp, and thread 12 or more inches of the cable through the connector, the hole in the box, and a locknut. **4** Tighten the locknut with a screwdriver. **5** Remove about 8 inches of the outer sleeve of the end of the cable, and strip the wire ends.

Insert the ends of the white (neutral) wire and the bare grounding wire into the holes along the bus bars at the side or bottom of the panel. Then tighten the setscrews, and note how the other circuits are connected. **6**

Adding the Circuit Breaker. Snap a breaker into its slot on the panel board. Loosen the setscrew on the breaker and insert the black wire of the cable into the hole below. Then retighten the screw to secure the wire end. **7** Screw the cover plate back onto the panel box and record the new circuit on the panel door. To prevent a power surge, turn off the individual breakers, turn on the main breaker, and turn on the individual breakers one by one. **8**

If you need to add a breaker for a 240-volt circuit, get a special breaker that occupies two slots in the panel box. The installation is similar to that just described, except the cable will have two hot wires—one black and one red. Insert one of the hot wires into each of two holes in the double breaker.

Adding A New Circuit

Difficulty Level:

Tools & Materials: ❖ Basic electrical tools ❖ Flashlight ❖ Cable (the type required by code) ❖ Cable clamps ❖ Circuit breakers of the required amperage and of the same make as your panel

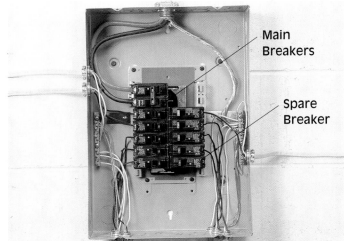

3 Check to see whether there are any breakers that are not in use or any spare slots. A breaker that is not in use will not have a cable attached to it.

6 Connect the end of the white wire to the neutral bus bar, where the other white wires are connected. Then connect the grounding wire to the grounding bus.

1 Open the door to the panel box, and turn the main breaker to the off position. Remove the cover plate by unscrewing the screws in the corners.

DIRECTORY 75300-24-00

1. Dishwasher — 13
2. Kitchen — 14
3. Family Room — 15
4. Water Pump — 16
5. Outside — 17
6. Small Bedroom — 18
7. Large Bedroom — 19
8. Washer — 20
9. Utility Room — 21
10. Dining Room — 22
11. — 23
12. — 24

2 Note the breaker arrangement. Each breaker in use is connected to a cable. A label on the door of the box should identify each circuit.

4 To run a cable into a panel, pry out a knockout from the side or top of the box. Thread the cable through a cable clamp and then through the locknut.

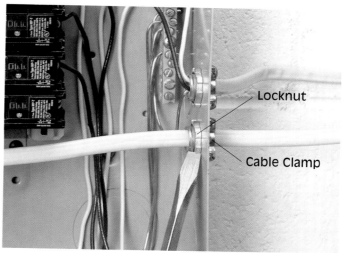

Locknut

Cable Clamp

5 When you have enough cable inside the panel, tighten the cable-clamp screws and the locknut with an insulated screwdriver.

Setscrew

On/Off Switch

7 A typical 120-volt circuit breaker has a clip in the rear that plugs into the hot bus of the panel and a hole in the side for inserting the black wire of the cable.

MAIN

8 Screw the cover plate back onto the panel housing, and record the new circuit on the panel door. Flip the main breaker to turn the power back on.

Putting in a GFCI Receptacle

When a ground-fault circuit interrupter (GFCI) senses a "leak" in the electrical circuit it is protecting, it cuts off the current in ⅟₂₅ to ⅟₃₀ of a second— 25 to 30 times faster than a heartbeat. A leak occurs when the amount of current entering a receptacle through its hot wire is not equal to the current carried away from the receptacle through the neutral wire. The current is not following its normal, safe path within the circuit, creating a dangerous situation. GFCIs are required by code for all receptacles that serve the countertop in a kitchen. But regardless of the code, GFCIs just make good sense.

There are three ways to get GFCI protection. (See "Three Ways to Protect with GFCIs," below.)

To install an outlet, go to the main panel box and turn off the circuit breaker that controls the outlet. Make sure you have tripped the right breaker by plugging a voltage tester or lamp into the outlet. **1** Remove the screws that hold the receptacle in the box. Unscrew the hot (black) wires from the brass terminals and the neutral (white) wires from the silver terminals. **2** Disconnect the ground wire, and discard the receptacle.

If there were two cables connected to the old receptacle, you must use a voltage tester to determine which is feeding power into the box and which is taking power out of the box. Make sure all of the bare ends of the wires are safely away from the walls and well separated from one another. Then turn the

Three Ways to Protect with GFCIs

The cheapest and easiest is a portable device that you simply plug into the outlet of the receptacle you want to protect. It protects only that outlet. At slightly more expense and effort, you can replace the receptacle with a GFCI receptacle, which offers the opportunity to protect receptacles downstream from the one you are replacing. Another way to protect all receptacles and devices connected to the kitchen is to wire them to circuits with GFCI breakers installed in the panel box. (See "Creating New Circuits," page 142.) This is also the most expensive way to achieve protection, as GFCI breakers cost about four times as much as an ordinary 120-volt breaker.

Portable GFCI Protector

GFCI Outlet

GFCI Breaker

Installing a GFCI Receptacle

Difficulty Level: 🗡🗡🗡

Tools & Materials: ❖ Screwdriver ❖ Voltage tester ❖ Plastic wire connector ❖ GFCI receptacle(s)

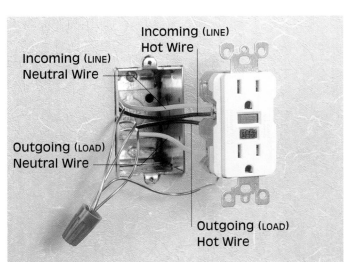

Incoming (LINE) Hot Wire

Incoming (LINE) Neutral Wire

Incoming (LINE) Neutral Wire

Outgoing (LOAD) Neutral Wire

Outgoing (LOAD) Hot Wire

3 Incoming hot and neutral wires are connected to their respective terminals marked LINE. Outgoing wires, if any, are connected to the LOAD terminals.

power back on. Touch one probe of the voltage tester to a black wire, the other probe to a bare grounding wire. All of the bare ground wires should still be connected together. If the tester lights, that black wire is the feed. Turn off the power. Label the feed black and white wires.

Connect the GFCI black and white leads labeled LINE to the feed wires of the same color. Connect the GFCI leads labeled LOAD to the outgoing wires in the box. **3** If there are no outgoing wires, tape a wire cap onto each GFCI LOAD lead. Connect the green GFCI grounding wire to the other bare grounding wires in the box. Fold the wires neatly into the box, position the new receptacle inside the box, and secure it with the screws that came

with it. Reattach the wall plate, and restore the power to the circuit. **4**

Now test your work. A GFCI that is installed incorrectly may still work as an electrical outlet, but it will not afford the protection it can offer. Some newer model GFCI outlets will not work at all if they are installed incorrectly.

Make sure the button marked "reset" is pressed all the way in. Then press the button marked "test." The reset button should pop out. If it does, push it back into position. **5** You are all set. The device you just installed will protect this outlet and any downstream of the outlet. But if the device does not work, turn off the power, open up the box, and check the connections.

1 Turn off the power at the panel. Insert a neon circuit tester to be sure that the circuit has been shut down. If the indicator light comes on, the circuit is still live.

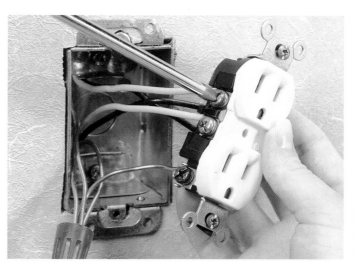

2 Use an insulated screwdriver to disconnect and remove the standard outlet from the box. Be sure to leave all wires and wire connectors in place.

4 After securing the new GFCI receptacle into the box, replace the wall plate using an insulated screwdriver and restore the power.

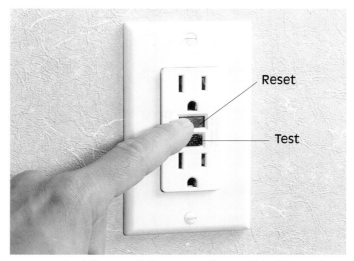

Reset

Test

5 To test the installation, press the reset button and then the test button. If the GFCI is working, the reset button should pop out.

Adding New Receptacles

Grounded receptacles accepted by the National Electrical Code contain three slots: two vertical slots of different sizes for the hot and neutral wires and a U-shaped slot for the ground wire. Don't install a three-prong plug on an ungrounded circuit. The circuit must be grounded back to the main panel through a grounding wire or a system of armored cable and metal boxes. Have a licensed electrician evaluate the circuit's wiring before substituting three-slot receptacles for old two-slot models.

High-Voltage Receptacles

Some appliances, such as electric ranges, require more power than the standard 120-volt circuit can deliver. These appliances need 240-volt receptacles to operate at full power, and most codes stipulate that they be the only receptacle on the circuit. In some cases, the circuit is wired directly to the appliance, but in many cases a high-voltage receptacle is mounted near the appliance.

A 240-volt receptacle uses a two-wire cable with ground. Both the black and white wires are hot (there is no neutral wire in this system). When wiring this type of receptacle, code the white wire as hot by applying some black electrical tape to it.

However, a high-voltage circuit that also requires 120-volt current to operate clocks, timers, and lights on the appliances does need a white neutral wire so that the appliance can split the entering current between 120 volts and 240 volts. These circuits use three-wire cable—black, red (also hot), and white—and a ground.

All receptacles of high-voltage appliances have specific slot configurations that can only mate with the corresponding type of plug.

To wire a middle-of-the-run receptacle, connect the two black wires to the two brass-colored screws and attach the two white wires to the silver-colored terminals. Connect the bare grounding wire as shown.

For an end-of-run receptacle, bring the incoming cable into the box. Connect the black wire to the brass screw and the white wire to the silver-colored screw. Connect the grounding wire to the green screw and pigtail as shown.

A 240-volt receptacle uses a two-wire cable with ground. Both the black and white wires are "hot," so be sure to code the white wire with black electrical tape to alert anyone working on the receptacle later.

A 120/240 receptacle uses a three-wire cable with ground. The black and red wires are connected to the brass screws; the white wire goes to the neutral screw; and the grounding wire goes to the ground terminal.

Wiring Switches

Switches control the flow of current through a circuit. If a switch has two terminals (plus a grounding terminal), it is a single-pole switch. It alone controls a particular circuit. The incoming hot wire is hooked to one terminal and the outgoing hot wire is attached to the other. A switch with three terminal screws (plus ground) is called a three-way switch. Two such switches control one fixture from two different locations, such as switches located at different doorways to the kitchen that control the same light. There are also four-way switches that control lights from three or more locations, and double switches that serve more than one circuit in the same switch box.

When wiring switches, remember that the circuit can run from the switch to the fixture or through the fixture to the switch; see samples below.

Switch Stamps

Switches are stamped with code letters and numbers detailing operating specifications and safety information. Learn how to read these so that you buy the right switch. The switch at right is rated for 15-amp, 120-volt circuits on alternating current (AC) only; CU/ALR (or CU/AL) shows that it can be used with copper or aluminum wiring; CU WIRE ONLY switches can be used only with copper wire. UL or UND. LAB. means that the switch has been tested by Underwriters Laboratories. (CSA is the equivalent Canadian organization.)

Amp/Volt Rating

UL Label

Wire Types

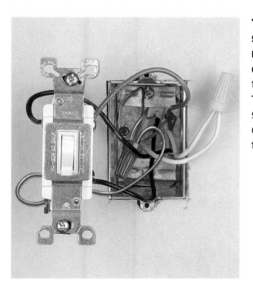

In a middle-of-the-run single-pole switch, connect black wires from both incoming and outgoing cables to the switch terminals. Splice together the white wires, and separately splice the green grounding wires, including a short grounding wire attached to the metal box.

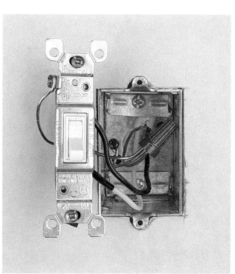

This switch is at the end of a circuit, which means the circuit actually passes through the light fixture before it gets to the switch. Both the black and white wires are hot, so be sure to code the white wire with black tape.

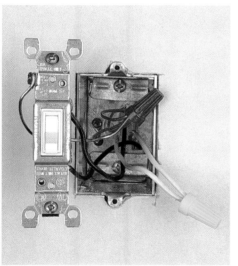

Three-way switches in the middle of a circuit have a red traveler wire. Two of these switches control one light from two locations.

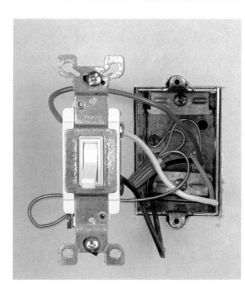

Three-way switches at the end of a circuit run still have a red traveler wire to connect switches—for example, at each end of stairs.

5 Construction Basics

Installing a Range Hood

The size of the hood you need depends on the size of your range. It should overlap the cooking area by at least 3 inches on each side. Some ranges come with downdraft ventilation, in which cooking vapors are sucked through a central or rear vent in the cooktop, and don't need a hood.

For the fan, allow a minimum of 40 to 50 cubic feet per minute (cfm) per foot of cooking area. However, the Home Ventilating Institute, a trade group of equipment manufacturers, recommends larger fans if you do a lot of cooking. HVI recommendations are 100 cfm per foot of cooking area for wall-mounted fans and up to 300 cfm for island fans. Downdraft ventilation requires a powerful fan.

Planning the Ductwork

Ductwork comes in various sizes and shapes to accommodate different pathways. Elbow and offset fittings let you change directions as you route ducts through a wall, ceiling, soffit (dead space over cabinets or under eaves), and/or roof. Depending on the fan size you use, you'll be limited in the distance the ductwork can run. Elbows and other turns in ductwork further limit the length of your run. For example, every 90-degree angle accounts for the equivalent of 5 linear feet of straight ductwork.

Wall and roof caps finish off the outside opening. Most ducting is made of sheet metal, but flexible ducting is also available. Rectangular-to-round converters connect ducts of different shapes.

The pathway you choose will depend on how the house is built and the hood's location. All range vents should be ducted to the outdoors and not into an attic or crawl space. If the range sits against an exterior wall, the shortest path is straight out the back of the hood. Most hoods can be adjusted to vent from either the top or rear. If the hood will be on an interior wall, avoid lengthy, twisted paths. Go straight up through wall space to the roof, if possible. If yours is a two-story house, pass ducting through a soffit over cabinets to an outside wall. Downdraft ventilators are often ducted through the floor, between floor joists.

Installation Process

If you are replacing an old hood with a new one, and the duct meets the specifications of the hood manufacturer, connect the new hood to the old ductwork. But if the old duct is damaged or filled with grease, remove it and install new duct. If you are installing a new hood in a different location, screw down the damper in the exterior wall and caulk it closed, fill the duct with insulation, and repair only the exposed interior opening.

For a new installation, mark the locations of the duct and electrical connections on the wall. Cut the holes, trying to avoid landing on a stud. **1** If you do hit a stud, some products allow you to shift the duct locations slightly. Pull the wiring into the vent hood, and make the necessary connections. **2** Follow the manufacturer's instructions for attaching the hood to the cabinets. **3** Connect the duct to the hood with sheet-metal screws. Use duct tape to seal the joints. **4** Cap the duct on the exterior. **5**

Ducting Options

If the duct comes out through the side of the house, install a duct cap. (See photo at left.) Embed the soffit vent in caulking compound. If the duct goes through a soffit, you'll probably need a transition fitting. (See photo at right.)

Installing a Range Hood

Difficulty Level: 🦇🦇

Tools & Materials: ❖ Range hood ❖ Electrical cable ❖ Basic carpentry tools ❖ Metal duct sized to fit unit ❖ Sheet-metal screws ❖ Duct tape

1 Cut the openings for the duct and the electrical cable. Depending on the hood you've selected, you may have to knock out openings in the hood.

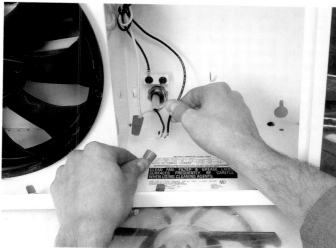

2 With the electric power off, pull the wiring into the range hood and fasten it with a cable clamp. Make wiring connections: like color wires to like color wires.

3 Attach the fan unit to the cabinets. Some models are screwed to the sides or bottom of the cabinets; others are attached to a nailer on the back wall.

4 Connect the ducts as per the manufacturer's directions. Attach ducts with sheet-metal screws, and seal the seams with duct tape.

5 If the duct passes through the roof, it should extend at least ¾ in. above the high side of the roof. Place the weatherproof cap over the opening.

5 Construction Basics

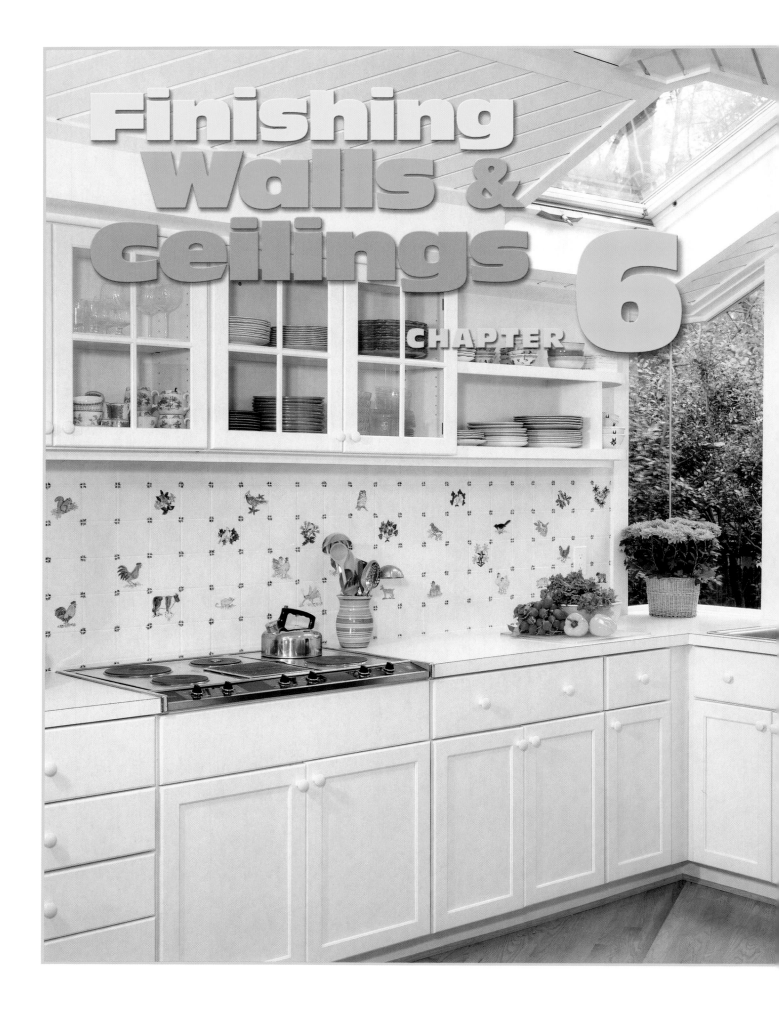

Finishing Walls & Ceilings

CHAPTER 6

Now that you've done all the preliminary construction work for your kitchen, it's time to turn your attention to the bare walls and ceilings. This is a rewarding phase of the project because you finally get to see how the paint colors and wallpaper patterns you've selected actually look on your walls and ceilings. But before you get started painting and papering, you must first repair any damage to the surfaces and make them as smooth as possible. The old saying is true: A good paint or wallcovering job depends on good prep work.

This chapter starts with the basics of repairing drywall, plaster, and wood surfaces and then takes you through painting and hanging wallcoverings. Once you have finished the walls and ceilings, you can begin to install the light fixtures you've selected for your new kitchen.

Preparing to Paint

Before you can start painting, you must make sure the walls and ceiling are free from blemishes and irregularities. Paint is an economical finish that is easy to apply, but you must take care to prepare the surface properly in order to achieve attractive, long-lasting results.

Scrape peeling paint from previously painted surfaces. **1** If you paint over a damaged section, the new paint will soon flake off of the wall. Scraping often leads to tearing the face paper on the drywall

Fixing Small Holes

Once a hole goes all the way through the drywall panel and is larger than ½ to ¾ inch in diameter, it won't hold the patching material you apply. To solve the problem, apply fiberglass mesh tape over the hole. The tape will keep the joint compound from falling into the hole.

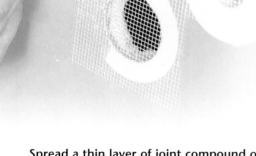

Spread a thin layer of joint compound over damaged area. Wait for it to dry completely before applying a second coat. You may need to spread on additional coats to completely repair the damage. As you work, feather the patch onto the surrounding drywall. Sand to a smooth finish, and apply a coat of primer.

panels. Repair torn drywall paper by cutting out the damaged portion with a utility knife. **2** Fill the depression with drywall joint compound. **3**

Wallcoverings that are torn or coming loose from the wall must be removed before painting. You will be able to peel strippable wallcoverings right off the wall, but others may require some elbow grease. Begin by misting walls with water, waiting a few minutes and then scraping. Another option is to spray or brush on a commercial wallpaper remover. You can buy an inexpensive wallpaper scoring tool that allows the wallpaper remover to penetrate the paper and dissolve the adhesive.

Wash the walls with trisodium phosphate (TSP) and water. If stains or marks remain after washing, apply a primer designed to hide stains. To remove any adhesive that clings after stripping off old wall-coverings, brush on a commercial wallpaper remover diluted with water according to the instructions.

Repairing Damaged Areas

Repair damaged areas by filling with joint compound. For deep depressions, apply several thin coats of compound rather than one thick coat. Allow each coat to dry, and then sand with 150-grit sandpaper, a sanding block, or a palm sander. **4** For larger holes, cover damaged area with fiberglass mesh and then apply joint compound. For holes larger than about 2 inches across, cut out the damage and replace with a drywall patch. Once a repair dries, prime the area with a latex primer. **5**

Preparing New Drywall

Finish new drywall by taping all joints and sanding the surface completely smooth. (See "Finishing Drywall," page 124.) Go over the surface, looking for popped nails, dents, and cracks in the drywall. Fix popped nails by driving a drywall screw 1 or 2 inches above and below the nail. Remove the popped nail, and cover the new screws with joint compound.

Run your hand along all of the taped seams. The surface of the wall should feel smooth and even. Use a sanding block or sponge to smooth out any ridges or bumps where the joint compound meets the surface of the wall.

A careless taping job often leaves small dents in the joint compound, especially in corners. Repair these with additional compound, let dry, and sand the surface even with the rest of the wall.

Prepping Drywall for Painting

Difficulty Level:

Tools & Materials: ❖ Masking tape ❖ Putty knives ❖ Basic carpentry tools ❖ Utility knife ❖ Drywall patching compound ❖ Fiberglass joint tape ❖ Sandpaper or sanding sponge ❖ Power palm sander (optional) ❖ Trisodium phosphate ❖ White shellac

1 Scrape off any cracked or flaking paint. Flaking paint is often a sign of water damage. Fix whatever is causing the damage before repainting.

2 Scraping often leads to torn face paper on the drywall. Pull the damaged section back to a sound surface, and then remove it with a utility knife.

3 Torn drywall, small dents, and cracks can be repaired with joint compound. Apply several thin coats rather than one thick application.

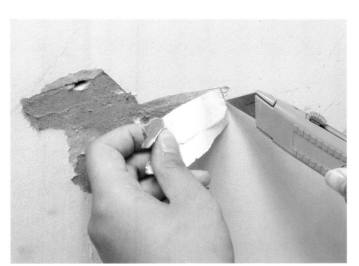

4 Once the joint compound has dried, use 150-grit sandpaper on the patches. Sand until the patch is smooth and even with the drywall surface.

5 Spot-prime all filled areas and unpainted surfaces. For stubborn stains, including watermarks, prime with white-pigmented shellac.

Preparing Old Plaster

Traditional plaster finishes aren't applied in many homes anymore, but they do still exist in older houses. If you have plaster walls in your home, take a hard look at their overall condition. If there are too many defects, such as numerous loose and crumbling areas or extensive cracks, you may be better off applying new drywall over the top or ripping the old plaster off and applying a new finish. (See "Gutting a Wall or Ceiling," page 114.) But if the plaster is in relatively good condition, there is no reason to rip it out and start over. Fix the minor problems, and get years of additional service from the finish.

Repair hairline cracks by enlarging the opening with a pointed tool such as a utility knife or can opener. Use the tool to undercut the sides of the crack, creating a small niche so that the new patching plaster will be held firmly in place once dry. Before patching, though, clean the joint with a dampened brush and let it dry. Apply the patching plaster, let it dry, and sand it smooth.

For larger cracks, clean the joint as above and fill it with patching plaster. **1** Then apply fiberglass mesh joint tape over the crack. **2** Apply the tape in short sections if the crack zigzags up the surface of the wall. Use a drywall taping knife to cover the damaged area with a thin layer of patching plaster. **3** Sand the dried plaster smooth, recoat, and sand it again. Spot-prime all filled spots.

Prepping Plaster for Painting

Difficulty Level:

Tools & Materials: ❖ Utility knife or can opener ❖ 6-inch and 12-inch drywall knives ❖ Patching plaster ❖ Fiberglass mesh drywall tape

1 After widening and undercutting the crack with a sharp tool, fill it with patching plaster. Once the patch is dry, sand it smooth.

2 Fill deep cracks with patching plaster and let it dry. Apply fiberglass mesh tape over the crack. Work with short sections of tape to keep it from bunching up.

3 Apply two or three coats of patching plaster to cover the tape. Feather the edges between each coat to blend the repair with the rest of the wall.

Preparing Woodwork

How you prepare woodwork and trim depends on its current condition and what you want to end up with. You can repaint previously painted woodwork after repairing surface defects. But if you want a natural finish, you need to start with raw wood or strip off any previous finish.

Set exposed nailheads by sinking them below the surface with a nail set. Fill the holes and cracks with a wood filler, and sand them smooth. If the wood is to be painted or repainted, use a premixed wood filler. **1** For natural-finish woodwork, you will want the filled spots to match the color of the wood when finished. Doing this is more art than science, and may take a few tries. Select the premixed wood-

filler color closest to that of the species of wood, and practice on a scrap piece of molding. When the filler is dry, apply the natural finish and evaluate the color. Try a darker or lighter filler as necessary to get a close match.

Professional painters know that a gap between woodwork and the wall can ruin any paint job. Avoid the problem by caulking any gaps you can find. **2** The caulk will not be exposed to the elements, so you can use an inexpensive latex caulk. Latex is easy to work with, cleans up easily with soap and water, and is paintable. Prime the woodwork with the appropriate primer. **3** Use a latex primer on clear wood but pigmented shellac on any knots to hide and seal them.

Prepping Woodwork for Painting

Difficulty Level:

Tools & Materials: ❖ Hammer and nail set
❖ Putty knife ❖ Wood filler ❖ Caulk and caulking gun
❖ Primer ❖ Narrow paint brush

1 Set nailheads below the surface of the wood with a hammer and nail set. Fill the holes with the appropriate wood filler.

2 Caulk the joints between the wood trim and walls with a flexible latex caulk. Smooth the caulk with a wet finger.

3 Prime woodwork with the appropriate first coat for a natural or paint finish. Use pigmented shellac on wood knots before painting.

Painting Walls & Ceilings

Choose high-quality latex or acrylic paints. The better the paint, the easier the application and the more durable the finish. Gloss and semigloss paints resist moisture and are easier to clean than more porous flat or eggshell paints. That is a big concern because kitchens generate large quantities of moisture and grease. Some manufacturers offer kitchen paints that contain mold and mildew inhibitors.

To get the best finish on new surfaces, apply one coat of primer and two coats of semigloss enamel. Most paint covers about 400 square feet per gallon, so estimate the amount you will need by first determining the square footage of walls and ceilings and multiplying by the number of coats. Protect fixtures and floor surfaces with dropcloths. The usual sequence is to do the large surfaces first and wood trim later. But if all surfaces are to be painted with the same color paint, begin with the brushwork and then cover the large surfaces with a roller.

Painting Woodwork

To get a clean job, remove any knobs from doors and cabinets before painting. Unless you need to paint large surfaces, use a small sash brush (1½ to 2 inches wide) to paint all wood. Paint the edges of doors first, ending with the larger surfaces. Use a paint shield to protect the floor while painting baseboards.

When painting a window sash, allow the paint to cover about ¹⁄₁₆ inch of glass to help seal the juncture between the glazing and the wood. Don't worry if too much paint slops over onto the glass. Go back after the paint dries, and scrape any spills off the glass with a razor blade. You can't remove paint quite so easily from tile, so if you are not confident of cutting a clean edge on wood trim next to tile, protect the tile with painter's tape.

Painting Sequence

It's tempting to try to paint around switch plates and fixture trim strips, but removing these items is usually easy, and you'll get a much better job for your efforts. When you remove the cover plates, place the screws back into the holes they came from or tape the screws to the outlet cover so that you won't lose them. **1**

Use a sash brush to cut-in around the ceiling perimeter and fixture openings. Overlap the joint where the ceiling meets the wall. **2** Use a roller to finish off the large surface (field) of the ceiling. **3** Begin at one wall, and work across the ceiling to the opposite wall. Try to start at a wall that contains a window. That way the light will shine on the

Painting Walls and Ceilings

Difficulty Level:

Tools & Materials: ❖ Screwdriver ❖ 1½- or 2-inch sash brush ❖ Roller pan ❖ Roller with ¼-inch nap cover ❖ Paint shield ❖ Masking tape (if necessary) ❖ Razor blade ❖ Dropcloths ❖ Roller handle extension (optional) ❖ Wall and ceiling paint

3 Begin rolling the ceiling at one wall, and work across to the opposite wall. Wear safety goggles, and work with a light source in front of you.

painted areas as you work back from the window, allowing you to catch missed areas before the paint dries. Use an extension handle on the roller so that you can reach the ceiling from the floor. After dipping the roller in the pan, roll paint onto the surface in a zigzag pattern about two roller-widths wide and 36 inches long. Finish off by rolling the spots between with smooth, straight strokes.

On walls, paint the corners and edges around open wall surfaces with a sash brush. If the wall color differs from the ceiling, let the ceiling dry completely, then cut in at the wall-ceiling joint. **4** Use a roller to paint the wall field. Start at one corner, and work across the wall, applying the paint to rectangular sections as described above. **5**

Sorting Out Wood Finishes

Wood/Finish	Undercoat
Bare wood, penetrating oil	Penetrating oil; one or more coats
Bare wood, clear finish	Stain (if desired); two coats clear surface finish
Bare wood, paint finish	Latex wood primer or white shellac
Painted wood, paint finish	Spot-prime filled areas with latex wood primer or white shellac

1 For a neater job, remove all cover plates and trim strips before painting. Shut off electrical power before painting around electrical boxes.

2 Begin by trimming the ceiling-wall joint with a sash brush. Don't worry about overlapping the wall—it's easier to cut a finish trim line on the wall than the ceiling.

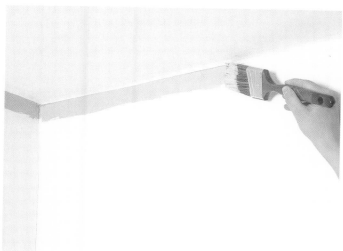

4 If the ceiling is a different color than the wall, cut the trim line on the wall with a sash brush, working the paint up against the ceiling line as shown.

5 Use a roller for large areas. Paint each section in a zigzag pattern; then finish off with straight, parallel strokes until all spots are covered equally.

Wallcovering Basics

Wallcovering includes a wide range of products, from traditional paper to treated fabrics and fabric-backed vinyl, paper-backed grass cloths, and even more exotic variations.

Several factors go into the choice of a wallcovering. For kitchens, look for a covering that withstands scuffs and cleans easily, such as solid vinyl, though vinyl-coated paper might be suitable for an eating area.

Preparing for a Project

Most wallcoverings now come prepasted, but some types still must be pasted strip by strip as they go up. If you have a choice, choose the prepasted paper. Installation is easier, and there is less of a chance of problems developing. Both types must be applied to a clean, smooth surface. Cover unfinished drywall with a wallcovering primer/sealer. If your kitchen's walls are already papered and the covering is still sound, you can probably scuff the surface with sandpaper to promote adhesion and apply a new wallcovering right over it. Check this with your wallcovering dealer before making a decision. It's frequently necessary to apply a wallcovering primer/sealer or to strip an old covering completely.

Planning the Job

Wallcovering is sold in rolls of various widths. Because patterned coverings must be matched side to side along the edges of the strips, there may be a fair amount of waste in trimming to keep the pattern repeating properly. To estimate material needs, determine the number of square feet in the area to be covered (less openings like windows, doors, and any wall space taken up by cabinets), then divide by 30—a number derived by subtracting the likely wastage from the standard 36 square feet in a roll. Round up to the nearest whole number for ordering standard rolls. If you're buying other than standard 36-square-foot rolls, consult your dealer about how many you need.

The repeating pattern in wallcovering also requires careful planning of where the covering job should start and end. Theoretically, you can start the first strip anywhere as long as the pattern lines up as you apply each strip. But it is often best to begin in an inconspicuous corner, say behind a door. That way any mismatch that comes when you try to

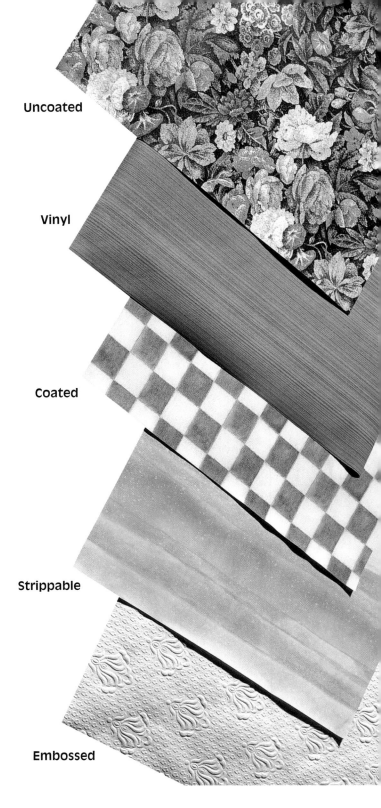

Uncoated

Vinyl

Coated

Strippable

Embossed

align the pattern from the last sheet with the one from the first strip will be less noticeable.

Cutting Wallcovering

Because wallcovering comes in rolls, it must always be cut to fit the height of the wall. Also, because full widths don't always fit exactly across a wall, wallcovering often has to be cut narrower along its length. Always use sharp cutting tools. To cut a piece of wallcovering to length, add about 2 inches to the wall height to allow for overlap at the top and bottom. The extra length lets you adjust a sheet up or down to match the pattern properly. You will trim it to fit exactly once it is on the wall.

Long cuts on wallcovering should be marked at both ends, measuring from the edge that will meet the piece already on the wall. Long cuts are usually made to fit the covering into corners. Measure at the top and bottom of the wall because corners are rarely plumb.

Applying Wallpaper Paste

Most residential wallcoverings come prepasted, but in some cases it will be necessary to paste the paper yourself. Wallpaper paste is available in liquid form and as a powder that you mix with water. **1**

To apply the paste, work on one-half of the sheet at a time. Place the sheet on the table flush with a long edge of the table. Work from about the middle of the sheet toward the side that is flush with the edge of the table. **2** Push the sheet across the table so that the unpasted half is now flush with the other edge of the table. Apply the paste. This helps keep the table clean. Any paste that ends up on the table will find its way to the surface of the wallcovering and need to be removed later. Fold the pasted section over on itself, a process called booking. **3** Apply the paste to the other half of the sheet in the same manner.

Pasting Wallcovering

Difficulty Level: 🐟🐟🐟 to 🐟🐟🐟

Tools & Materials: ❖ Pasting brush ❖ Clean, flat work table ❖ Wallpaper paste

1 To mix your own paste, work the powder into the water until it has a smooth, viscous consistency. Paste is also available premixed.

2 Spread paste with a pasting brush. To keep paste off of the table, align the strip with the table's edge and work from the middle toward the edge.

3 Fold the pasted section of the strip over on itself— a process called booking—and paste the remaining section as described previously.

Hanging Wallcovering

Measure out from the corner the width of a sheet. One method is to use a sample strip of paper to determine where to draw the starting line. **1** Another good method, especially for corners that are not square, is to measure out from the corner the width of one sheet at the top, bottom, and middle of the wall. Subtract ½ inch from the mark closest to the corner, and draw a plumb line there using a plumb bob or level. **2**

Following the manufacturer's directions, dunk the paper in the water trough and book it. **3** Some professionals feel that using the water trough is messy and that parts of the paper remain dry, failing to activate the glue in those areas. An alternative is to lay the paper on a worktable and apply water using a sponge. Then book the sheet by folding the paper onto itself. **4** This helps the glue in the paper set up for installation.

Unbook the paper against the ceiling, leaving about 2 inches of overlap, and shift it into position along the vertical guideline. **5–6** This first piece must be placed precisely. Pull the strip free, and adjust it if necessary.

Once the strip is in position and laid reasonably flat, use a wallpaper brush to smooth out any wrinkles. **7** Brush from the middle of the sheet toward the edges. Use the brush to tuck the covering into corners and along the ceiling and baseboard. Finish the installation of the sheet by wiping it with a damp sponge.

Hanging Wallcoverings

Difficulty Level:

Tools & Materials: ❖ 48-inch level or chalk-line box with plumb bob ❖ Measuring tape ❖ Pencil ❖ Long straightedge ❖ Scissors ❖ Utility knife with extra blades ❖ 6-inch taping knife ❖ Smoothing brush ❖ Sponge ❖ Seam roller ❖ Seam adhesive ❖ Prepasted wallpaper ❖ Wallpaper trough and water

1 Use a sample strip with a folded edge for corner overlap to determine where to draw the starting line or measure the width of a sheet minus ½ in.

4 Fold the soaked or pasted paper onto itself—a process called booking—to make it easy to carry and place the strips.

5 After the paper sets up according to the manufacturer's directions, unbook and position it on the wall. The paper should turn the corner slightly.

Vinyl wallcoverings make a good choice for kitchen walls. There are numerous colors and patterns from which to choose, and the paper itself is easy to keep clean. Consider a complementary border treatment.

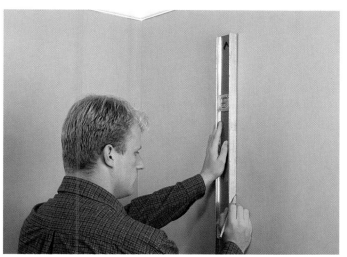

2 Use a level or chalk-line box with a plumb bob to mark where the first seam will fall. Plan the complete layout before cutting and pasting paper.

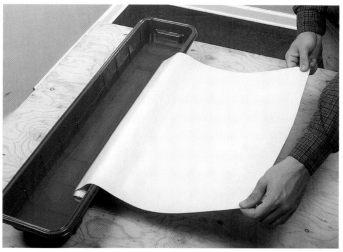

3 Dunk prepasted wallpaper in a pan of lukewarm water. Apply adhesive to unpasted paper with a pasting brush. (See "Pasting Wallcovering," page 159.)

6 Align the strip with the plumb line. There should be excess material at the baseboard and the ceiling that will be trimmed later.

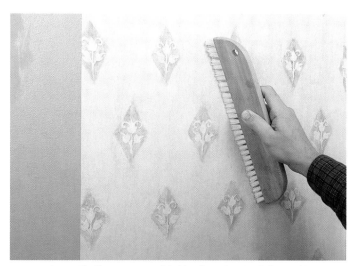

7 Smooth the paper with the brush. Work from the center of the paper toward the edges to remove air bubbles.

Continued on next page

8 Trim the sheet by firmly pressing a wide taping knife into the corner to form a crease. Then cut along the knife using a sharp utility knife or razor trimmer.

9 The glue won't set up immediately so you can raise the seams to make small adjustments, shifting the panel slightly to match the pattern.

10 On overlapped panels, use a sharp razor knife to cut through both strips at once, creating a perfect match.

11 Finish edges with a wallpaper roller. Use a dampened sponge to wipe away excess adhesive that squeezes from the seam.

When you've hung and brushed out the wall-covering strip, trim it with a razor trimmer. Hold a 6-inch or larger taping knife where the wallpaper meets the ceiling, floor, or corner to act as a guide for the razor trimmer. **8**

At windows, hang a sheet over the window around which the covering must be cut. Notch the corners back to the edge of the window casing, and then trim the covering as described above.

Position a second strip along the edge of the first so that the pattern lines up and the edges of the sheets are butted together tightly—not overlapped or pulled apart—with a slight ridge at the junction. (This will flatten out when the wallcovering dries.) Wallpaper glue is somewhat forgiving, so if you find

that a sheet isn't quite straight, peel it from the wall and align as necessary. **9** If sheets do overlap, use a sharp razor knife to cut through both strips at once to create a perfect match. **10**

After the paste has started to dry and the edges have shrunk back to the wall, use a seam roller to flatten the seam and press the edges of the wallcovering sheets firmly into the paste. Roll once up and down. **11** Don't roll over the seam repeatedly. You could create an indentation or a shiny track on the wallcovering.

Go over the surface of the wall once again with the slightly dampened sponge. A small amount of wallpaper paste may appear along the seams. Clean the seams with the sponge.

Turning Inside Corners

When you come to a corner, measure from the edge of the last full sheet into the corner at the top, middle, and bottom of the wall. **1** Add ⅛ inch to the largest of these measurements, transfer it to a sheet, and cut the wallcovering lengthwise. Hang the sheet against the edge of the previous sheet, letting the other edge turn the corner. Brush the sheet out, and tuck it into the corner. **2**

Measure the width of the remaining section of the cut strip. Transfer this measurement to the uncovered wall at the corner by drawing a line that's absolutely plumb. Hang the second, remainder strip against the plumb line, and brush the wallcovering. **3** Use the brush to smooth the edge that meets the corner. Run a bead of wallcovering seam adhesive along the corner to be sure you secure any overlap that occurs.

SMART TIP

For wrapping outside corners, follow the same procedure you used for inside corners, but add ½ inch to the measurement. Place the paper in position, but before wrapping it around the corner, make small slits in the waste portions of the paper near the ceiling and the baseboard. The cuts will allow you to turn the corner without wrinkling or tearing the paper. Hang the remainder of the cut sheet so that it overlaps the first portion.

Dealing with Corners

Difficulty Level: 🔧🔧

Tools & Materials: ❖ 48-inch level or plumb bob ❖ Measuring tape ❖ Pencil ❖ Long straightedge ❖ Scissors ❖ Utility knife with extra blades ❖ 6-inch taping knife ❖ Smoothing brush ❖ Sponge ❖ Seam roller ❖ Seam adhesive

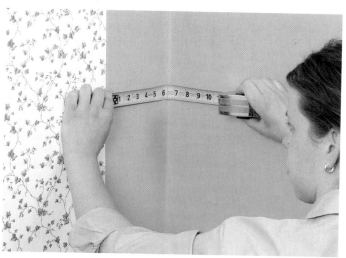

1 Measure from the edge of the last full sheet into the corner at the top, middle, and bottom. Cut the sheet ⅛ in. wider than the largest measurement.

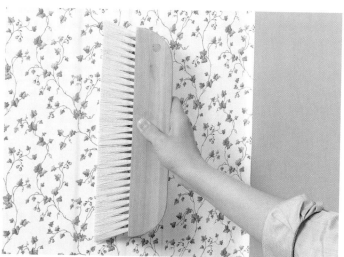

2 Install the cut section, and smooth it into place with a wallpaper brush. The piece should turn the corner slightly.

3 Draw a plumb line a distance from the corner equal to the width of the remainder of the strip. Install the wallpaper.

Wallcovering Options

Wallcoverings enhance any room but work particularly well when used with simple cabinet designs and neutral finishes.

DESIGN IDEAS

See "Wall Treatments," page 37

See "Color Basics," page 78

Bright colors provide a rich background when paired with white or neutral cabinets and appliances.

Paper or paint? The pattern in the wallcovering complements the French country style of this kitchen (left). A painted finish is better suited for the casual feeling of this homey kitchen (above).

The formal feeling of this breakfast area is reflected in the wallcovering pattern and the floral border.

Light Fixtures

No matter what their size, kitchens need a variety of lighting fixtures. For example, even a small kitchen may have a ceiling fixture to provide general, ambient light to the room, and a series of fixtures with fluorescent bulbs mounted to the underside of wall cabinets to provide task lighting for anyone working at the counter. Deciding on the types and locations of light fixtures should be part of the design phase of your remodeling.

Types of Bulbs

Kitchen light fixtures use incandescent, fluorescent, or halogen bulbs. The bulbs, or lamps, come in a variety of shapes and sizes to meet your lighting needs.

Incandescent Bulbs. The old-fashioned incandescent light bulb hasn't changed much in the last century, yet remains the most popular bulb among homeowners. However, these bulbs waste enormous amounts of energy when compared with other types available. To cut energy costs, replace incandescent bulbs with the newer compact fluorescent bulbs.

Fluorescent Bulbs. Fluorescent bulbs use far less energy than incandescent lights. But choose carefully. Many fluorescent bulbs distort colors. Seek the advice of a lighting expert when buying fluorescent fixtures for the kitchen.

Halogen Bulbs. Halogens are a special kind of incandescent bulb. Halogen bulbs produce more light and use less energy than the standard incandescent bulb, but they require special fixtures.

Ceiling-Mounted Light Fixtures

These fixtures are attached to a ceiling box. If you are simply replacing an existing fixture, turn off the power, remove the old fixture, and install the new light, making the connections as described below.

When installing a new box you may need to attach it to the ceiling joist to support the weight of the fixture. You will also need to bring a power supply cable to the fixture and wire in a switch. You can run the power cable through the switch and into the fixture (in-line wiring) or run the cable to the fixture first, then to the switch (switch loop).

Mounting a new light is fairly straightforward. After turning off the power, use a neon circuit tester to confirm that the power to the circuit is off. Pull the cable from the switch into the fixture's electrical box, secure it in place, rip the cable sheathing, and strip the wires in the cable. **1** If the box does not have a built-in hanger stud, attach a mounting strap to the box tabs. **2** Screw a threaded nipple into the collar of the crossbar to support the weight of the light fixture. Make certain that it will extend through the suspended fixture to engage the mounting nut. **3**

Using wire connectors, splice the hot black wire from the switch to the hot black lead wire from the fixture. Next, connect the neutral white wire coming into the box to the neutral white wire from the fixture. Then splice together the grounding wires, and pigtail them to the green terminal screw in the electrical box or on the mounting strap. **4** Push the completed wiring neatly into the box, and install the fixture cover over the threaded nipple. Lastly, tighten the mounting nut. **5**

Cut-in Boxes

Cut-in or old-work boxes are designed for installation in a finished wall or ceiling. Although you will still need to fish cable to the box, installing the box does not damage the finished surface. To install, cut an opening with a keyhole saw, pull the cable into the box, and then insert the box.

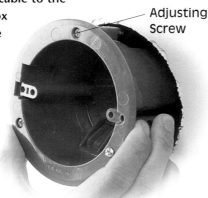

Adjusting Screw

Tighten the adjusting screws to set the wings against the back of the finished wall. Usually these boxes will not support fixtures that weigh more than 15 pounds, but check the manufacturer's literature.

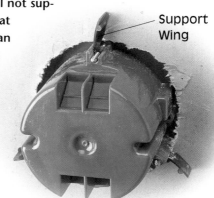

Support Wing

Installing a Ceiling-Mounted Fixture

Difficulty Level:

Tools & Materials: ❖ Insulated screwdriver ❖ Electrical box ❖ Knockout punch ❖ Cable ripper ❖ Needle-nose pliers ❖ Wire stripper ❖ Cable clamps ❖ Wire connectors ❖ Light fixture ❖ Threaded nipple ❖ Mounting strap

1 After making sure the power is off, pull the cable into the box; cut away the cable insulation; and strip the individual wires.

2 If the fixture box does not have a hanger to hold the light fixture, attach a metal mounting strap to the ceiling box.

3 Screw a threaded nipple into the collar of the support. A retaining nut will hold the fixture to the threaded nipple.

4 You may need a helper to hold the fixture near the ceiling as you connect the wiring. Pigtail the grounding wires to the terminal screw.

5 Place the fixture cover over the nipple, and tighten the retaining nut. Install bulbs recommended for your fixture.

Recessed Ceiling Lights

Recessed lights are characteristically used where spot lighting is needed and/or low-hanging fixtures are not desirable. In kitchens they are most often used to illuminate a work area or are used with other fixtures to provide ambient light to the room. It often makes sense to have one switch control a series of recessed lights.

Some recessed systems must be installed before the ceiling is closed or from above if you can gain access to the space, such as an attic over a kitchen. If that is not possible, buy lights that you can install from below through a finished ceiling. Whichever type you select, be prepared to run cable between the fixture and the switch and from the power source to the fixture or the switch.

Installing the Fixture

Once you have determined where in the attic you will mount the light fixture housing, pull out the extension bars on the housing to reach the adjoining ceiling joist. **1** Make final adjustments to the housing position by sliding the fixture along the bars. Be sure that the face of the unit extends below the framing so that it will be flush with the finished ceiling. Then using nails or screws, fasten the extension bars to the joists.

Recessed fixtures come with their own prewired box. Take the cover off the electrical box, and use a screwdriver to remove a knockout for the switch-leg cable. **2** Pull the cable into the box, and secure it in place using a cable clamp. Leave about 10 inches of cable extending from the box. Rip the cable sheathing to within ¼ inch of the cable clamp, and remove the ripped-back sheathing. Then using a multipurpose tool, strip the wires in the cable and cut away excess wire. Repeat this procedure for each cable entering the box. **3**

Wiring the Box

Using wire connectors, splice the white switch-leg wire to the white wire from the fixture. Next, connect the black switch-leg wire to the black wire from the fixture. Pigtail the grounding wires from the switch-leg and fixture cables to the green grounding screw in the electrical box. **4** Attach the box cover. **5**

Replace any insulation you disturbed in accordance with the type of fixture you are installing. When the ceiling is finished and painted, install a light bulb with the recommended wattage into the fixture socket. Attach the decorative housing cover.

SMART TIP

Rather than moving insulation to drill through joists when running cable in an unfinished attic space, place two 1×4 guard boards over the joists and run the cable between them. Staple the cable to the top of each joist.

Installing Recessed Light Fixtures

Difficulty Level: 🪶🪶🪶

Tools & Materials: ❖ Insulated screwdrivers ❖ Nails or screws ❖ Hammer (if necessary) ❖ Power drill-driver ❖ Cable ripper ❖ Needle-nose pliers ❖ Multipurpose tool ❖ Cable clamps ❖ Recessed lamp housing ❖ Wire connectors

3 Pull the power cable coming from the switch into the junction box; clamp it securely in place, and strip the sheathing from the wires.

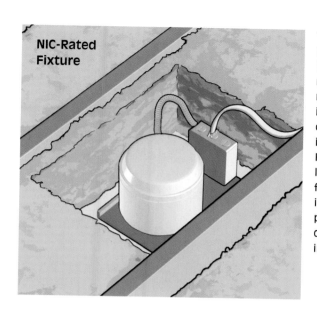

NIC-Rated Fixture

Types of Recessed Lights. Recessed light housings are rated for either non-insulated ceilings (NIC), at left, or insulated ceilings (IC), at right. Keep insulation at least 3 in. away from any NIC housing. IC housings are permitted to be in direct contact with insulation.

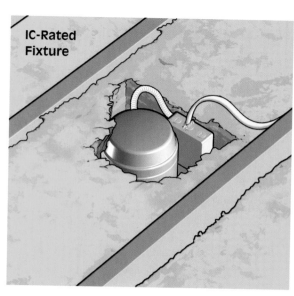

IC-Rated Fixture

1 Position the lamp between two joists, adjusting the extension bars as necessary. Attach the bracket with screws.

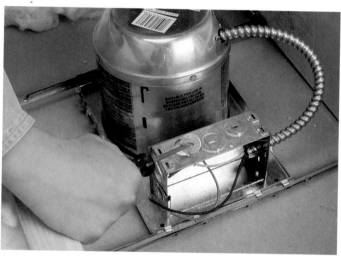

2 Use the screwdriver to remove the cover to the box and one of the knockouts to accommodate the power cable.

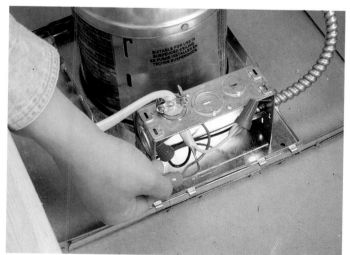

4 Connect like-colored wires from the switch-leg cable to the wires in the fixture (black to black and white to white) using wire connectors.

5 Pigtail the grounding wires to the green grounding screw mounted in the electrical box. Reattach the cover to the box.

The soft glow near the ceiling is not only decorative, it also helps to separate the eating area from the rest of the kitchen.

Fixtures should match the style of the room. Hanging fixtures (above) are a good choice for tables and breakfast nooks. Pendant lights (right) provide task lighting.

DESIGN IDEAS

See "Lighting," page 40

See "Developing a Style," page 74

Task lighting makes kitchen work areas more efficient. The track lighting system at left illuminates all of the counter space. The decorative fixture below lights this snack counter.

Track Lighting

If you're fortunate enough to have a switch-controlled ceiling box in the right place, installing track lighting isn't much more difficult than changing a single fixture. You simply start at the existing box and run the track from it.

Turn off power to the electrical box where the track lighting will be connected. Use a neon circuit tester to verify that the power is off, and disconnect the existing fixture. Measure and draw guidelines out from the ceiling box to center the new track lighting. **1** Then wire the track lighting power connector to the electrical box. **2** Using wire connectors, splice the neutral white wire from the cable to the neutral white fixture wire and the hot black switch wire to the hot black fixture wire. Next, splice together the grounding wires, and pigtail them to the green terminal screw in the electrical box, if the box is metal. (Some nonmetallic boxes are provided with a grounding plate and green terminal screws.)

Fasten the power connector plate to the electrical box, and screw or bolt the first section of lighting track temporarily into place. **3** Insert the power connector into the first section of track. Twist-lock the connector in place, and attach the power box cover. Install additional lengths of track to the first section, using T-connectors and L-connectors, if needed. **4** Cover all connections using connector covers. Mark the positions for screws or toggle bolts on the ceiling. Then take down the temporary track sections, and drill pilot holes as needed. Install the track, and tighten all fasteners. Set the lighting fixtures into the track; slide them into place; and lock them in position. **5**

Track fixtures can be used for general lighting or to provide task lighting to specific areas.

Installing Track Lights

Difficulty Level:  to

Tools & Materials: ❖ Track lighting kit ❖ Insulated screwdrivers ❖ Basic electrical tools ❖ Pencil ❖ Straightedge ❖ Drywall fasteners or screws ❖ Power drill-driver

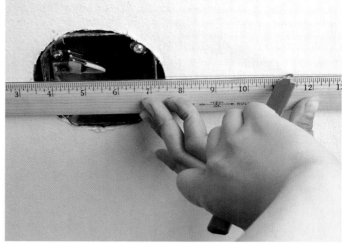

1 Turn off the power at the service panel, and remove the old fixture. Draw guidelines for the precise placement of the track lighting.

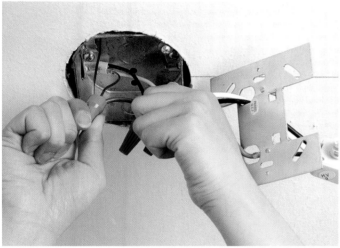

2 Splice the wires from the power connector to the like-colored wires coming from the ceiling-mounted electrical box.

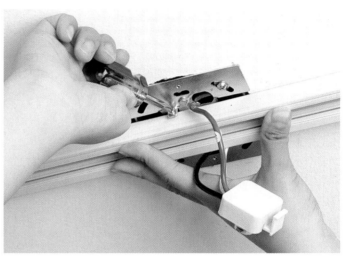

3 Fasten the power-connector plate to the electrical box; then temporarily attach the first section of track to the ceiling.

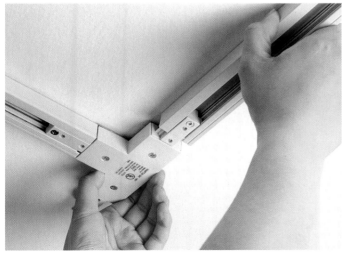

4 Lock the connector to the track, and install additional sections of track as needed, using the appropriate connectors.

5 When the layout is complete, attach the track permanently, slide the lighting fixtures into the track, and lock them into the desired position.

Under-Cabinet Lighting

Installing fluorescent or halogen fixtures on the bottom of wall cabinets is a great way to provide task lighting for the countertop. The fixtures are also a good choice if the walls are already finished because you can install the switch and fixture with a minimal amount of damage to the wall. Place the fixture toward the front of the cabinet so that its light illuminates as much of the counter as possible.

Cut out an opening for the switch box in the wall above the counter, and drill a hole for the cable in the rear of the cabinet frame. Bring the power leg of the cable into the box. Fish the section of cable that will connect the switch with the fixture between the new opening and the hole you drilled. **1** Screw the fixture to the underside of the cabinet, and make the necessary connections at the fixture. **2** In the project below, the light fixture is at the end of the circuit run. To wire the switch, attach the power leg black wire to the power terminal on the switch. Then connect the black wire from the fixture to the other terminal. Splice together the white wires from the power cable and the cable running to the fixture. Splice together the green or copper grounding wires, and pigtail them to the green grounding screw on the switch. **3** Push the wires into the box; screw the switch into the box; and test your work.

Installing Under-Cabinet Lighting

Difficulty Level: 🔧🔧

Tools & Materials: ❖ Drywall saw ❖ Needle-nose pliers ❖ Cable ripper ❖ Wire stripper ❖ Wire connectors ❖ Insulated screwdrivers ❖ Cable ❖ Fixture ❖ Single-pole switch

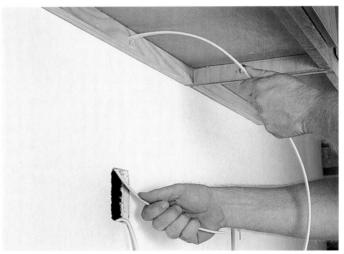

1 Fish the power leg of the cable into the new opening. Run a new section of cable through the hole in the cabinet to the wall opening.

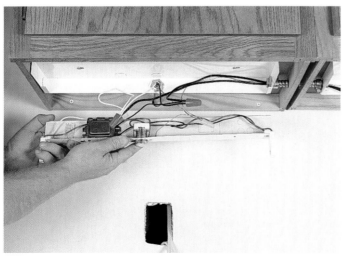

2 Attach the fixture base to the cabinet. Splice together the like-colored wires from the switch-leg cable to the fixture wiring.

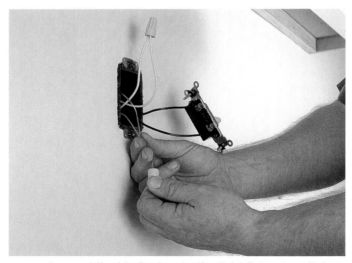

3 Connect the black wires to the light fixture's switch. Splice together the white wires, and pigtail the grounding wires.

Hanging Fixtures

Hanging fixtures, such as chandeliers and pendant lights, provide light to a specific area, such as the work surface of an island or a dining table. Install a ceiling box to support a hanging fixture. Most fixtures are too heavy for cut-in boxes and must be supported by a box that is attached to the ceiling framing. You can also replace an existing ceiling-mounted fixture with a new hanging light.

Turn off the power to the circuit, and unscrew the fixture housing from the ceiling. Support the old fixture or have a helper hold it as you disconnect the wiring. Screw a short threaded stud into the center knockout at the top of the box to support a hickey (a threaded fitting). Inside the box, screw a hickey onto the stud. Then screw a threaded nipple into the hole at the bottom of the hickey. Secure the hickey and threaded nipple using a locknut. **1**

Wiring the Fixture

Pull the fixture's wires through the nipple and into the box. Splice the black wire from the chandelier to the black wire from the box. Do the same with the white wires. Pigtail the grounding wires to the green grounding screw in the box. **2** Tuck the wiring into the box; screw the fixture support to the nipple; and slide the escutcheon plate up to the ceiling box. Attach the fixture's collar nut to the nipple protruding from the escutcheon. **3**

Installing a Chandelier

Difficulty Level: 🔧🔧🔧

Tools & Materials: ❖ Cable ripper ❖ Wire stripper ❖ Stud ❖ Hickey ❖ Threaded nipple ❖ Insulated screwdrivers ❖ Wire connectors • Needle-nose pliers

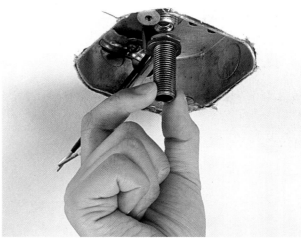

1 Install a stud in the box and then screw a hickey onto the stud and a threaded nipple into the hickey to support the fixture.

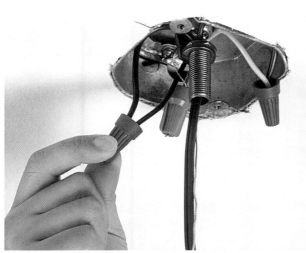

2 Pull the chandelier wires through the nipple and into the box. Connect the fixture wiring to the wires in the box.

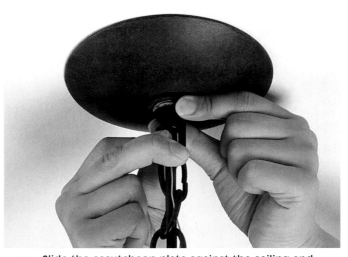

3 Slide the escutcheon plate against the ceiling and screw the collar nut onto the nipple protruding from the plate.

Flooring

In This Chapter

nstalling the finished floor is usually one of the last major construction components of a project. You
will find it easier to protect the floor
if you wait until most of the other
messy work is completed before you
install the finished flooring.

If you already have a wood floor
that you like, you may be able to repair and refinish it to look like new.
If not, it may be necessary to make
repairs to the floor framing, such as
reinforcing damaged joists. It is also
a good idea to check insulation levels
at this point. You may need to insulate the floor or the foundation walls
of an unheated crawl space. At the
very least, you'll have to prepare the
subfloor and install underlayment to
get the floor ready for a new surface.
In addition to wood, common choices
for kitchens include resilient vinyl
tile, vinyl sheet flooring, laminate
flooring, and ceramic tile.

Insulating Crawl Spaces

Kitchens located over crawl spaces or uninsulated basements often feel uncomfortable because the floor may be cold. Solve the problem by adding fiberglass batts between the floor joists or insulating the foundation walls.

Insulating the Floor

Cut sections of unfaced insulation to fit snugly between the floor joists. Keep them in place by stapling sheets of house wrap or polyethylene plastic to keep the material from falling down.

Protect pipes from freezing and ductwork from losing energy by wrapping them in insulation. Buy insulation designed for these jobs, and seal all joints with duct tape. If the ducts also serve the air conditioning system, the insulation will help save energy during the summer as well.

Insulating the Foundation

The most important part of this project is to keep moisture vapor generated in the ground from migrating into the house and the house framing. Spread a 6-mil sheet of polyethylene plastic over the exposed ground in the crawl space. Staple sheets of polyethylene to the sill plate, and let the plastic drape down the wall and overlap the sheet on the ground by about 12 inches. (See the drawing below.) Each sheet of plastic attached to the rim joists should overlap the one next to it by 12 inches.

Measure the distance from the top of the rim joist to the ground, and add 36 inches. Cut insulation to this length. Push the cut batts against the rim joist and between the floor joists. Staple the batts in place with the kraft paper covering facing into the crawl space. The batts should overlap the ground by about 36 inches. Hold them in place with 2×4s. Connect the batts together, creating a good seal, by stapling the seams together every 8 inches.

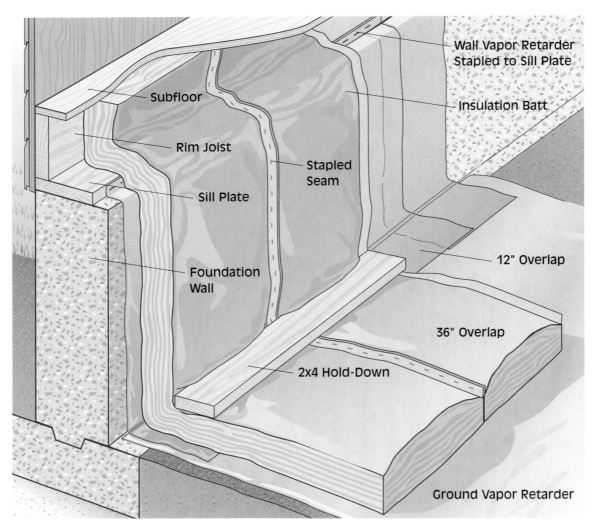

Subfloor
Rim Joist
Sill Plate
Foundation Wall
Stapled Seam
2x4 Hold-Down
Wall Vapor Retarder Stapled to Sill Plate
Insulation Batt
12" Overlap
36" Overlap
Ground Vapor Retarder

Insulating Crawl Spaces. If your kitchen sits above a crawl space, prevent cold feet by making sure there is enough insulation in either the floor or on the surrounding foundation. If you insulate the floor by installing fiberglass batts between the joists, be sure to wrap water pipes and ductwork in the crawl space with insulation. An alternative is to insulate the foundation walls and install a continuous vapor retarder as shown at left.

Reinforcing the Subfloor

If an existing floor feels spongy or excessively flexible when you walk on it—or if it squeaks over a large area—chances are that you will need to reinforce it. If the floor sags noticeably, you will need to level it.

Start by renailing or screwing the subfloor to the floor joists. **1** If you have an older, board-type subfloor, you can shim individual loose boards with shingles. Gently tap shims into the space between the joists and the subfloor to prevent movement. Do not drive the shims too forcefully, or they will cause the boards to rise, resulting in a wavy floor. Then nail or screw the boards to the joists.

Reinforcing Old Floors

Difficulty Level:

Tools & Materials: ❖ Power drill-driver and screwdriver bit ❖ Galvanized screws ❖ 4-ft. level ❖ Lumber to match existing joists ❖ Construction adhesive ❖ Caulking gun

If a large area of the subfloor is weak, the cause could be damaged joists. The best way to assess the damage is to examine the joists from below. Weak or sagging joists are a telltale sign of structural problems that should be corrected. Check joists with a 4-foot level. **2** This procedure will tell you whether a joist has twisted out of position or one is sagging below the others. For difficult problems, solicit the opinions of a contractor or licensed structural engineer.

Repair a minimally damaged joist by adding a sister joist to its side. Install sister joists of the same depth and length as the originals. Put them into place, and fasten them to the sides of existing joists with construction adhesive and 12d (3¼-inch) nails or 3-inch galvanized screws. **3**

1 Check the subfloor before installing underlayment. Remove popped nails, and drive screws through the subfloor into the joists.

2 Locate weak or sagging joists by checking across several with a 4-ft. spirit level. It will rock over the lowest joist and where one dips.

3 Strengthen a weak joist (after propping it up if necessary) by adding a second joist secured with construction adhesive and screws.

7 Flooring

Underlayment

Installing the proper underlayment helps ensure that your new floor covering will lie flat and level and will resist wear for several years. Selecting the right thickness will help you match the new floor level to that of an adjacent floor or at least minimize the difference between the two.

It's important to match the floor covering to a compatible underlayment. (See "Underlayment Options," facing page.) Most flooring materials are compatible with a number of different underlayments. Always avoid particleboard, especially in the kitchen: it swells when wet, causing floor coverings to separate or bubble.

Types of Underlayment

Underlayment-grade plywood made from fir or pine is available in 4 × 8-foot sheets in thicknesses of ¼, ⅜, ½, ⅝, and ¾ inch. Because it can expand when damp, plywood is not as good a choice for ceramic tiles as cement board.

Lauan plywood, a species of mahogany, is often used under resilient flooring. It is available in 4 × 8-foot sheets. The usual thickness for underlayment is ¼ inch.

Cement board is also called tile backer board. It is made of a sand-and-cement matrix reinforced with fiberglass mesh. It is usually available in 3 × 5-foot sheets in a thickness of ½ inch. This is the preferred base for ceramic tile and stone floors in wet areas.

Installing Plywood and Hardboard Underlayment

Difficulty Level:

Tools & Materials: ❖ Basic carpentry tools ❖ 1-inch ring-shank nails or galvanized screws ❖ Wood filler ❖ Circular saw with plywood blade ❖ Underlayment ❖ Power drill-driver

1 Cut the underlayment so that when installed the joints of the underlayment are staggered from one another and offset from the subfloor joints.

2 Leave a gap of about ¹⁄₁₆ in. between the sheets and about ¼ in. between the sheets and the wall. The gap allows the material to expand.

3 Drive screws long enough to reach through the subfloor and about 1 in. into the joists below. Place screws about every 4 in.

If the old flooring is not in good condition, remove it and smooth down the old underlayment before installing the new floor covering. If you can't remove the old floor covering, just apply the new underlayment over it.

Installing Plywood Underlayment

To prevent popping nails, let the underlayment acclimate to the room for a few days before installation. Measure and cut each section of underlayment into lengths that will allow the joints to be staggered. **1** It's also important that the joints of the underlayment do not line up with the joints in the subfloor.

Leave a ⅟₁₆-inch gap between sheets. **2** Attach the underlayment to the subfloor with ring-shank nails or screws. **3** Space fasteners in rows no more than 4 inches apart and ½ inch in from the edges. Fill any holes or imperfections with a plastic-type wood filler. Sand the filler smooth after it sets.

Underlayment Options

Floor Covering	Acceptable Underlayments
Resilient floor coverings	Old vinyl or linoleum flooring in sound condition Underlayment-grade plywood Lauan plywood
Wood parquet flooring	Old vinyl or linoleum floor in sound condition Underlayment-grade plywood Lauan plywood Hardboard
Laminate flooring	Any sound surface
Solid wood flooring	Underlayment-grade plywood
Ceramic tile and stone	Old ceramic tiles, if sound Concrete slab Cement board Underlayment-grade plywood

7 Flooring

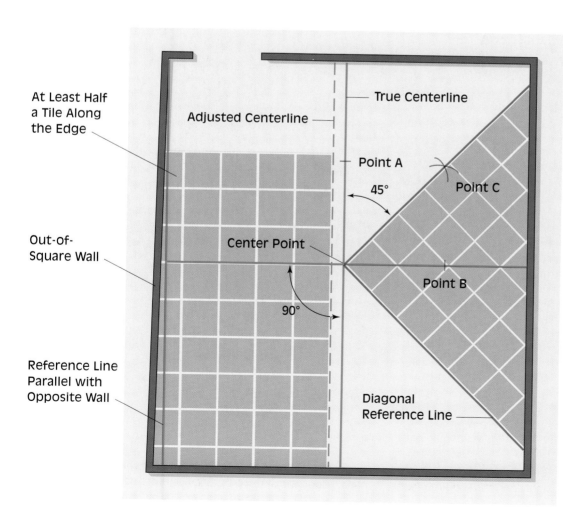

At Least Half a Tile Along the Edge

Adjusted Centerline

True Centerline

Point A

45°

Point C

Out-of-Square Wall

Center Point

Point B

90°

Reference Line Parallel with Opposite Wall

Diagonal Reference Line

Creating Layout Lines.
When installing any type of tile floor, it is best to create layout lines to guide the installation. For a standard layout, snap chalk lines in the middle of opposite walls. To create diagonal layout lines, measure out an equal distance along any two of the original perpendicular lines, and drive a nail at these points, marked **A** and **B** in the drawing. Hook the end of a measuring tape to each of the nails, and hold a pencil against the tape at a distance equal to that between the nails and the center point. Use the tape and pencil as a compass to scribe two sets of arcs on the floor. The arcs will intersect at point **C**.

Snap a diagonal line between the center and point **C**, extending the lines in each direction. Repeat the process for the other corners. Do a dry run, setting the tiles on the diagonal.

Vinyl Floor Tiles

Installing vinyl or resilient floor tiles is fairly simple and requires only a few tools. For a professional effect, though, you'll need to plan the layout and prepare the substrate properly.

Most resilient floor tiles come in 12-inch squares. Trim strips in various accent colors are available in ¼- to 6-inch widths. When ordering, figure the areas in square feet to be covered (length times width) and add 5 to 10 percent for waste.

Start with the Right Base

When you pick out a resilient flooring material, check the manufacturer's instructions for acceptable substrates. This will guide you as to the type of underlayment to put down and the corresponding adhesive. Here are some commonly acceptable substrates for resilient tile and sheet flooring and what to watch out for:

Plywood that bears the stamp "Underlayment Grade" (as rated by the American Plywood Association) is the best underlayment for resilient flooring. Use only material of ¼-inch or greater thickness. Lauan, a tropical hardwood, is also used, but make sure you get Type 1, with exterior-grade glue. All plywood should be firmly attached, with surface cracks and holes filled and sanded smooth.

Wood strip flooring will serve as an underlayment only if it is completely smooth, dry, free of wax, and has all joints filled. Even then, the wood strips can shrink and swell, so a better bet is to put down an underlayment of ½-inch underlayment-grade plywood or ¼-inch lauan plywood.

Old resilient tile, sheet flooring, and linoleum should be clean, free of wax, and tightly adhered with no curled edges or bubbles.

SMART TIP

Always check with the manufacturer when selecting an underlayment material. Two that most manufacturers reject:

• *Particleboard* because it swells greatly when wet. If you have particleboard on the floor now, remove it or cover it with under-layment-grade plywood.

• *Hardboard* because some tile manufacturers do not consider it a suitable underlayment for their products.

Ceramic tile must be clean and free of wax. If the surface is porous, make sure it is completely dry. Joints should be grouted full and leveled.

Concrete must be smooth and dry. Fill cracks and dimples with a latex underlayment compound.

Preparing the Layout

Set tiles working from the middle of the floor outward. Begin by finding the middle of each wall and snapping a chalk line between opposite walls. Use a framing square to make sure the intersection of the lines is square. If not, change one chalk line, which will mean cutting the tiles along one wall at a slight angle. For a diagonal pattern, see "Creating Layout Lines," page 181.

Setting Resilient Floor Tile

Difficulty Level:

Tools & Materials: ❖ Framing square ❖ Chalk-line box ❖ Measuring tape ❖ Scribing or utility knife ❖ Rolling pin or floor roller ❖ Pencil ❖ Resilient tiles ❖ Adhesive ❖ Solvent ❖ Notched trowel (notch size as specified by adhesive manufacturer)

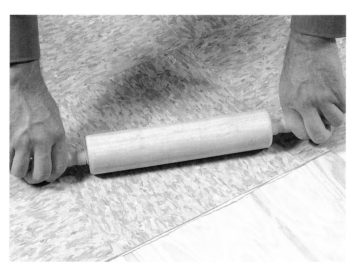

3 Drop the tiles into place; don't slide them into position. Embed the tiles in the adhesive by going over them with a rolling pin or a floor roller.

Place a row of tiles along each of the chalk lines to check your layout. **1** If the last tile will have to be cut down to the size of a skinny strip, move the appropriate chalk line up one way or the other a few inches.

Setting the Tiles

Begin at the intersection of the perpendicular chalk lines, and spread adhesive with a notched trowel held at about a 45-degree angle. **2** Leave part of the line exposed for reference. Set a row of tiles in place—dropping them rather than sliding them into position. Starting at the center, set intersecting rows of tiles, then fill tiles in the spaces between the two guide rows. Use a rolling pin to apply pressure to the tiles in each row as you set them. **3**

To trim the edge tiles, place a dry tile on top of the last set tile from the wall. Then put a third tile over these two tiles, pushed to the wall. **4** Using the edge of the topmost tile as a guide, scribe the middle tile with a utility knife and snap it in two to make a trim piece.

Trimming Outside Corners

Put a tile directly above the last set tile at the left side of a corner. Place a third tile over these two and position it ⅛ inch from the wall. **5** Mark the edge with a pencil, then without turning it, align it on the last set tile to the right of the corner. Mark it the same way. Cut the marked tile with a knife to remove the corner section. Fit the remaining part around the corner.

1 Lay the tiles out on the work lines. If the fit isn't right, adjust the lines. Place a row of tiles along each of the chalk lines to check your layout.

2 Spread adhesive in a relatively small area, so you can lay the tiles before the adhesive dries. Apply with a notched trowel held at a 45-deg. angle.

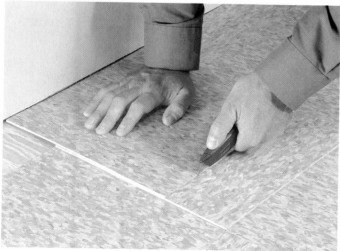

4 To cut a border tile, place a tile over the last full tile, and place another tile on top of it, butted against the wall. Cut where the top two meet.

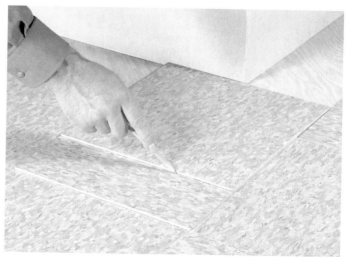

5 To cut around a corner, repeat step 4; then move to the other side of the corner, and realign the pieces to make the second cut.

7 Flooring

Vinyl Sheet Flooring

Unlike setting tiles, putting down sheet flooring will require you to manipulate large rolls of material. Before you begin the installation process, create a scale drawing of the room on graph paper, showing the exact outline of the flooring. A day or two before you begin work, place the roll or rolls of flooring in the kitchen to allow it to acclimate to the room's temperature and humidity. Remove edge trim, such as the base shoe.

Some sheet flooring requires no adhesive, some requires adhesive around the outer edge, and some is stuck down with double-sided tape. The method described here is for adhesive-applied flooring.

Installing Sheet Flooring

Difficulty Level:

Tools & Materials: ❖ Linoleum roller (rent one from your flooring supplier) ❖ 6- or 12-foot-wide roll of resilient flooring ❖ Notched trowel ❖ Framing square ❖ Chalk-line box ❖ Measuring tape ❖ Marker ❖ Utility knife ❖ Straightedge ❖ Seam roller ❖ Rolling pin ❖ Adhesive ❖ Solvent

Cutting and Fitting

Unroll the flooring in a room big enough to lay out the whole sheet. With a marker, draw the kitchen's edges on the flooring; add an extra 3 inches on all sides. Cut the flooring to the marks with a straightedge and a utility knife. **1** Position the piece so that about 3 inches of excess goes up every wall.

For layouts that require more than one sheet, put the first sheet in position and measure and cut the second piece as you did with the first one, allowing for a 3-inch overlap at the seam.

To trim outside corners, cut a slit straight down through the margin to the floor. **2** Trim inside corners by cutting the margin away with increasingly lower diagonal cuts on each side of the corner. **3**

1 Make the rough cut with a knife and straightedge in an area where you can lay out the entire piece of flooring.

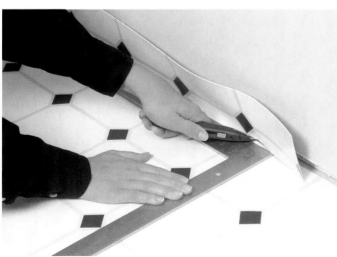

4 To trim along the wall, use a framing square to guide your cuts. Leave about a ⅛-in. gap between the edge of the flooring and the wall.

5 Roll half the floor covering back to the center of the room; apply adhesive; and roll the covering back down. Repeat for the other half of the flooring.

Crease the flooring into the joint at the wall with a 2×4. Then place a framing square in the crease, and cut with a utility knife, leaving a gap of ⅛ inch between the wall and the flooring. **4**

Use a handsaw to cut a recess in the wood door casing that is wide enough to slide the flooring beneath. Trim the flooring to match the angles and corners of the door casing; allow about ½ inch of the flooring to slip under the casing.

Adhering the Flooring

Roll back the flooring to the center, and apply adhesive to the exposed half of floor with the smooth edge of a notched trowel, following the manufacturer's directions. Comb it out with the notched edge. **5** Roll out the flooring immediately onto the adhesive. Repeat for the other half of the flooring.

If a second or third sheet of flooring must join the first, stop the adhesive about 2 inches short of the edge to be seamed when installing the first sheet. Spread adhesive on the floor to receive the second piece, stopping about 2 inches from the first sheet. Position and align the second piece carefully, allowing it to overlap the first piece slightly. With a sharp utility knife, cut through both sheets along the seam line. **6** Remove the waste. Peel back both edges, and apply adhesive. Press the flooring into place. Use the seam sealer recommended for your flooring. Press the flooring firmly into the adhesive with a roller, working from the center outward. **7**

7 Flooring

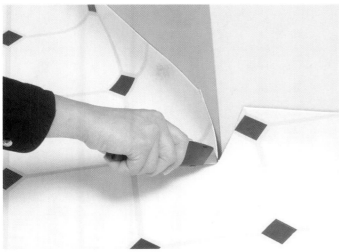

2 To trim outside corners, slit the margin down to the floor with a utility knife. Be careful not to cut too far, or the mark will be visible on the finished floor.

3 On inside corners, cut diagonally through the margin until the flooring lies flat. Then trim the excess as described in the next step.

6 To make a seam, apply adhesive up to 2 in. from the edge of the first piece. Overlap the two pieces by 2 in. Cut through both pieces, and remove the waste.

7 Use a rented seam roller to force out any ridges and air bubbles in the flooring; roll from the center of the room to the edges.

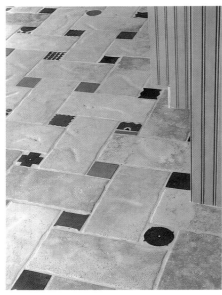

Mixing shapes of tiles adds visual interest to a floor design.

Inlaid designs, such as medallions and borders, help define space.

Real wood is still one of the most popular kitchen flooring options.

DESIGN IDEAS

See "Flooring," page 38

See "Color Basics," page 78

Set the tone for your kitchen with the flooring material and color you select. The natural stone tiles above offer a fresh, clean look. The tile pavers at right provide a rustic, natural feeling to this family kitchen.

It looks like tile, but it is really vinyl sheet flooring. Most vinyl flooring products have long-lasting, no-wax finishes.

Sophisticated designs are the latest trend from the manufacturers of vinyl sheet flooring.

Ceramic Tile

Ceramic and stone floor tiles are installed much the same way as vinyl tile, described on page 182. But there are differences, and it's the differences that make tiling more difficult than setting a vinyl floor. Tile is set in thinset adhesive, and cutting tiles is more difficult than trimming vinyl products. (See "Cutting Tiles," opposite.) You must also grout the spaces between tiles, a step that takes some time and

practice to get right. However, the results are well worth the extra effort and will provide a durable, long-lasting floor.

You can start your tile installation in a corner or from the center of the floor, using chalk lines as described on page 181. In either case, it is best to lay out the tiles in a dry run. Use tile spacers to indicate the width of the grout joint; if using mesh-backed tile sheets, you don't have to worry about joint spacing. Try to lay out the tiles to avoid narrow pieces of tile (less than 1 inch) abutting a wall. If this happens, adjust the layout.

If the corners in the room are not square or if you must install cut tiles around the perimeter of the room, make guide strips by temporarily nailing 1×2 or 1×4 battens to the underlayment. If you are tiling to concrete, weigh down the ends of the guides with heavy weights, such as a few stacked bricks. Place a strip parallel to each of two adjacent walls, with their leading edges positioned on the first joint line. Begin your installation here and then go back and fill in the space between the first full row of tiles and the wall by cutting each tile to fit.

To make sure the strips are at right angles, use the 3-4-5 method. Measure 3 units (3 feet, if the room is big enough) from the corner along the guideline (or strip), and mark the spot. Measure out 4 units (4 feet) along the long guide line, and mark the spot. Now measure the diagonal between the two points. If the diagonal measures 5 units (5 feet), then the two guides are at right angles. If not, adjust the lines (or strips) as necessary.

Laying a Threshold

The transition from the tiled kitchen floor to an adjacent floor of a different material, and possibly different height, is made with a saddle, or threshold. Choose from among the following: trim pieces of tile that come with a molded edge, solid-surface material (cultured marble), metal, or hardwood. A hardwood threshold offers the chance to cut and shape the piece to blend floors of two different heights. Apply adhesive to the floor and bottom of the saddle. Then screw or nail the saddle in place. Conceal the screw or nailheads with putty or plugs. Allow space between the saddle and tile for a grout joint.

Ceramic tiles provide beautiful, long-lasting floors. Notice how the counter material complements the tiles.

Cutting Tiles

Wet Saw

You can make a straight cut on most thin glazed tiles by scoring the surface with a glass cutter and then snapping the tile over a small dowel. This works fine in a pinch but for larger projects use a snap cutter. The cutter consists of a metal frame that holds the tile in position, a carbide blade or wheel to score the tile, and a lever to snap the tile along the score line. You can buy or rent snap cutters, but many tile dealers loan these tools to their customers for the duration of the project. If you do buy or rent one, make sure it can handle the tiles with which you will be working. Some models will not cut thick, unglazed quarry tiles or pavers.

Snap Cutter

A wet saw is a step up from the snap cutter. This is a stationary circular saw with a water-cooled carbide-grit blade. You can rent this tool, but many dealers keep them on hand to make cuts for a fee. Don't use this tool on floor tiles coated with a slip-resistant abrasive grit, because the grit will dull the blade.

Tile nippers take small bites out of tiles. They are good for cutting out curves and other irregular shapes to fit tiles around pipes or openings. The cuts will not be as smooth as cuts produced by the other tools, so plan on hiding the edges of these tiles under molding or some other type of trim.

Tile Nippers

7 Flooring

Basic Tile Shapes and Patterns

The basic floor tile measures 12 x 12 in. with a ⅛ in. to ¼ in. grout joint.

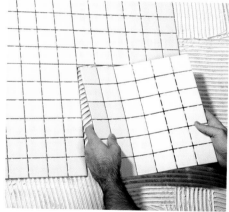

Sheet-mounted tile will look like individual mosaic tiles when installed.

Rectangular tiles can be used to create basket-weave patterns.

Combining different shapes allows you to create a variety of patterns.

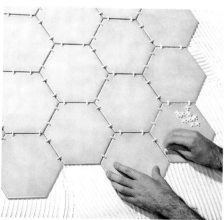

Hexagon-shaped tiles create an interlocked pattern.

Multi-color and multi-size tiles are available in sheets.

Setting the Tiles

Spread adhesive over a 16 × 16-inch area of the substrate with the smooth side of a notched trowel, following the manufacturer's directions. **1** Comb out with the notched edge. Note that you may have only a limited time to work before the adhesive sets up. If you are not using wood strips as guides, take care not to cover the chalk lines with adhesive.

Press each tile or sheet of tiles into the adhesive. **2** Set mosaic tiles by rolling each sheet up loosely, then setting one edge and rolling the rest of the sheet out. Insert a spacer (except with mosaics), and lay up the next tile or sheet. If you notice that the tiles are getting progressively out of line with each other, wiggle them into position instead of lifting them out of the adhesive. Make frequent checks for alignment—every two sheets with mosaic tiles, every row with individual tiles. Before the adhesive dries, wipe off any excess from the surface of the tiles.

After laying several rows of tile, embed them into the adhesive with a carpet-wrapped 2×4. **3** As you move the board around, tap it firmly with a hammer. Use the edge of a framing square or level to make sure the surface is flush, row to row.

Grouting the Joints

Allow the adhesive to dry for the length of time recommended by the manufacturer before filling in the joints with grout. Premixed grout is ready to apply. If you buy the grout as powder, mix it as directed.

Setting Ceramic Floor Tiles

Difficulty Level:

Tools & Materials: ❖ Hammer ❖ Rubber float ❖ Pail ❖ Sponge ❖ Soft cloths ❖ Tiles ❖ Tile spacers ❖ Grout ❖ Jointing tool or toothbrush ❖ 1x2 or 1x4 battens ❖ Notched trowel (notch size as recommended for the tile and adhesive you want to use) ❖ Tile cutter (rented from supplier) ❖ Tile nippers (rented from supplier) ❖ 12-inch piece of 2x4 wrapped with carpet ❖ Adhesive (type and quantity as recommended by supplier) ❖ Solvent (as recommended for the adhesive) ❖ Sealant ❖ Roller and pan ❖ Small brush (for grout lines)

1 Spread the adhesive evenly with a notched trowel, leaving your work lines visible. Work in small areas, so you can apply the tile before the adhesive sets up.

4 After the tile adhesive sets, clean out the grout lines. Mix the grout, and force it into the joints with the edge of a rubber float.

5 Remove excess grout by working the rubber float diagonally across the joints. Be careful not to pull the grout out of the joints.

Grout may be white or colored to match or complement the tile color. Ask your tile dealer to show you the range of colors available.

Spread the grout over the tiles, and press it into the joints using a rubber float held at a slight angle. **4** Work diagonally over the tiles, taking care to fill all joints. **5** After the surface is well covered, remove any excess grout with the rubber float. To avoid removing too much grout, work across the tiles diagonally.

Wipe the surface with a wet sponge, squeezing it out frequently in a pail of water. **6** Get as much of the grout off the surface of the tiles as you can without eroding the joints. Then wait 30 minutes or so until the residue dries to a thin haze. Wipe off the residue using a clean damp cloth followed by a dry cloth.

For large tiles, you may want the joints to be smoother than they appear after the grouting and cleaning steps. Tool the joints with a jointing tool, which you can obtain from your tile supplier, or use the end of a toothbrush.

To prevent moisture from penetrating the grouted joints and any unglazed tiles, seal the surface with a sealant recommended by your supplier. **7** Some sealants are applied with a roller; others come in a spray can. Allow two weeks for the grout to dry, and then apply one coat of sealant. Apply another coat after the tiles have been down for two years, or more frequently if specified by the manufacturer.

2 Press tiles into the adhesive, giving them a slight wiggle and making sure their backs are completely covered. Keep tiles aligned as you work.

3 Embed the tiles into the adhesive by tapping them with a padded board, or bedding block. Use the block after installing every two or three rows.

6 Wipe the remaining grout off of the tiles using a dampened sponge. Rub in a circle, and rinse out the sponge often. Clean the resulting haze with a clean cloth.

7 Seal unglazed tile and grout with a sealant made for that purpose. For glazed tile, apply sealer to the grout only.

Laminate Flooring

Laminate floors are installed as floating floors, which means the planks or tiles in the system are glued to one another but not to the subfloor. This allows them to expand and contract at a rate that is different from the rest of the structure without cracking.

As with any flooring system, the subfloor should be clean and sound. Leave flooring material in the room for 2 or 3 days before installation to allow it to acclimate to the temperature and humidity. If you are installing laminate over an existing floor, there usually isn't a need for a special underlayment. As long as the floor is in fairly good condition and there is no structural damage, you can apply the material right over the existing flooring. The only exception is carpeting, which must be removed.

Undercut door trim, as discussed on page 195. Make sure the walls of the room are straight and the corners square. If they are not, compensate by finding the midpoints of the two walls between which the planks will run, and snap a chalk line. From this line, measure equal distances to within about ¼ inch of the end wall where you will begin laying strips. Snap a chalk line between these two points, and let this be your work line for the first course of flooring.

Installing the Flooring

Unroll the foam padding to cover the floor. **1** Test-fit the first three rows of flooring, beginning with the groove toward the wall and staggering the joints as necessary. **2** Use spacers to maintain the gap between the flooring and the wall. The gap will be covered by baseboard molding.

Follow the manufacturer's gluing instructions carefully. Be sure to apply a continuous bead of the approved glue along either the groove or the tongue of the plank. **2** (inset) Push the planks together, and tap them into position with the tapping block. **3** Driving the planks together forces excess glue to rise to the surface. Look for a bead that follows the seam—it means you applied the glue properly. Remove the beaded glue using a plastic putty knife.

After laying at least three complete rows, use strap clamps to hold them firmly together. **4** Many manufacturers require that you allow the glue used in the first three rows to set up for about an hour before you can continue with the rest of the floor. After an hour, the first rows will provide a good base against which you can lay the rest of the floor.

Using the strap clamps is an important component of the installation. If you stop work, even for a brief period during the installation, use the clamps on the floor. Failure to provide tension on the just-glued seams will allow the seams to open, and they will be visible in the finished flooring.

Trim the final row of planks as you would any type of strip flooring or tile. Place a plank over the last completed row; insert another plank or scrap plank against the wall spacers. **5** Use this line to scribe a cut line. Glue as described previously. Be sure to use the clamps or to drive shims between the spacers and the wall to keep the just-installed seams together until the glue dries.

Wait 12 hours before removing the spacers and moving furniture into the room. Cover gaps along the wall with base molding, attaching the molding to wall studs. Do not nail through the flooring.

Protect Your Knees

Many homeowners feel that they don't need knee protection. They know the pros wear knee pads, but they reason that contractors work on floors day-in and day-out. The average do-it-yourself project is short enough that it won't put a serious amount of stress on their knees. Many homeowners find out how wrong they are an hour or two into the project. Kneeling for an extended period can be slightly uncomfortable to extremely painful for someone with problem knees. Protect yourself with knee pads such as the ones shown here, or at the very least roll up a towel to use as a cushion while working.

Installing a Laminate Floor

Difficulty Level: 🗲🗲🗲

Tools & Materials: ❖ Laminate flooring
❖ Foam underlayment padding ❖ Spacers ❖ Glue
❖ Hammer ❖ Installation tapping block ❖ Plastic putty
knife ❖ Strap clamps ❖ Circular saw or handsaw
❖ Chalk-line box

1 Roll out the foam padding. Some manufacturers require a polyethylene vapor retarder under the padding in basements.

2 Test-fit the first three rows, stepping the planks. Apply a continuous bead of glue to the entire length of the tongue or groove on the edges and ends (inset).

3 Use a tapping block to drive the planks into position. Look for excess glue that beads up along the seam of the plank, and remove it with a plastic putty knife.

4 Use strap clamps to hold just-glued planks together. Lay at least three complete rows, and allow the glue to set up for about one hour before continuing.

5 To cut final planks, lay a plank over the last installed one. Use a third plank or a piece of scrap to scribe a cutting line on the good piece.

Hardwood Floors

Many wood species are used for flooring, and there are various wood grading systems in use. It's important to remember that wood grades for flooring are based on the appearance of the milled product and not on the strength and durability characteristics.

Layout

Remove the baseboard and shoe molding. **1** Tack down any loose boards in the subfloor, setting all exposed nailheads. Lay a covering of 15-pound asphalt-saturated felt building paper over the subfloor. Lap the seams slightly and cut the edges flush with the walls.

Lay work lines based on either a wall that is square or on the center of the room. Find the midpoints of the two walls that are parallel with the joists and snap a chalk line between them. From this line, measure equal distances to within about ½ inch of the end wall where you will begin laying strips. Snap a chalk line between these two points, and let this be your work line for the first course of flooring. Any gap between the first course and the wall can be covered with the baseboard and shoe molding.

Installing the Flooring

Undercut doorways by using a sample of flooring as a guide. **2** Lay out the starter course (the first row of strips) the full length of the wall along the work line. Drill holes along the back edges of the strips and into the joists, slightly smaller in diameter than the nails. Drive nails to attach the strip flooring. **3** Next, predrill holes through the tongue of the first course of strips into the joists. Then drive and set finishing nails.

Lay out several courses of strips. Plan as much as six or seven rows ahead. **4** Stagger the end joints so that each joint is more than 6 inches from the joints in the adjoining rows.

You can nail each strip of flooring individually, but you will be much more productive if you rent a floor nailer. **5** For boards that won't slip into position, nail a temporary block to the floor and use a wedge to force the flooring into position. **6**

At the end of rows, try to keep end pieces at least 8 inches long. **7** For gaps of more than ½ inch between the final strip and the wall, remove the tongue sides of the strips, cut them to width, and wedge them into place using a pry bar. **8**

Installing Wood Strip Flooring

Difficulty Level: 🔧🔧🔧

Tools & Materials: ❖ 15-pound felt building paper ❖ Chalk-line box ❖ Basic carpentry tools ❖ Backsaw ❖ Wood flooring ❖ Electric drill with assorted bits ❖ Flooring and finishing nails ❖ Nail set ❖ Pry bar ❖ Rented nailing machine ❖ Circular saw or handsaw ❖ Dust mask

3 Use shims or blocks as spacers. Set the first row of strips. Predrill holes along the back edge of the wood. Face-nail the strip in place.

6 Some strips have a crook and won't fit easily. Coax them into place by driving a wedge between the strip and a nailed block.

1 Use a flat pry bar to remove moldings and baseboards. If you plan on reusing the moldings, label them for easier reinstallation.

2 Use a piece of flooring as a guide to undercut doorway casings. Lay felt building paper, and establish a straight working line at the starting wall.

4 Test-fit several rows of strips. This will help you stagger joints and match variations in the natural wood tones.

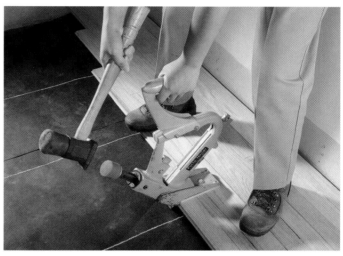

5 Rent a floor nailer to edge-nail flooring. Place the tool over the tongue of the strip, and strike the plunger with a mallet.

7 To finish rows, mark the required length on a full strip next to the end gap. Use a spacer block to maintain wall clearance.

8 To close up the joint on the last row, use a pry bar against a wood block on the wall to tighten the joint. Cover the perimeter gaps with baseboard molding.

Refinishing Wood Floors

There is no need to tear up or cover an old wood floor with another material if the original suffers from only minor damage. If you like the look and feel of wood, consider sanding out the imperfections and refinishing with polyurethane.

This job will generate more dust than you thought possible, and it is bound to work its way to other parts of your house. Do your best to contain the dust by sealing doorways, pass-throughs, and heating registers with heavy plastic.

Go over the entire floor looking for popped nails or uplifted boards. Drive nails back into place be-cause they can damage a sanding belt. Use a sharp chisel to reduce raised edges on slightly uplifted boards. **1** Cut out and replace sections with deep gouges or other imperfections that can't be sanded out. Fill minor dents and nicks with wood putty.

SMART TIP

To revive a polyurethane finish over an un-damaged floor, go over the floor with a sanding screen. Attached to a rotating floor polisher, the screen removes the old finish without cutting into the floor as traditional sanding with a drum sander does. Do not screen floors with wax top coats.

Refinishing a Floor

Difficulty Level: 🐟🐟🐟

Tools & Materials: ❖ Hammer (or nail puller if necessary) ❖ Sharp wood chisel ❖ Drum sander ❖ Edge sander ❖ Hand-held sander ❖ Medium-grit sanding belt and pad ❖ Fine-grit sanding belt and pad ❖ Hand-held floor scraper ❖ Lamb's wool applicators ❖ Vacuum ❖ Rotary buffer ❖ Tack cloth ❖ Polyurethane

1 Inspect the floor for popped nails and uplifted boards. Remove or set nails, and use a sharp chisel to shave down raised edges.

4 Use a hand-held scraper and elbow grease to remove the protective finish from corners and other hard-to-reach areas.

5 After two passes with the sanders, vacuum completely and apply either a stain or the first coat of polyurethane.

Sanding Floors

You can rent a large drum sander for the main part of the floor and a special orbital edge sander for working on areas up close to walls. You will also need a sharp hand-held floor scraper for reaching into corners. In addition, it is a good idea to pick up paper dust masks or a respirator with replaceable filters.

Drum sanders are powerful tools and can easily gouge out a trough in your floor if you keep it in one place. Once the drum is going, keep moving at a steady pace. Follow the direction of the grain. **2** When you reach a wall, tip the machine up so that the sanding belt is not in contact with the floor.

Use the edge sander to remove the finish from areas near the wall. **3** The edger rotates, so you need to blend the circular pattern of the edger with the straight pattern of the drum sander. Switch to the hand scraper to get into corners and other hard-to-reach areas. **4** Vacuum the floor, and make a second pass with the sanders (using a finer-grit sandpaper). This should be sufficient for most floors.

The Final Finish

Vacuum again to remove any dust, and wipe with a tack cloth. Apply the first coat of polyurethane with a lamb's wool applicator. **5** Rather than apply the polyurethane at this point, you could apply a stain to the floor. When it dries, apply polyurethane. You may need to buff the finish with a rotary buffer. **6** Apply a final coat of polyurethane. **7**

7 Flooring

2 Load a medium-grit belt on the sander, and sand in the direction of the wood strips. Keep the tool moving to avoid damaging the floor.

3 Switch to the edge sander to work close to the wall. The sander has rotating disks that create a circular pattern on the floor.

6 Allow the polyurethane to dry, and then buff with a steel wool disk attached to a rotary buffer. Follow the grain of the wood when buffing.

7 Make sure the floor is completely clean (you may want to run a tack cloth over it), and apply at least one more coat of finish.

Putting It All Together

CHAPTER 8

In This Chapter

At this stage everything comes together and becomes a real kitchen. You've installed new wiring and plumbing and worked on the walls, ceiling, and floors. The new light fixtures you've selected should be in place and in working order. It's now time to install the cabinets and appliances. There is a lot left to do, but when you are finished you will finally reclaim the kitchen for your family.

Preparing for Cabinet Installation

Wall materials such as plaster and drywall don't have the strength to support heavy cabinets, so plan on attaching all cabinets, especially heavy wall-hung cabinets, directly to the studs with screws.

A magnetic stud finder is one of the simplest and least expensive ways to find studs. These nifty gadgets detect the nails or screws used to attach the wallboard to the wood. A bit more expensive but even better are electronic stud finders available in home centers and hardware stores. In the absence of a stud finder, probe the wall with a small nail. Find the studs, and mark their location on the wall.

Go over the walls with a straightedge to locate low and high spots. Fill depressions with joint compound; sand down high spots. The repairs will be hidden by the cabinets.

In many cases, the floor will not be perfectly level, so find the high spot on the floor where the cabinets will go. To do this, set a level on the floor and check whether the floor is level. If it isn't, slide the level along to the high side until the bubble shifts to the other side of the vial. Mark that spot as the high point of your floor.

Installing Wall Cabinets

If you are installing both base and wall cabinets, work on the wall cabinets first. You will find it eas-

Installing Wall Cabinets

Difficulty Level: 🦅🦅🦅

Tools & Materials: ❖ Stud finder ❖ Cabinets and hardware ❖ 48-inch level ❖ Measuring tape ❖ Pencil ❖ Wood shims ❖ Utility knife ❖ 3- and 3½-inch wood screws ❖ Handsaw ❖ Power drill-driver with assorted bits ❖ C-clamps or adjustable bar clamps ❖ Screwdrivers (flat-bladed and Phillips) ❖ Lumber for ledger ❖ Shims

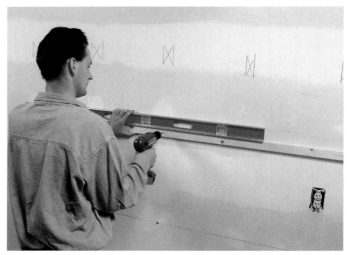

1 Screw a 1x2 ledger directly to the wall studs. The ledger will help you during the installation process. You will remove it when finished.

4 Attach 3-in. wood screws through the cabinet's top and bottom cleats. Drive the screws through the cabinet backing strip into the wall studs.

5 Install the second cabinet, securing it loosely to the wall. Clamp adjoining cabinets together, and fasten them together with screws through their stiles.

ier to work close to the wall with the base cabinets out of the way.

Measure down from the low point on the ceiling. (See page 98 for typical cabinet measurements.) Using a level, draw a line along the wall indicating the bottom of the wall cabinets. Secure a temporary one-by ledger along that line using 2-inch screws. **1** Make sure that you've screwed into studs and that the board is perfectly level. Begin a run of cabinets with an end or corner unit. **2** The first cabinet determines the alignment for the entire run, so be extra careful leveling and shimming it. **3** Drive two 3-inch screws through the hanging cleat just tight enough to hold the cabinet in place. **4** Check for level from front to back and side to side. You may have to add shims.

Secure the bottom of the cabinet to the wall by driving two 3-inch screws through the lower cleat and into the studs.

Lift each succeeding cabinet onto the ledger, and position it as close to the wall as possible. After you've installed two or more adjacent cabinets, clamp them together at their face frames. **5** Bore through the stiles with a 3/32-inch bit, and connect them using #6 wood screws at the top and bottom. Attach each cabinet through its hanging cleat. **6** Remove the ledger, and install cabinet hardware. **7**

Depending on how flat and plumb the walls are, there will probably be gaps between the walls and the cabinet. You can easily conceal the gaps by installing quarter-round or other molding.

2 If possible, begin by installing a corner unit. With a helper, lift the cabinet into position and rest it on the temporary ledger.

3 Position the cabinet so that it is plumb and level, using shims if necessary. A level first cabinet helps ensure that the others will also be level.

6 Check each cabinet to make sure it is plumb and level as you install it. When you are satisfied, drive screws through the hanging cleats.

7 Unscrew and remove the ledger, and install cabinet hardware. Some cabinets come with hardware holes already drilled.

Installing Base Cabinets

Measure up the wall from the floor's high point, and make a mark at cabinet height. See page 98 for typical cabinet measurements. Use a long level to scribe a level line along the wall for the full length of the cabinet or cabinets. You may need to install a ledger along this line when cabinets, such as some corner units, do not have back panels. **1** The ledger will support the countertop.

Slide a cabinet against the wall, and check it against the level line. **2** Use wood shims at the base of the cabinet where necessary. The cabinet should be plumb and level.

Place additional cabinets in position. In some situations you may need to install shims between cabinets, such as between a corner unit and the next cabinet in line. **3** Attach cabinets to each other by screwing through the stiles. Drill and countersink holes for two #8 × 2½-inch wood screws at each juncture. Once the cabinets are level and plumb, attach them to the studs using 3½-inch screws. **4** Trim the shims with a utility knife or chisel. As you tighten the screws, watch to be sure that the face frames remain square and on exactly the same plane. As you continue to install cabinets, be sure to leave spaces for appliances, such as a dishwasher, refrigerator, and range.

If your layout calls for a filler strip at one or both ends of the cabinet run, install them before attaching the cabinets to the wall. Cut the strips to fit where needed. Then pull the end cabinet or cabinets out, clamp each strip to a stile, and bore two pilot holes for screws through the edge of the stile into the filler. Counterbore these holes so the screw heads won't protrude above the surface. Drive the screws, slide the cabinet or cabinets back into position, and check again to be sure the cabinets are level.

At a corner you'll probably need a filler strip. Install one cabinet, attach a filler to the second cabinet with screws, then butt the two together and drive a second set of screws into the filler. Offset these screws from the first ones.

Cover the gaps between the bottom of the cabinets and the floor by installing vinyl cove molding or trim that matches the cabinets. Use contact cement or construction adhesive to attach it. Or for a more finished look, you can install wood base molding along the bottom of the cabinets. Install molding with finishing nails. Set the nailheads, and fill the holes with wood putty. **5**

Installing Base Cabinets

Difficulty Level:

Tools & Materials: ❖ Stud finder (or nail) ❖ Cabinets and hardware ❖ 48-inch level ❖ Measuring tape ❖ Pencil ❖ Wood shims ❖ Utility knife ❖ 2½-, 3-, and 3½-inch wood screws ❖ Handsaw ❖ Power drill-driver with assorted bits ❖ C-clamps ❖ Screwdrivers (flat-bladed and Phillips) ❖ Vinyl or wood kickplates ❖ One-by ledger material ❖ Quarter-round molding

3 You may need to shim between units, such as when a corner cabinet meets another cabinet. Attach cabinets to one another by screwing through stiles.

Toe-Kick Heaters

Toe-kick heaters have a short profile designed to slide into the normally empty space under kitchen cabinets. They are a good solution for providing auxiliary heat when needed or to provide spot heat on particularly cold days. To install one, you will need to bring power from an existing junction box to a new switch, and pull cable from the switch to the heater—similar to the method used for installing under-cabinet lighting. (See page 174.) Cut out the opening in the toe-kick space; then pull the cable into the room. Make the necessary electrical connections and slide the heater into position.

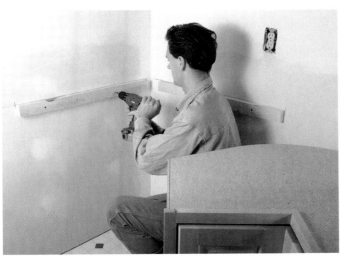

1 For backless corner units, measure up from the floor and attach a ledger to the wall studs to help support the countertop.

2 Place cabinets in position, and check that units are square and level. Use wood shims as necessary to make cabinets level.

4 Double-check that cabinets are level. When you're satisfied, attach them to the wall studs by screwing through the back frame or cleat.

5 Use vinyl cove molding or wood molding along the toe kick to hide any gaps between the cabinets and the floor.

8 Putting It All Together

Open storage puts items on display. The cabinet above stores dishes and bowls near the prep and cleanup areas. Shelving under the cooktop at left holds pots and pans.

DESIGN IDEAS

See "Cabinets," page 12

See "Types of Storage," page 18

Unusual configurations can help meet storage needs. The cabinet above combines drawers with shelves for appliances and wine storage. The baskets below hold cooking ingredients.

Dealing with necessities is central to a storage plan. Pull-out pantries (above) allow owners to stock up on packaged goods. Recycling cabinets (below) help organize a room.

8 Putting It All Together

Islands

No matter how complicated they may look, islands are really nothing more than cabinets and counter-tops—and perhaps fixtures and appliances—installed in the middle of the floor rather than against a wall. The island shown here consists of ordinary base cabinets that receive some finish work on their backs and sides because these areas will be exposed. You can create a small island like this one or use it as a starting point to create a more complicated feature.

Planning the Island

Place the base cabinets where you want the island located. Good design calls for a 42- to 48-inch space between the island and a bank of cabinets or appliances installed against a wall. Draw an outline of the cabinets on the floor. Measure in from the outline a distance equal to the thickness of the cabinet frames, and draw another line. **1** Line 2x4 cleats against the inside line, and screw them to the floor. **2** You'll need cleats at both ends of the island as well as along its long sections. If you use short cleats, be sure to mark their position on the floor with tape so that you'll know where they are located when it comes time to attach the cabinets.

Installing the Cabinets

Slip the cabinets over the cleats, and fasten them through the cabinet frame using wood screws or

Installing an Island

Difficulty Level: 🐟🐟

Tools & Materials: ❖ Base cabinets or island cabinets ❖ Straightedge ❖ Pencil or marker ❖ 2x4 cleats ❖ Power drill-driver ❖ Wood/utility screws ❖ Plywood veneer ❖ Hammer ❖ Contact cement ❖ Finishing nails ❖ Wood molding ❖ Countertop materials ❖ Corner molding

1 Draw an outline of the island on the floor. Measure in from the outline a distance that equals the thickness of the cabinet frame plus the toe kick.

4 Cover the unfinished sides and back of the island with furniture-grade plywood veneer. Use contact cement and finishing nails to attach the plywood.

5 Secure a plywood base for a tile or laminate counter-top to the island by screwing up through the cabinet mounting blocks.

nails. **3** These fasteners will be hidden by trim later.

Many manufacturers sell cabinets with finished backs and sides for islands and peninsulas. If the cabinets you've selected do not have finished backs, you will need to cover them. One option is to cut furniture-grade plywood veneer slightly larger than needed. Attach the veneer to the backs of the cabinets with contact cement and finishing nails. **4** Use a router to trim the excess veneer from the edges. Do the same for the sides.

The new island will require a countertop. If you're installing a laminate counter or one that requires a plywood substrate, put it in place and screw through the support blocks from inside the cabinet. **5** Set solid surfacing or natural stone counters in adhesive caulk following manufacturer's directions. If you install a substrate, finish the counter with the material of your choice. **6**

Install wood molding to cover the corners where the back and sides meet. **7** You can also install base molding at the bottom of the island.

CAUTION Most building codes require that islands be equipped with electrical outlets. Here's the reason: If you have an outlet on the island, you will not be tempted to place a countertop appliance on the island and then drape the cord across the aisle to a wall outlet, creating a potential hazard.

2 Align 2x4 cleats to this new line, and screw them to the floor with 3-in. screws. Screw into floor joists where possible.

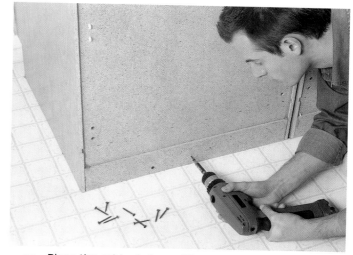

3 Place the cabinets in position over the cleats. Screw or nail through the frame of the cabinets into the cleats to secure the island.

6 Finish the countertop if necessary. Apply cement board over the plywood for tile. Set solid surfacing material in caulk.

7 There may be small gaps where the veneers on the side and back of the island meet. Hide them and the visible nailheads by installing corner molding.

8 Putting It All Together

Reviving Cabinets

Sometimes it is not necessary or practical to replace existing cabinetry. Cabinets that are in reasonably good condition can be painted or refaced.

Painting Cabinets

A fresh coat of paint is often a good short-term solution. Begin by removing cabinet hardware and filling any dents and gouges with wood putty. Clean the surfaces with a strong detergent or trisodium phosphate, a cleaner sold in paint and hardware stores. Sand the cabinets with 150 grit sandpaper.

You will get the smoothest finish if you remove the doors and spray paint them. If you can't spray paint them, use a good-quality brush. Most jobs will require the application of a primer and two top coats. Choose either alkyd or water-based latex paint. In either case, use the best quality primer and paint available.

Refacing Cabinets

Refacing cabinets includes replacing doors and drawer fronts and covering the frames and sides with matching wood veneer, rigid thermofoil (a vinyl product molded over fiberboard), or plastic laminate. Refacing is a good option if your existing kitchen is well designed and the cabinets structurally sound but a little worse for wear. It is also a good alternative if you want to refresh the look of the kitchen but want to put off a major gutting-and-rebuilding job for the future.

Refacing can cost about half of what replacing cabinets would cost. And you can reface the face frames and replace the doors and drawers in a few days as opposed to the weeks a full-scale remodeling usually takes.

However, refacing cannot correct an inefficient layout or improve low-quality cabinets. It is also a difficult job that is beyond the scope of most home-owners. For local refacing companies, check your phone book or our resource guide.

Before

After

Refacing cabinets consists of removing old doors and drawer fronts (above) and replacing them with new ones (right), and covering the cabinet frames with a matching material. Refacing is a good solution for updating a kitchen that has an efficient layout.

To begin a refacing project, remove the doors, drawers, and hinges from your existing cabinets. Take any drawer-pull hardware off the drawer fronts. Scrape and sand old peeling finish from the cabinet face frames and sides. Fill all holes, gouges, and scratches with wood putty. Then sand all the patched surfaces with 150-grit sandpaper. If you intend to paint the cabinet interior, do it now.

Use flexible veneer with pressure-sensitive adhesive backing on the cabinet face frames. You can use the same material on the exposed sides of cabinets, or you can apply ¼-inch plywood veneer, which is stiffer and easier to lay flat on large surfaces.

Cover the sides first by cutting the veneer slightly larger than the surface. Attach it by first spraying the surface with contact cement. **1** Roll the panel to get a secure bond. **2** Trim any overhang with a router.

Veneering the Stiles and Rails

Start with the stiles. Measure the stile, and then add ½ inch. Cut the veneer with a sharp utility knife. The width should equal the width of the face frame plus the thickness of the frame on each side. If the stile is 1¾ inches wide and ¾ inch thick, the veneer should be 3¼ inches wide.

To help keep the veneer straight as you put it in position, draw reference lines on the rails at the top and bottom of the stile. Make the lines ¾ inch from the stile. Line up the veneer with the reference lines, remove the paper backing, and press into position. **3**

Refacing Cabinets

Difficulty Level: 🔧🔧🔧

Tools & Materials: ❖ Screwdriver ❖ Scraper and sandpaper ❖ Putty knife ❖ Wood putty ❖ Paint and brushes (if necessary) ❖ Utility knife ❖ Veneer ❖ Contact cement ❖ Laminate roller ❖ Hinges ❖ Power drill-driver and assorted bits ❖ Spring and/or C-clamps ❖ Router ❖ Handsaw

1 After preparing the cabinets, mask off surfaces adjacent to the cabinets and apply contact cement to the cabinet sides.

2 Cut a section of veneer plywood to cover the area with a slight overlap. Press into place with a laminate roller. Trim the overage with a router.

3 Make layout marks at the top and bottom of the stile (the vertical section). Measure out from the stile the distance equal to the thickness of the face frame.

8 Putting It All Together

Continued on next page

4 Line up the cut section of veneer, remove the paper backing, and press into place. Cut the veneer at the top and bottom of the stile with a sharp utility knife.

5 Fold the veneer in to cover the edges of the face frame. Use a straightedge to trim the excess veneer that overhangs the rail.

6 Cut the section for the rail. Measure up from the rail by the thickness of the frame, and make a layout mark on tape. Butt the pieces together.

7 After folding and smoothing the veneer, fill any open seams with matching wood putty. Install doors and drawer fronts to complete the project.

Make horizontal cuts in the veneer where the stile meets the rail, and then wrap the veneer along the sides of the stile. **4–5**

Follow the same procedure for the rails, but draw reference lines on pieces of tape rather than marking up the newly veneered stile. **6** Sand the surface lightly, and use matching wood putty to fill seams.

Doors and Drawers

If the hinges aren't attached to the doors, set the new hinges 2 inches from the top and bottom of the doors, and mark the screw holes. If the hinges will be hidden, lay the door face down. If the hinges will be fully visible, lay the door face up. Drill pilot holes, and attach the hinges with the supplied screws. Hold the doors in the openings, and mark the hinge locations on the cabinet face frame. Be sure that the door overlaps the opening by an equal amount around the perimeter. Hang the doors. **7**

Install the drawer fronts. If the existing fronts are one-piece, clamp them face down to a work table and cut off the overhanging edges with a handsaw. If they're made from two pieces, with a decorative false front attached to the drawer carcass, remove the front panel and throw it away.

Lay the new drawer fronts face down. Set a prepared drawer box on a panel, centered with an equal overlap around the perimeter of the drawer front. Drill pilot holes through the front of the drawer into the decorative panel, and secure it with screws.

Repairing Doors and Drawers

Not all kitchen remodeling jobs include installing or even refacing cabinets. New countertops and plumbing fixtures, new appliances, and fresh finishes on floors and walls can revitalize a kitchen, and often these improvements work well with existing cabinets. But if cabinet doors are warped and drawers have begun to fall apart after years of use, make the repairs a part of the remodeling project.

Fixing Doors. There are a number of reasons why a cabinet door gets out of alignment. Sometimes the solution is as simple as tightening the hinge screws. If your doors bind, tighten the opposite hinge screws. So if the door binds at the top, tighten the bottom screws. If the door continues to bind, you may also need to plane the area where it's tight.

Warped wood doors stick and are difficult to open and close. Find out where the warp occurs by coating the edge of the door with powdered chalk. **1** (inset) Close and open the door once or twice. The powder will rub off where the door is warped. Use a block plan to remove the high spots. **1**

Upgrading Drawers. Replace worn-out wooden guides on drawers with metal ones. These products vary, but you may need to add a one-by side rail to the side of the cabinet to support the guide. Attach the rail, and then screw the track of the guide to the rail. Attach the mating roller guides to the sides of the drawers. **2** Remove old drawer fronts, and replace them with new decorative panels. **3**

Repairing Doors and Drawers

Difficulty Level: 🃏🃏

Tools & Materials: ❖ Powdered chalk ❖ Block plane ❖ Screwdrivers ❖ Wood/utility screws ❖ Metal drawer guides

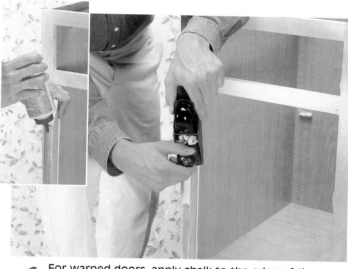

1 For warped doors, apply chalk to the edge of the door (inset). Open and close the door. Areas where the powder rubs off indicate high spots.

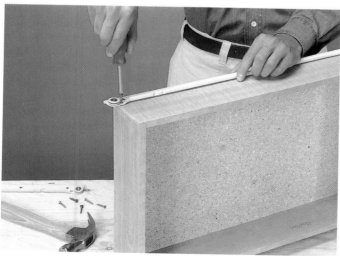

2 Replace worn-out slides with new metal ones. Attach the track to the side of the cabinet or side rail, and screw the guides onto the drawer.

3 Add new drawer fronts by predrilling through the front of the drawer into the decorative panel. Attach the drawer to the panel with screws.

Customizing Cabinets

Cabinet manufacturers offer dozens of storage options to make their products more efficient and useful. Lazy Susans turn the wasted space of a corner cabinet to a valuable storage area; appliance garages keep countertop appliances out of sight; and tilt-down bins and drawer fronts accommodate specialty items.

If you choose not to install new cabinets, you can still outfit your existing ones with a variety of storage options. These products range from door-hung shelves that put frequently used items where you can reach them quickly to slide out units that make a cabinet's contents easily accessible.

Rollout Shelves

Items stored in base cabinets are often difficult to reach. To put those items at your fingertips, install rollout shelving. The installation shown here is for a two-tier storage rack, but the same hardware can be used for multicompartment storage or as a base to hold tall recycling containers.

To install, attach the baskets to the uprights using the metal screws provided. **1** On some models you may have to extend the bracket and lock it into position. Place the template in the cabinet, and mark the locations for the screws. **2** Be sure that the door can close easily. Screw the roller glides to the bottom of the cabinet. **3** Tilt the basket assembly up, and slide it into the glides.

Installing Rollout Shelves

Difficulty Level: 🔧🔧

Tools & Materials: ❖ Shelving kit ❖ Tape measure ❖ Screwdrivers ❖ Power drill-driver with screwdriver attachment ❖ Wood screws (if not provided) ❖ Metal screws (if not provided) ❖ Masking tape

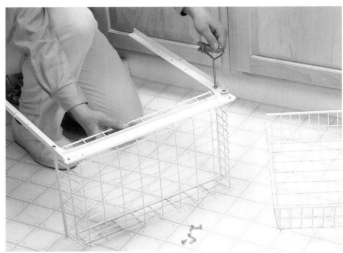

1 Attach the baskets to the uprights and side rollers. Lock the upright into position, place the basket in the roller groove, and secure it with metal screws.

2 Place the template in the cabinet, making sure it is square to the front of the cabinet. Tape it to the cabinet, and mark the locations for the screws.

3 Install the roller guides with the wood screws. Place the basket into the glides by tilting the front up and sliding the basket assembly into position.

Pullout Platforms

You may want some appliances, such as a mixer, bread maker, or even a television for catching your favorite show while working in the kitchen, stored out of sight until it is time to use them. But rather than lift them to the counter, you can install them on a slide-out shelf placed in a cabinet. Many of these items are sold as kits that include the slides, the platform, and a shelf. Some kits have shelves that swivel so that you can rotate the shelf when it is extended. Before installing such a kit, make sure the shelf and hardware are strong enough to hold the weight of whatever it is you want to store there.

Installing the Platform. Some kits come with a template to make installation easier. If the kit you purchase does not, mark the center of the pullout platform and align it with the center of the cabinet that will hold it. **1** Be sure to leave enough room to allow the doors to close. Pull out the shelf to expose the guides, and screw them to the bottom of the cabinet. **2** Measure the width of the shelf that will attach to the platform by extending the platform and holding the shelf in position. If the shelf you are installing swivels, make sure that it swivels easily in the cabinet opening. If the cabinet is not large enough to accommodate the shelf, trim the shelf as much as necessary. Install the shelf by extending the platform, placing the shelf in position, holding it there with clamps, and screwing up from the bottom of the platform. **3**

Installing Pullout Platforms

Difficulty Level:

Tools & Materials: ❖ Shelf kit ❖ Wood screws (if not provided) ❖ Clamps ❖ Tape measure ❖ Power drill-driver with screwdriver attachment ❖ Screwdriver

1 Place the kit template in the cabinet. If you don't have a template, mark the center of the pullout platform and align it with the center of the cabinet.

2 Install the pullout platform first. Extend the platform to expose the glides. Make sure they are square to the front of the cabinet, and install them with wood screws.

3 Trim the shelf, if necessary, to fit in the cabinet. Position it on the platform, and hold it in place with clamps. Screw up from the bottom of the platform.

Molding & Trimwork

Besides the added beauty it brings to your kitchen, molding can conceal the gaps between cabinets and walls or ceilings and hide nailholes, screw holes, and other blemishes that are inevitable in construction. If the original kitchen contained intricate moldings that you want to keep, remove them carefully and reinstall them later.

Starting at the end of a wall, coax the existing molding away from the wall with a pry bar. Pry as near the nails as possible, and use a thin scrap of wood behind the pry bar to protect the wall. After you've pried part of the trim away from the wall, move to the next nail. Continue this process until you gradually pry away the entire length of material. If a strip of molding won't come loose, drive the nails through the piece with a nail set. It's much easier to patch these holes later than to fix broken trim.

If you plan on installing new molding, you do not need to be careful with the old wood, but you should protect the surface of the drywall around the molding. Trying to get some leverage with the pry bar placed between wall studs can lead to large holes in the drywall.

Molding Joints

When installing molding, you'll have to fit pieces together around corners. Miter joints are the way to go for outside corners. For these joints you will cut two adjoining pieces of molding at 45-degree angles. When you place them together you create a 90-degree turn around a corner. You can use a back-saw and portable miter box or a power miter saw for accurate cuts. Apply carpenter's glue and finishing nails to join the molding.

But for inside corners, it is better to create coped joints. Done properly, a coped joint looks seamless, allowing the profile to continue smoothly through the corner. Coped joints are less likely to open up than inside miter joints.

To make a coped joint, cut the first piece so that it butts into the corner. **1** The idea behind a coped joint is to make the second piece of molding fit snugly around the profile of the first piece. Measure for the second piece, but add a couple of inches to the rough measurement. Cut the second piece at a 45-degree angle, leaving the face of the cut exposed. **2** The type of tool you use will determine how to place the molding. Place crown molding in a basic miter saw bottom up with the top side resting squarely on the table. With a compound miter saw, place the molding flat on the table. Use a coping saw to back-cut the molding. **3** It takes some practice, but try to maneuver the thin blade of the saw along the profile of the miter. Use a file to finish up the cut. **4** The simpler the molding profile, the easier it is to create a coped joint. Baseboard, for example, usually requires a simple straight cut. Intricate crown molding requires some finesse with the coping saw.

Test-fit the molding, and make necessary adjustments with files or rasps. Predrill holes for finishing nails to avoid splitting the wood. Place carpenter's glue on the cut end, and place the molding in position. Drive and set finishing nails. Fill the holes; then sand and finish the molding. **5**

Upgrading Base Molding

To replace vinyl cove molding with real wood, first remove the vinyl. Insert a pry bar or screwdriver into the corner to peel a small section back. Once it is free and you can grip the vinyl, pull back as you work the pry bar behind the molding. Use a hand scraper to remove the old adhesive. Don't use chemical adhesive removers.

Attach the new molding to wall studs with finishing nails. Set the nails, and fill the holes with putty. You can install a simple one-piece molding or build up the profile with a decorative top bead and quarter-round installed along the floor.

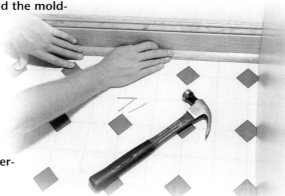

Making a Coped Joint

Difficulty Level: 🐟 🐟 🐟

Tools & Materials: ❖ Molding ❖ Backsaw ❖ Combination square ❖ Pencil ❖ Miter box or power miter saw ❖ Coping saw ❖ Round file and half-round files ❖ Utility knife or small chisel ❖ Power drill-driver and ¹⁄₁₆-inch bit ❖ Hammer and nail set ❖ Glue ❖ Sandpaper

1 Butt the first section of molding into the corner. Measure out from the corner (plus an extra couple of inches) to find the rough length of the coped molding.

2 Cut the coping miter on another board. Note how the bottom of the molding is facing up and the piece is leaning against the fence.

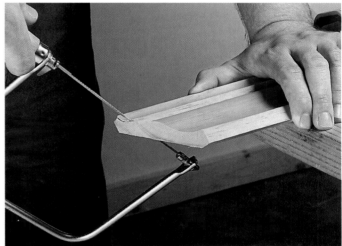

3 Use a coping saw to back-cut the coped piece. Rotate the saw as needed to maneuver the thin blade along the profile of the miter.

4 Use files and rasps to clean up the cut or to increase the back-cut angle. Test fit the coped piece. If the angle fits, trim the board to length.

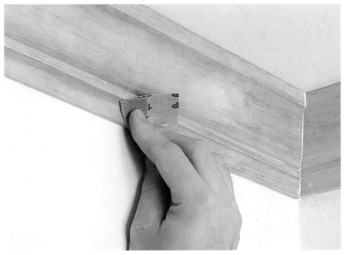

5 Apply glue to the coped end, and attach the molding to the wall. Drill pilot holes to avoid splitting the wood, and drive and set the finishing nails.

8 Putting It All Together

Molding & Trimwork Options

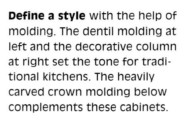

DESIGN IDEAS

See "Cabinets," page 12

See "Developing a Style," page 74

Define a style with the help of molding. The dentil molding at left and the decorative column at right set the tone for traditional kitchens. The heavily carved crown molding below complements these cabinets.

Molding completes a room's design. The rope molding above adds a distinctive touch to this cabinet. Top and bottom molding (right) define this corner unit. Baseboard molding (below) protects and frames this half wall.

8 Putting It All Together

Countertops

There are a number of countertop options available to you, including laminate, ceramic tile, solid surfacing, natural stone, stainless steel, and concrete. Of this list, laminate and ceramic tile counters are best suited for the do-it-yourselfer because the tools and materials are widely available. Setting a solid-surface countertop in place is relatively easy, but fabricating the actual countertop requires skill and expertise. Besides, most manufacturers sell their products only to professional countertop fabricators and do not deal directly with the public.

If you have decided on a laminate countertop, you can either fabricate one yourself by attaching the laminate to a substrate or by purchasing a pre-fabricated countertop that you install. There have always been ready-made countertops available in standard lengths that you cut to fit your needs. Called post-formed countertops, they come with integral rounded backsplashes and are available in a limited range of colors. But an increasing number of home centers and dealers are serving as the middle men between countertop fabricators and homeowners. You can order a countertop cut to your specifications in any one of a wide range of laminate colors and textures. You can also specify edge treatments and backsplash configurations. If you go this route, have the retailer or fabricator take the measurements for the countertop. That way, if the countertop doesn't fit when the fabricator delivers it to your house, he is responsible for fixing the problem.

Making a Plastic Laminate Countertop

The substrate for the laminate countertop can consist of two layers of ¾-inch exterior-grade plywood or particleboard. Another method is to use one layer of material and build up the edges to achieve the 1½-inch thickness. Attach the layers to one another with 1¼-inch screws. For a standard-size counter, cut the substrate 24¾ inches wide and ¾ inch longer than the run of the cabinets. This will cover standard-size cabinets and allow for a ¾-inch overhang.

Cut laminate for the edge strips about ¼ inch wider than you will need. You will trim the excess with a router and a flush-trimming bit. Rough-cut laminate for countertops and other flat surfaces about ½ inch larger on all dimensions. **1**

Applying the Laminate. Apply contact cement to the countertop surface and the bottom of the laminate. **2** Apply the edge strips first, and trim them with a flush-trimming bit. **3** For the horizontal surface of the counter, pour cement directly onto the surface and the back of the laminate, and spread it out with a short-napped paint roller, a large brush, or a scrap of laminate. When the cement is dry to the touch, cover the substrate with small strips of lattice. Leave about ½ inch of exposed surface along one edge of the substrate. Carefully lay the laminate on the lattice. **4** Don't allow the laminate to touch the substrate yet, or it will stick immediately.

Align the laminate, and press it into place where you left the exposed cement. Gradually remove the

Making a Laminate Countertop

Difficulty Level: 🔧🔧🔧

Tools & Materials: ❖ ¾-inch plywood and cement backer board (optional) ❖ 1½-inch screws ❖ Basic carpentry tools ❖ Laminate ❖ Contact cement and brush ❖ Brown wrapping paper or lattice strips ❖ Laminate roller ❖ Router with carbide flush-trimming bit and roller-guided bevel bit

3 Apply the edges first. Carefully position the strip over the edge, and roll edge strips firmly into place with a laminate roller. Trim the strips with a flush-trimming bit.

lattice one strip at a time, and press the laminate in place to work out any bubbles. Use a laminate roller or a rolling pin to ensure that the laminate lies flat. Trim the overhang with a router fitted with a bevel bit with a ball-bearing guide. **5** If your router does not have a ball-bearing guide, friction from the high-speed rotation may scorch the laminate.

CAUTION Use contact cement only in well-ventilated areas. Exposure to its fumes can irritate your nose, throat, and lungs. Be sure to wear eye protection and rubber gloves as well.

Solid-surface counters are installed by professional counter fabricators. Each countertop is custom made.

1 Rough-cut the laminate by scoring it with a utility knife or a laminate scoring tool held against a straightedge. Snap along the score line.

2 Brush contact cement onto the substrate and the back of the laminate. Read the label, and observe all safety precautions.

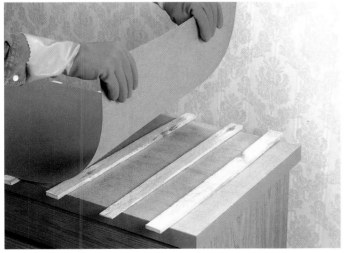

4 Position the main sheet over a series of lattice strips. The sheet should overlap the edges slightly. Remove the lattice one at a time.

5 Press the laminate into the substrate, and roll it with a laminate roller. Use a router and a roller-guided bevel bit to trim the slight overhang.

8 Putting It All Together

Installing Prefabricated Countertops

Whether you are installing a post-formed counter-top you pulled off the rack or laminate countertop built by a fabricator, the process is the same. The supporting cabinets should be level. Even if you are using existing cabinets, check them for level because old cabinets can settle over time. **1**

If the counter will turn the corner, you must assemble the two sections. Lay the pieces upside down on a soft surface. Apply adhesive caulking to the edges of the miters, press them together, slip I-bolts into the slots, and partially tighten the bolts. **2** Check alignment before snugging up each bolt.

It's a good idea to measure to be sure there is at least 34½ inches between the underside of the counter-top and the floor. This is the minimum rough-in height for under-counter appliances. If the counter-top is less than 34½ inches above the floor or if its front edge interferes with the operation of drawers, you'll have to raise the countertop with riser blocks. **3** You'll probably need a helper to set the assembled countertop in position. **4** Push the backsplash up against the wall so that it fits as snugly as possible. To identify high spots on the wall that will cause a gap, hold the shaft of a short pencil against the wall, with the point on top of the backsplash. **5** Pull the pencil along the length of the countertop to scribe a line along the top of the backsplash. At any point where the line bows, you will need to sand or file the rear of the backsplash. If the countertop isn't level, place shims beneath it at the base cabinets' corner braces.

Have a helper hold the countertop firmly against the walls while you drill pilot holes up through the cabinets' corner braces into the top's underside. **6** Take care that these holes don't penetrate more than two-thirds of the countertop's thickness. Drive #10 wood screws through the braces into the top. Run a bead of tub-and-tile caulking along the joint between the backsplash and the wall. **7**

Ready-made post-formed countertops that you cut to size should be finished with an edge cap. Build up the end of the countertop to equal the front edge. Cut a section of laminate to cover the exposed area, and attach it using wood glue or contact cement. A warm iron helps the glue to set up. **8**

Installing a Prefabricated Countertop

Difficulty Level: 🐟🐟🐟

Tools & Materials: ❖ Countertop ❖ 48-inch level ❖ Shims (if necessary) ❖ Caulking gun and adhesive caulk ❖ Pencil ❖ Sandpaper or file ❖ Power drill-driver and assorted bits ❖ Wood screws as needed ❖ Tub-and-tile caulk ❖ Iron (optional)

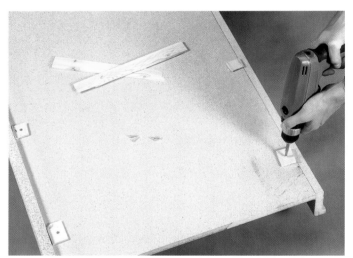

3 If the bottom of the countertop isn't at least 34½ in. from the floor (the rough-in clearance for under-counter appliances), screw riser blocks along its edges.

6 While a helper holds the countertop in place, screw up through the cabinet's corner braces into the bottom of the countertop.

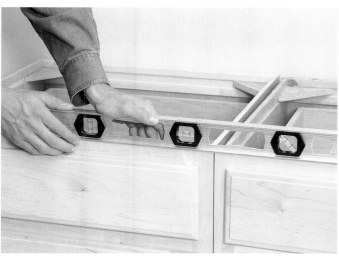

1 Even if you are installing a new countertop over old cabinets, check to be sure that they are level. Cabinets can settle over time.

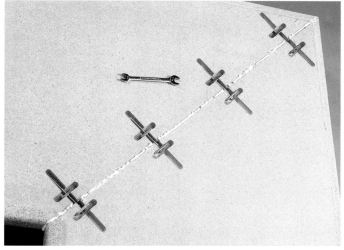

2 If the counter will turn a corner, join the mitered edges before installation. Apply adhesive caulk to the seam, and attach the two sections with I-bolts.

4 Work with a helper or helpers to lift the countertop into position. Support any area where two sections of countertop are joined together.

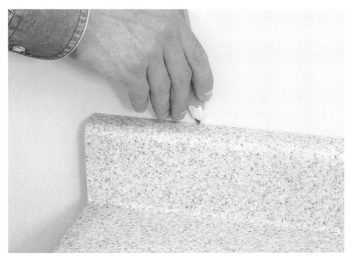

5 Scribe the top of the backsplash by running a pencil against the wall. Sand or file the back of the backsplash where the line bows out.

7 Caulk the line between the backsplash and the wall. This will prevent moisture from getting behind the countertop, causing the substrate to swell.

8 If you need to cut a post-formed countertop to size, finish the exposed edge by installing a strip of matching laminate. The iron helps set the cement.

8 Putting It All Together

Tile Base Basics

Ceramic tiles require a smooth, level, and rigid substrate for a durable installation. If the tile base flexes or moves, it could cause cracks in the tile grout. You could install tile over a double layer of exterior grade plywood. But the best approach is to install a layer of plywood, reinforced with perimeter strips and topped by a layer of cement backer board. The plywood is typically ¾-inch exterior grade with one finished side. The backer board is typically ½ inch thick.

Adding Strength

Before you install the counter, strengthen the base cabinets to resist even slight shifting. You may need to add shims on the cabinets, construction adhesive, and some screws to make sure that separate components are tied together and locked into the wall studs. On new corner units, which often contain lazy Susans and may have open backs, you may need to add nailers along the wall. This supporting framework should be level.

When attaching the substrate to the cabinets, first run a bead of construction adhesive at all contact points. **1** Settle the substrate on the cabinets, and make sure it is level. From inside the cabinets, drive screws up through cabinet braces into the bottom of the plywood. **2** Cabinets generally have either hardware fittings or triangular pieces of wood at the corners.

Installing a Backer Board Substrate

Difficulty Level: 🐟🐟

Tools & Materials: ❖ Utility knife ❖ Power drill-driver and bits ❖ Square ❖ Template ❖ Pencil or marker ❖ Screwdriver ❖ Notched trowel ❖ Construction adhesive ❖ Caulking gun ❖ Thinset adhesive ❖ 4-mil polyethylene ❖ Stapler ❖ Backer board ❖ Screws ❖ Fiberglass mesh tape

1 Lay a bead of construction adhesive along the top of the cabinets to help secure the countertop. Also cover the partition frames between components.

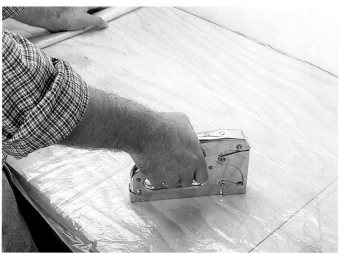

4 Install a moisture-resistant membrane over the plywood countertop. You can use 15-lb. felt paper or 4-mil polyethylene sheeting, as in the photo.

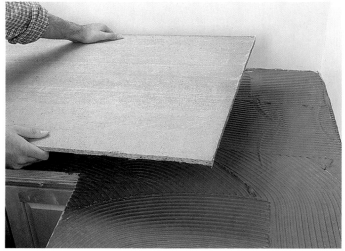

5 Spread an embedding layer of thinset, and install a layer of cement backer board. Leave about a ⅛-in. gap between the panels.

Substrate Options

On countertops that won't get wet, you can affix tile directly to the plywood substrate. Use an organic adhesive, generally called thinset.

You can instead apply a mortar bed substrate to the top of the counter. This is called thickset and consists of a ¾- to 1-inch-thick bed of metal-reinforced cement mortar leveled over a membrane such as roofing felt. It's a solid system, but it's time-consuming and challenging to float a smooth and level mortar bed.

The alternative and easier system is a built-up substrate made of plywood and cement backer board. Before installing the backer board, create cutouts for sinks and other appliances in the plywood. **3** Then attach a moisture-resistant membrane to the ply-

wood—either 15-pound roofing felt or 4-mil polyethylene. **4** There are also liquid membranes. The poly works well, because you can drape sheets over the cabinet fronts for protection and trim the membrane before you tile the counter edge.

Next comes a layer of cement-based backer board set in a bed of thinset combed out in a ribbed pattern with a notched trowel. **5** You can cut the heavy panels to size with a diamond blade, but it's faster and easier to score and snap them. Leave a ⅛-inch gap between panels.

Cut strips of backer board to fill in around the cutouts. **6** Drive corrosion-resistant screws along the edges of the cement board. Use fiberglass mesh tape on the seams and along the exposed edges. **7**

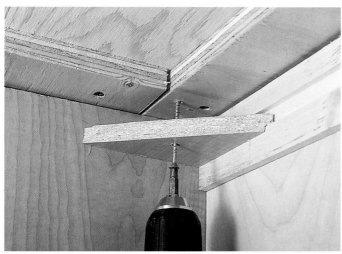

2 Put the plywood base in position, and drive holding screws up through corner braces inside the cabinets. Do not drive through the plywood.

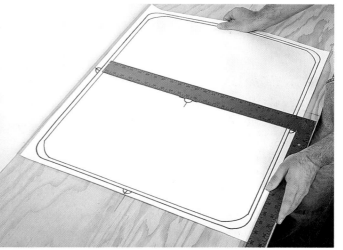

3 Use a template and framing square to position the sink cutout. If you trace the sink outline, measure in from the lip overhang to mark the actual line.

6 Using corrosion-resistant screws, install sheets of cement backer board up to the edges of the cutout. Add narrow strips front and back.

7 Fill the ⅛-in. gaps between backer board panels with thinset, and embed a layer of fiberglass mesh tape over all of the panel seams.

Tiling a Countertop

Arrange the tiles on the countertop in the desired pattern. In some cases, it's best to start from the center of the counter and work to the sides. If there is a sink or some other type of cutout in the counter, install full tiles on each side and work out. The object of the dry run is to position the tiles to minimize narrow cuts. If one layout does not work, try another. If you are using V-caps or similar trim tiles along the edges, mark a line to allow for the edges of the trim tiles, and start the field from that line. **1**

To install the field tiles, lift some of the dry-laid tiles and apply adhesive to the countertop with a notched trowel. **1** (inset) Take care not to spread adhesive over too great an area, so you have time to set the tiles before the adhesive begins to harden. Press each tile firmly in place with a slight wiggle to ensure a good bond. **2** To mark a partial tile, set a full-size tile so that it overlaps one of the field tiles. **3** Cut and then install the partial tile. Make sure you install the cut edge against the backsplash. Install the trim tiles by applying adhesive to the edges of the counter and buttering the back of each tile. **4–5**

Grout the Joints

Wait 24 hours. Apply a strip of wide masking tape along the underside of the front trim tiles to prevent the grout from falling out of the joints. Also mask any surrounding walls you want to protect.

Then mix the grout according to the manufacturer's directions (using colorant if desired), and press it into the joints with a rubber float. When the grout is firm, but not dry, clean the surface with a damp sponge. When the grout dries to a hazy residue on the surface of the tiles, clean the haze off with a dry cloth.

Tiling a Countertop

Difficulty Level: 🐟🐟🐟

Tools & Materials: ❖ Chalk-line box ❖ Pencil ❖ Framing square ❖ Sponge ❖ Tile cutter (rent from supplier) ❖ Tape measure ❖ Tile nippers (rent from supplier) ❖ Hammer ❖ 12-inch 2x4 wrapped with carpet ❖ Rubber float ❖ Masking tape ❖ Tiles ❖ Plastic spacers ❖ Grout solvent (as recommended for the adhesive) ❖ Squeegee ❖ Dry cloth ❖ Adhesive (type and quantity as recommended by supplier) ❖ Notched trowel (notch size as recommended for the tile and adhesive you want to use) ❖ Putty knife

Great Looking Granite

Granite countertops are usually installed by professionals, but you can get the same look by installing granite tiles. The installation procedure is similar to the one shown at right. Use special granite and marble mortar rather than tile thin-set. Seal the stone before grouting to prevent staining.

3 Mark a tile for cutting by overlapping a full-size tile on field tiles and butting it against the wall. Embed partial tiles in the adhesive with a firm pressure.

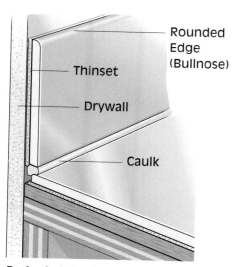
Rounded Edge (Bullnose)
Thinset
Drywall
Caulk

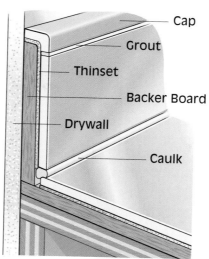
Cap
Grout
Thinset
Backer Board
Drywall
Caulk

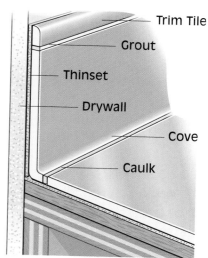
Trim Tile
Grout
Thinset
Drywall
Cove
Caulk

Backsplash Options. One of these three designs can be used to create a simple tile backsplash. Only the center option requires a backer board or plywood substrate. Be sure to caulk the joint between the field tiles and the vertical backsplash.

1 Use the edge tiles to establish a working line for the main field of full tiles. Spread adhesive over the backer board surface using a notched trowel (inset).

2 Work your way along the counter to set all of the full-size tiles. Check the surface with a straightedge to be sure the tiles lie flat.

4 Butter the back of V-caps or other edge tiles with adhesive. Fiberglass mesh tape on the counter edges will improve the bond.

5 Set the edge tiles to align with the grout joints of the field tiles. Work the edging pieces slightly side to side to embed them firmly.

8 Putting It All Together

Sink Options

The installation method you choose not only depends on the type of sink you purchase but also on the countertop. Laminate and ceramic tile countertops consist of substrates that cannot be exposed, so the sink should rest on the countertop. For these countertops choose either a self-rimming or metal rim sink. Solid surfacing and natural stone are not necessarily installed on substrates, and their edges may be exposed. This gives you the opportunity to install an undermount sink.

Installing a Rimmed Sink

Set the rim over the sink, and use a screwdriver to bend the tabs inward on the sink rim. With a cast-iron sink, install supporting corner brackets.

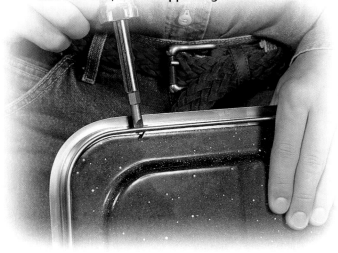

Use a sink-clip wrench (or a long nut driver or screwdriver) to drive the clip bolts against the underside of the countertop. Space clips about 8 inches apart. If the corners do not draw down, use an extra clip at each corner.

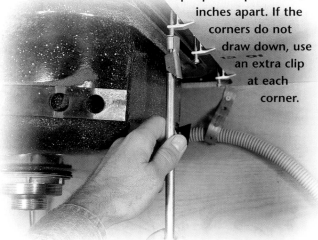

Undermount sinks have a distinctive appearance that looks best when used with natural stone or solid surfacing. Some manufacturers offer special mounting hardware.

Installing a Self-Rimming Sink

Some sinks come with a template for marking the cutout on the countertop. **1** If your sink does not have a template, place it upside down on the counter and trace around the edge. Remove the basin and mark the actual cutting line inside the outer line. Determine the dimensions of the cutout from the sink or the manufacturer's instructions.

Drill ¼-inch-or-more holes at the corners to establish the extent of the cutout. Use a saber saw to cut through the countertop. **2** In many cases the counter will support the weight of the sink, but check the manufacturer's directions. For heavy sinks, install braces to support the sink on the underside of the countertop.

Before placing the sink in the hole, attach the faucet and any other deck-mounted items. You can also attach the sink drain, but you may find it easier to keep the drain holes empty to use as a handhold when lifting the sink into position. Place a bead of silicone caulk along the underside of the sink rim. **3** Then position the sink in the opening, and press it into the sealant. **4** If your sink comes with clips, install them on the underside of the sink. Install the drain by pressing plumber's putty formed into a rope on the underside of the drain flange. Put the drain through the sink opening, and attach the rubber and paper gaskets. Hold everything in place by tightening the spud nut with large groove-joint pliers or a spud wrench. **5** After hooking up all the plumbing, run a thin bead of caulk around the edge of the sink.

Installing a Self-Rimming Sink

Difficulty Level:

Tools & Materials: ❖ Pencil ❖ Template ❖ Saber saw ❖ Power drill-driver with bit ❖ Spud wrench or groove-joint pliers ❖ Utility knife ❖ Caulking gun ❖ Silicone caulk ❖ Basin ❖ Drain kit ❖ Plumber's putty ❖ Gloves

1 Lay the template on the countertop, and trace the opening for the sink. You can also place the sink on the countertop and trace around the rim.

2 Cut out the opening for the sink by drilling holes at the corners of the outline and using a saber saw to make the final cuts.

3 Attach the faucet while the sink is still on the countertop. Run a bead of caulk around the underside of the sink's rim.

4 Lift the sink into the hole. Cast-iron sinks are heavy and will be held in place by their weight. You may need help getting one into position.

5 Place a roll of plumber's putty on the underside of the drain flange. Insert the drain through the opening, attach the gaskets and spud nut, and tighten the nut.

8 Putting It All Together

Plastic Pipe

Lightweight plastic pipe ranges in diameter from 1½ to 6 inches. Most plastic DWV lines are installed with just a few simple tools. Making connections is easy and straightforward, but it requires a little practice. After cutting the pipe with a handsaw, clean up the ends with a utility knife, apply pipe primer and solvent cement, and join the pieces. Be sure to match the solvent cement to the type of plastic used in the pipe. You can even join a new section of plastic pipe to an existing cast-iron waste line with compression clamp fittings consisting of flexible gaskets and metal rings that screw-tighten.

Plastic waste pipes are made of ABS (black) or PVC (white) plastic. Check with the local plumbing inspector to find out which type is acceptable for your project.

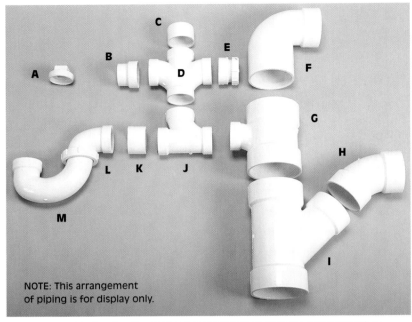

NOTE: This arrangement of piping is for display only.

Basic plastic drainage piping includes (A) cleanout plug, (B) threaded adapter, (C) coupling, (D) cross, (E) ground-joint adapter, (F) street 90-deg. elbow, (G) 3 x 1½-in. T-fitting, (H) 45-deg. elbow, (I) 3 x 2-in. Y-fitting, (J) sanitary T-fitting, (K) coupling, (L) trap arm, (M) trap.

Working with Plastic Pipe

Measure the lengths required, allowing for the fittings. (Assume the pipe will fit all the way inside the sleeves of the fittings.) Unless you are cutting pipe already in place, put the lengths you're planning to cut in a miter box. Make a straight cut with a backsaw or hacksaw. **1** Use a utility knife or emery cloth (or both) to remove burrs from the cut ends and to dull the outer cut edge so that it will slide smoothly into the fitting.

After cutting the pipes, test-fit the parts that will be joined. **2** If the new pipe is too long, simply trim it to the correct size. If the pipe is too short to fit completely in the fittings, cut another piece of pipe, which you can add to the first piece, or start over with a new section of pipe. Use PVC primer to clean the ends of PVC pipe and fittings. **3**

Thoroughly coat the ends of each pipe and the inside of the fittings with the solvent cement. **4** Be sure to use the type of solvent cement intended for the type of plastic pipe you are using. Immediately after applying solvent cement, insert the pipe into the fitting, and twist the two parts against each other about one-quarter turn. **5** Hold the pieces together for about ten seconds. If you fit the joint properly, the solvent cement will form a continuous bead around the joint.

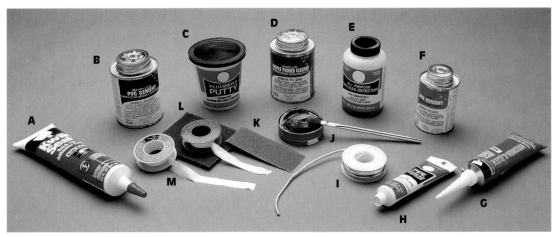

Basic plumbing supplies include (A) latex tub-and-tile caulk, (B) PVC solvent cement, (C) plumber's putty, (D) PVC primer, (E) leak-detection fluid, (F) ABS solvent cement, (G) silicone caulk, (H) pipe joint compound, (I) solder, (J) flux, (K) grit cloth, (L) abrasive pad, (M) pipe-thread sealing tape (yellow spool: gas, blue spool: water).

Cutting and Joining Plastic Pipe

Difficulty Level:

Tools & Materials: ❖ Plastic pipe ❖ Backsaw or hacksaw ❖ Miter box ❖ Work gloves and goggles ❖ Pipe primer ❖ Pipe ❖ Solvent cement ❖ Compression clamp fittings (when working with cast iron) ❖ Utility knife ❖ Emery cloth

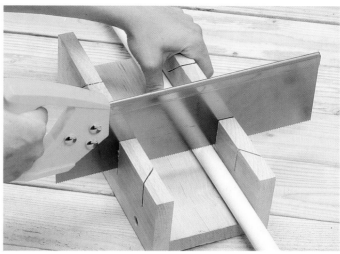

1 Place the pipe in the miter box, and hold it against the side of the box. Remove burrs from the cut ends with a utility knife or emery cloth.

2 Test-fit the pipe sections before assembly, and adjust to the correct size. If the pipe is too long, trim it; if it's too short, add another piece.

3 Clean the end of the pipe and fittings with pipe primer. Use the type of primer specifically made for the type of pipe you are using.

4 Coat the ends of the pipes and the inside of the fittings with the appropriate solvent cement. Be sure to use the correct type for the pipe you're using.

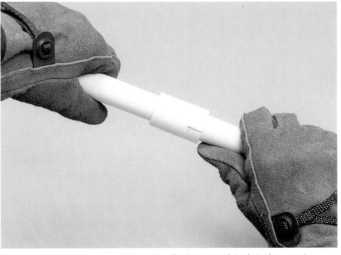

5 Insert the pipe into the fitting, and twist the parts against each other about one-quarter turn. Hold the pieces together for about 10 seconds.

8 Putting It All Together

Copper Pipe

Copper pipes come in either rigid pipes or flexible tubing. The advantage of the flexible version is you can bend it to snake around curves in existing walls and floors without making joints. The downside is that the curves must be gentle and without kinks; making bends requires a little practice. Each joint in rigid tubing requires a joint with a soldered or threaded coupling.

Soldering Copper Connections

From a home center or hardware store, buy a small torch that screws to a disposable propane canister. Also buy self-cleaning flux and solder. Use only lead-free solder (nickel or silver) for pipes that carry drinking water. When soldering with a torch, you can endanger both yourself and your house. Protect your eyes with safety goggles and your hands with work gloves. Get a 12 × 12-inch piece of sheet metal to insert between the joint to be soldered and any nearby wood to protect your house from catching fire.

Use a small brush or toothbrush to coat the joint ends with flux. **1** Slide the fitting over the pipe ends so that half of the fitting is on each pipe. **2**

Light the torch, and heat the joint by running the flame over the fitting, taking care to avoid burning the flux. When the pipe is hot enough to melt the solder, take the torch away, and feed solder into the joint. **3** Continue until the joint stops drawing

Using a Propane Torch

If you're going to be working with metal pipe—whether copper, steel, or cast iron—you'll need to become familiar with the propane torch. Although it has the potential to be a dangerous tool, a few precautions and the proper safety gear will keep you safe from harm. Use a sparking tool to safely ignite the gas. Turn on a gentle supply of gas, and squeeze the sparker handle. Once you ignite the gas, increase the flow to enlarge the flame. It's wise to wear gloves when you handle heated pipes.

Before you try to heat up a pipe with a torch—to thaw a frozen section or to resolder a joint—first drain the line. You can't get copper hot enough to make solder flow when it is filled with water. Also, open a faucet just beyond the repair so that any steam that develops can escape. Be careful when using propane torches in tight spots where the flame may lick past the pipe and heat up building materials nearby. Use extra care working in framing cavities, particularly in older homes where the wood is very dry.

Soldering Copper Pipe

Difficulty Level: 🃏🃏🃏

Tools & Materials: ❖ Copper pipe ❖ Bristle brush ❖ Flux (soldering paste) ❖ Solder ❖ Propane torch ❖ Sparker ❖ Sheet metal ❖ Work gloves ❖ Clean rag ❖ Pipe fitting ❖ Coupling

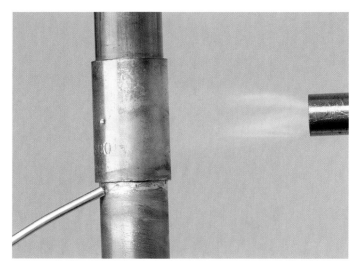

3 Light the torch, and begin to heat the fitting. Heat the fitting until it is hot enough to draw solder into the joint. Continue until the joint is filled.

in the solder and there are no gaps in the solder.

If the solder around the rim of the joint stays puddled and does not draw in as it cools, reheat the joint until the solder liquifies; then try again. If the solder joint beads up and does not flow evenly, the fitting and pipe may need to be cleaned with an emery cloth and resoldered. Practice with some scrap pipes and connectors until you feel confident enough to solder your new supply lines. If you're soldering near combustible materials, place the piece of sheet metal between the soldering area and the material to prevent fire. **4**

Cool the pipe with a wet rag; then test the joint for leaks. **5** If more solder doesn't stop the leaks, melt the joint apart and start over.

Insulating Pipes

For pipes that will carry hot water, it's smart to save a little on your energy costs with pipe insulation. Fit preformed polystyrene insulation tubes around hot-water pipes, and tape them in place. You can also wrap the pipes in strips cut from fiberglass batts. Either system will not only conserve heat loss but also prevent pipe sweating in the summertime. If you have pipes running through an unheated crawl space, insulate (or protect with a heating cable) both hot- and cold-water pipes to keep them from freezing.

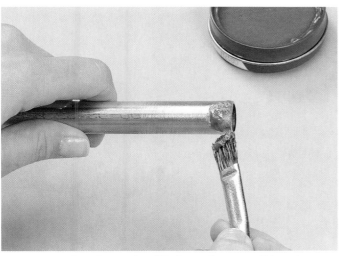

1 Coat the pipe ends with flux using a small brush or toothbrush. Make sure the ends of the pipe have been cleaned with an emery cloth.

2 Insert the fitting over one pipe end so that half of the fitting is on the pipe. Twist the fitting to spread the flux. Then connect the second pipe to the fitting.

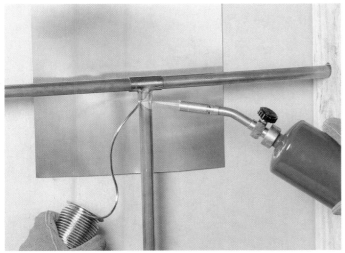

4 To prevent fire, place a small piece of sheet metal between the area you are soldering and any combustible material.

5 Wipe the pipe with a rag to clean the joint. Check your work for leaks. Stop leaks with more solder. If that doesn't work, melt the joint apart and try again.

8 Putting It All Together

Faucets & Drains

If possible, attach the faucet and strainer to the sink while it is sitting on top of the counter. You will avoid the problem of making those connections from inside the cramped quarters of the sink cabinet. If you do need to work under the sink, use a basin wrench to make the connections up behind the bowl of the sink.

Installing Faucets

Installation methods vary depending on the type of faucet. In addition to the single-handle model shown below, where the supply lines are bundled together, some have individual supply hookups, called tailpieces, at either end of the base plate.

Clean the surface of the sink, and install the gasket that came with your faucet. Secure the base plate by fastening the jamb nuts snug against the bottom of the sink deck. **1** On some models, the base plate is held in place by fastening nuts alongside the brass tailpieces.

Place the faucet through the hole in the base plate. Mounting hardware varies. The faucet shown here has a plastic spacer, a steel washer, and a brass nut. Slide the assembly up the column and tighten. **2**

If you were working on the sink on top of the counter, now is the time to install the sink. Complete the installation by hooking up the water supply. **3** Most newer faucets use compression fittings to make the connections.

Installing Faucets

Difficulty Level: 🐟🐟

Tools & Materials: ❖ Screwdriver ❖ Basin wrench ❖ Adjustable wrench ❖ Plumber's putty ❖ Pipe joint compound ❖ Faucet

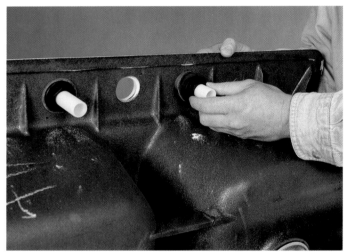

1 Install the base plate gasket, put the plate in position, and then hand-tighten the jamb nuts on the base-plate supports.

2 Insert the faucet into the hole, and slide the mounting hardware up the faucet column. Tighten the hardware bracket.

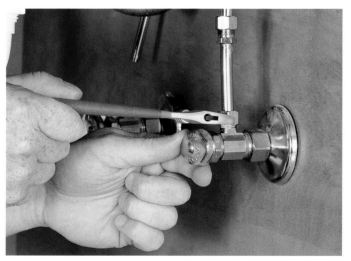

3 Connect the riser to the water outlet near the shut-off valve. Most new faucets make connections with compression fittings.

Installing the Drainline and Trap

With the sink and faucet installed, it's time to hook up the drainage system. As is the case with faucet installations, it is easiest to attach the strainer before installing the sink. However, many people like to use the empty drain hole to hold the sink when settling the sink into position.

If you haven't mounted the strainer, place a roll of plumber's putty under the drain flange and install the drain in the sink opening. Put the drain gaskets in position, and tighten the spud nut.

Most kitchen sink drainage systems are made of plastic and consist of a tailpiece that connects the sink to the trap, the P-trap, and a trap arm to connect the trap to the permanent drain that enters the cabinet from the wall or floor. For multibowl sinks, buy drain kits that include the extra extension tubes and T-fittings you'll need.

Place a nylon insert washer into the tailpiece flange. **1** (inset) Push the tailpiece into the drain opening, slide a metal coupling nut onto the tailpiece, and tighten it over the threads on the drain spud. **1** Connect the tailpiece to the trap or to a T-fitting for multiple-bowl sinks. Use a nylon washer and compression nut. **2** Connect the trap to the extension arm in the same manner. If your permanent drainpipes are plastic, cement a ground-joint adapter to the pipe stub. **3** The adapter allows you to connect the piping to the permanent drain with a screw-on coupling nut.

Installing Drains

Difficulty Level: 🦇🦇 🦇

Tools & Materials: ❖ Hacksaw ❖ Sink trap kit ❖ Groove-joint pliers ❖ PVC primer and cement

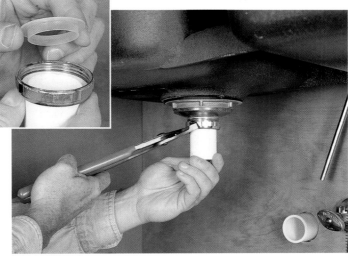

1 Press a nylon washer into the flanged tailpiece (inset), and use a metal coupling nut to tighten the tailpiece onto the drain spud.

2 Slide a compression nut and a beveled nylon washer onto the tailpiece. Push the T-fitting or the trap against the tailpiece, and tighten the nut.

3 Connect the trap assembly to the permanent drain. If necessary, cement a ground-joint adapter to the plastic drain stub.

8 Putting It All Together

Waste-Disposal Units

It is easier to begin the installation before the sink is in place. Roll a ½-inch diameter rope of plumber's putty and place it around the underside of the sink flange. **1** Slip the sleeve into the sink hole, and press down on the sink flange to make sure it's seated.

Flip the sink over, and attach the disposal unit's mounting assembly, which usually includes gaskets and mounting flanges, onto the drain spud. **2** Follow the manufacturer's directions for the correct order of installation. Tighten the three screws so that the mounting assembly is seated firmly and evenly with the sink.

Installing the Disposal Unit

If you are installing a built-in dishwasher, the dishwasher will drain through the disposal unit. Use a screwdriver to remove the drain knockout plug in the unit. **3**

Lift the disposal unit into position, lining up its mounting tabs or ears with the mounting ring on the sink assembly. Turn the unit's lower mounting ring (with the ears) to the right using the small wrench that comes with the unit or a screwdriver. Keep turning until the ears engage the flanges on the upper mounting ring. **4**

If you are installing a new sink along with the disposal unit, now is the time to hook up the drain system. Connect the trap and tailpiece to the main sink drain as shown on page 233. Connect the drain to the disposal unit with an extension tube that connects with a T-fitting to the main drain above the trap. **5** Attach the dishwasher drain hose to the disposal unit, and secure it with a hose clamp. **6**

Attach the wiring by removing the electrical cover plate from the disposal unit, and locate the black and white wires coming from the unit. **7** Pull the power cable through the access hole in the bottom of the unit, and secure it with a clamp. Make the connections by joining the black wires to black wires and white wires to white ones. Attach the grounding wire to the grounding screw on the appliance.

With the power off, install the switch box near the sink. Pull power cable into the box, and attach the black wire to the switch. Attach the black wire on the cable that connects the switch and disposal to the other terminal. Splice together the white wires, and pigtail the grounding wire. **8**

Installing a Waste-Disposal Unit

Difficulty Level: 🔱 🔱 🔱

Tools & Materials: ❖ Waste-disposal unit ❖ Plumber's putty ❖ Screwdrivers (flat-bladed and Phillips) ❖ Plastic wire connectors ❖ Pliers ❖ Wire stripper ❖ Cable ❖ Switch

3 If you're installing a dishwasher, lay the disposal unit on its side, and use a screwdriver and hammer to remove the drain knockout.

6 Run the drain hose from the dishwasher to the disposal unit. Connect the hose with a hose clamp. The dishwasher will drain through the disposal unit.

1 Roll plumber's putty into a rope that is about ½ in. thick and about 10 in. long. Press the putty under the drain flange.

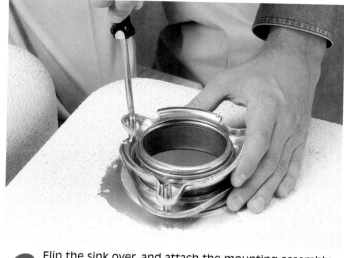

2 Flip the sink over, and attach the mounting assembly (gasket, sealing flange, mounting flange, and split ring) onto the drain spud.

4 Lift the disposal unit into position under the drain fitting, and engage the mounting ring. Rotate the unit clockwise to secure it.

5 Connect the drain system. Use an extension tube to connect the disposal unit to the main drain above the trap. Tighten all fittings.

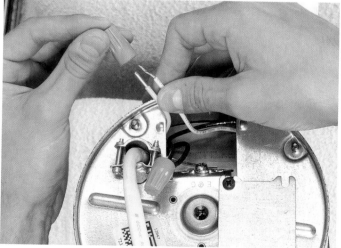

7 Remove the electrical cover plate. Pull the cable from the switch into the unit. Make splices between the white, black, and grounding wires using wire connectors.

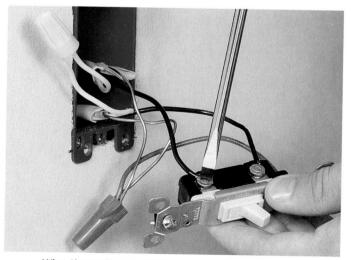

8 Wire the switch that will control the unit. Connect black wires to the terminals, and splice together white wires. Pigtail the grounding wires.

8 Putting It All Together

Dishwashers

Before sliding the dishwasher into its space, tip it onto its back to give you easier access for making connections. Remove the access panel, and set it aside. Attach the discharge hose to the appliance's pump with a hose clamp. **1** Apply some pipe-thread sealing tape to a dishwasher elbow, and thread the ½-inch side onto the solenoid valve. Tighten it until the elbow points toward the appliance purge pump.

Cut a 1½-inch hole in the cabinet wall leading to the sink to accommodate the water supply line and the drain hose. You will also need to bring electrical power to the dishwasher. All require a dedicated 20-amp circuit.

For the water supply, you can remove the existing shutoff on the hot-water line and replace it with a dual-stop valve. **2** Another option is to remove the shutoff and install a T-fitting and separate shutoff valves for the hot-water line and the dishwasher. If you need to repair the dishwasher, you can shut off the water on that branch without interrupting water to the faucet.

Installing the Dishwasher

Run the drain hose and the supply line from the dishwasher to the sink. You will need about 5 feet of ⅜-inch soft copper line to make the connection in a normal installation. Carefully slide the dishwasher into position. Connect the line to the dishwasher

Installing a Dishwasher

Difficulty Level: 🐟🐟🐟

Tools & Materials: ❖ Dishwasher ❖ Compression T-fitting ❖ Compression-fitting shutoff valve ❖ Copper tubing (⅜-inch or larger) ❖ Adjustable wrench ❖ Bucket ❖ Rubber or plastic drain line ❖ Backflow preventer ❖ Hose clamps ❖ 12-gauge electrical cable ❖ Basic electrical tools ❖ Wire connectors ❖ 1-inch wood screws

1 With the dishwasher unit lying on its back, attach the discharge hose to the appliance pump using the supplied hose clamp.

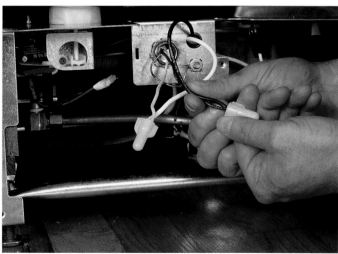

4 Join like-colored wires with twist connectors to make the electrical connection. Attach the grounding wire to the green ground screw.

5 Slide a compression nut and ferrule onto the supply line, and connect the line to the new dual-stop valve. Apply pipe-thread sealing tape to the fitting.

elbow. **3** Make the electrical connections by joining the like-colored wires from the circuit to the lead wires from the dishwasher. **4**

Under the sink, connect the supply line to the dual-stop valve. **5** Most codes require some method of backflow prevention be used in dishwasher drain installations. You must either install a backflow preventer on the sink deck or loop the hose up near the top of the sink cabinet. **6** Either method prevents a backed up drain from spilling into the dishwasher.

If you have a waste-disposal unit, connect the dishwasher drain hose to the unit's nipple with a hose clamp. **7** For installations that do not involve a disposal unit, take the existing drain apart and replace a section above the trap with a waste T-fitting designed for this type of installation. **7** (inset)

Level the dishwasher by adjusting the leveling legs with a wrench. The top of the dishwasher will have mounting clips. Screw these clips into the bottom of the countertop. Replace the access panel.

SMART TIP

Most dishwashers come with a discharge hose. If the unit you buy does not have one, you'll need to supply the hose. Appliance supply stores may have what you need, but if they don't, automotive heater hose is a reasonable substitute. It can handle prolonged exposure to heat and detergent.

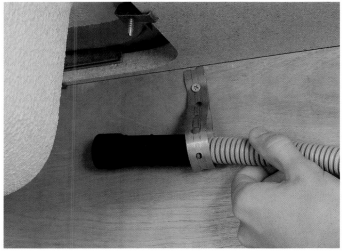

2 Remove the existing hot-water shutoff valve from under the sink and install a new dual-stop valve. Use compression fittings for the connection.

3 Slide a compression nut and ferrule onto the water supply line, and connect the line to the dishwasher elbow. Tighten the fitting with an adjustable wrench.

6 To prevent a clogged drain from backing up into the dishwasher, install a backflow preventer or, if allowed, loop the drain hose up near the top of the cabinet.

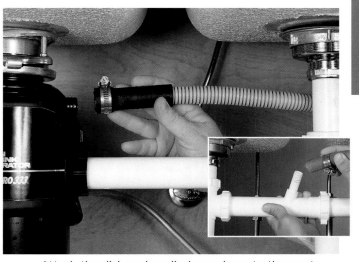

7 Attach the dishwasher discharge hose to the waste-disposal unit's nipple. If you do not have a disposal unit, attach the hose to a waste T-fitting (inset).

8 Putting It All Together

Slide-In Ranges

Check with the local building department for applicable codes before hooking up either a gas or electric range if you're changing what you already have. With electric ranges, codes specify the type and length of appliance cord you must install. With gas ranges, most codes permit use of special flexible brass tubing from the gas-line shutoff to the range; a few, however, require that this connection be made with rigid steel gas pipe.

Some ranges come with an anti-tip bracket. The bracket, which is screwed to the floor, surrounds one of the rear legs and prevents the appliance from tipping forward.

Installing Gas Ranges

Purchase a flexible connector that's only slightly longer than you need. To hook up the connector, coat the threads with pipe joint compound or wrap them with plumber's tape. Thread the connector nuts onto the shutoff and the stove inlet. **1** Overtightening can crack soft brass gas fittings, causing a gas leak. Check for leaks by turning on the gas and brushing the fittings with soapy water. **2** Bubbles indicate a gas leak. To fix, turn off the gas and try tightening the nut again. If you can't stop the leak, turn off the gas, and call a plumber.

Slide the range into its final position. Place a level on top of the range, and make necessary adjustments by turning the nuts on the appliance leveling legs. **3**

Installing a Gas Range

Difficulty Level:

Tools & Materials: ❖ Gas range ❖ Flexible gas connector ❖ Adjustable wrenches ❖ Groove-joint pliers ❖ Pipe joint compound ❖ Brush and soapy water

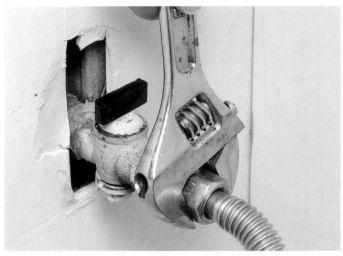

1 With the gas off, connect the flexible gas connector approved for your range to the appliance and to the gas shutoff valve.

2 Test your work by turning on the gas and brushing the fitting with soapy water. Bubbles indicate a leak that must be corrected.

3 Slide the range into position, and plug in the electric cord to operate clocks and lights. Level the appliance by adjusting the leveling legs.

Electric Cooktops

Some cooktops are installed on top of the counter with their weight holding them in place. Others are installed in a fashion similar to that of self-rimming sinks: Placed in a cutout in the counter and held by a lip that rests on the counter.

Installing Cooktops

Electric cooktops require permanent electrical connections. You will need a dedicated 240-volt, 30-amp circuit and an approved junction box.

Trace the outline of the appliance template onto the counter. Use a saber saw to make the counter cutout just as you would for a sink. **1** Place the unit in the cutout, and secure it from below with clips. **2** Install the junction box on the cabinet wall, and bring the cable into the box. Run the cable from the cooktop, and secure it with a conduit connector. Make the necessary connections. **3**

CAUTION Check with your local building inspector before attempting this type of installation. The latest version of the National Electric Code states that if the circuit is new, the appliance must be wired hot to hot, neutral to neutral, and ground to ground. The wiring shown below is wiring for an existing circuit.

Installing an Electric Cooktop

Difficulty Level:

Tools & Materials: ❖ Cooktop ❖ Junction box ❖ Electrical cable ❖ Wire connectors ❖ Tape measure ❖ Template and pencil ❖ Saber saw ❖ Power drill-driver ❖ Drill bits

1 Place the template on the counter, and trace the outline of the opening. Use a saber saw to cut through the countertop material.

2 Place the cooktop into the cutout. From inside the cabinet, attach the clips that came with the unit to the underside of the countertop.

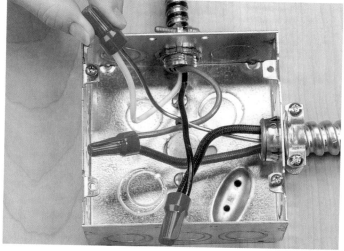

3 Pull the power cable into the junction box, and make the electrical connections. This wiring sequence hooks up the appliance to an existing circuit.

Side-by-side refrigerators (left) offer a variety of options, such as through-the-door water and ice.

Built-in appliances offer a sophisticated look to a kitchen. The refrigerator above is designed to fit narrow spaces. Sleek finishes and distinctive handles help the dishwasher at left and refrigerator at right stand out.

DESIGN IDEAS

See "Food Preparation," page 22

See "Dishwashers," page 32

Cooking options include restaurant-style ranges (above) that provide higher than normal burner temperatures; unique AGA cookers (right) that are always on; and modular cooktops (below) that combine gas and electric burners.

8 Putting It All Together

Water Filtration

There are a variety of types of water treatment systems available, but no one system can solve all of the possible water-related problems. To narrow the choices, test your water to identify any harmful elements. Use either a do-it-yourself test kit, or for a more thorough analysis, send samples to a testing laboratory.

Types of Treatment

Water treatment systems can be divided into two broad categories. In point-of-entry systems, the equipment is located where the water enters the home, treating all of the water used. Point-of-use (POU) systems are located at the sink, and only water that is used for drinking and cooking actually receives some treatment. POU systems are relatively inexpensive and easy to install, and the equipment is easy to handle.

The most popular POU systems are activated carbon filters, reverse-osmosis (RO) filters, and distillation units.

Carbon Filters. These have been around for some time and are effective at eliminating a great variety of odors, tastes, and contaminants that can affect your health. They are available in filter canisters such as the one installed at right. Some faucet manufacturers now offer faucets that have an integral filter built into the faucet spout.

Carbon filters must be changed regularly. Better-quality filtration systems have warning lights that let you know when it is time to change the filter.

RO Systems. In RO filters water is forced through a semipermeable membrane that allows water molecules through but traps a wide range of contaminants. Once filtered, the water is held in a storage tank until used. The typical system can filter between 5 and 15 gallons per day. Most RO systems include pre- and post-filters for improving the taste and smell of water.

Distillation. These systems don't filter the water but rather boil it and capture the steam in a condensing coil. The impurity-free water collects in a holding tank until used.

Installing a POU Filter

Difficulty Level:

Tools & Materials: ❖ Filtration system ❖ Filtration system installation kit (saddle valve, water lines with compression fittings if not included with the system) ❖ Screwdriver ❖ Adjustable wrench or appropriate open-end wrenches ❖ Pliers

POU Systems

Problem	Possible Solutions
Bacteria	Activated carbon, distiller, RO
Low suds	RO
Rusty stains	Activated carbon
Rotten egg smell	Activated carbon
Yellow/brown tinge	Activated carbon, distiller, RO
Chlorine odor	Activated carbon, RO
Pesticides, volatile organic compounds, benzene	Activated carbon, distiller, RO
Lead, mercury	RO, distiller
Nitrates, sulfates	RO, distiller

3 Place the dedicated faucet in the hole you just created. Secure the faucet in position by tightening the mounting nut under the sink.

Installing the System

Although procedures may vary slightly from product to product, many manufacturers have simplified installation for the homeowner by using fittings designed for quick installation. Filter kits come with the filter canister and all the necessary plumbing fittings you will need.

Clear a space under the sink for the unit. Some reverse-osmosis systems consist of a large tank holding the RO membrane and two or three filter canisters, taking up a good portion of the under-sink cabinet. Screw the hanging bracket to the back or side of the cabinet under one of the unused sink knockouts. Attach the unit to the bracket. **1**

Remove the knockout in the sink. **2** If you don't have a knockout in the sink, you can drill through the countertop to install the faucet. If you have an integral solid-surface sink, you can drill through the sink deck. Place the dedicated faucet in the opening, and tighten the mounting nut from below. **3**

Install the self-piercing saddle valve on the cold-water riser. **4** Back the tapping pin out as far as it will go, and with the rubber tapping seal in place, bolt the two halves of the assembly together over the riser. Draw the two bolts down alternately, a little at a time, until they feel snug. Use a compression fitting to attach the supply tube to the valve. **5** Make the necessary connections between the valve and the filter and between the filter and the dedicated faucet.

1 Clear a space under the sink for the filtration unit. Install the mounting bracket near the cold-water riser and under a sink knockout.

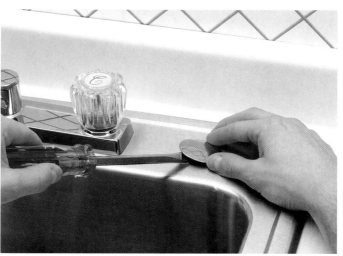

2 Use a screwdriver to remove the knockout in the sink deck. You can drill through the countertop or a solid-surface sink if no hole is available.

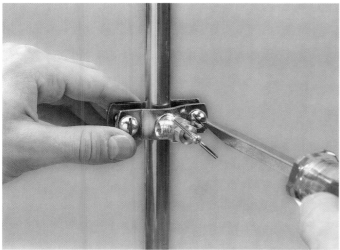

4 Make the water connection by installing the supplied saddle valve on the cold-water riser. Draw the bolts down until they feel snug.

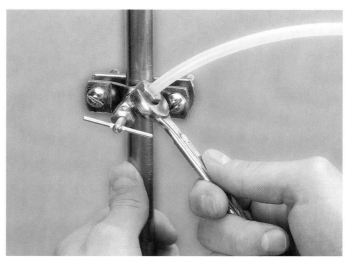

5 Connect the water line between the filter and the faucet and then between the cold-water riser and the filter. Tighten the compression fittings.

8 Putting It All Together

Instant Hot-Water Dispensers

Hot-water dispensers deliver 190-degree water for brewing tea, making instant soups, and blanching vegetables. The heating unit mounts in the sink cabinet and comes with a three-prong plug. If you already have an outlet in the cabinet, the hardest part of the installation is already complete. If not, you will need to get electrical service to the location.

These units do not require a dedicated plumbing line. You simply tap into a copper cold water riser using a self-piercing saddle valve. For brass or galvanized pipes, you have to shut down the system and drill a tap hole into the line.

Installing an Instant Hot-Water Dispenser

Difficulty Level:

Tools & Materials: ❖ Dispenser and fittings ❖ Flat-blade screwdrivers ❖ Groove-joint pliers ❖ Open-end wrenches ❖ Tubing cutter (optional)

Installing a Hot-Water Dispenser

Mount the saddle valve onto the cold-water riser. With the rubber seal in place, bolt the two halves of the assembly over the riser. **1** Draw the two bolts down alternately until they feel snug. Feed the threaded shank of the heater up through the sink hole, and screw the mounting nut onto it from above. **2** (inset) Then tighten the jamb nut from below. **2** If the unit you buy has a detachable spout, screw it in place on the faucet body. Connect the water line from the heater to the saddle valve using the compression fitting. Test for leaks. Use a thermometer to measure the temperature of the water. If it does not register 190 degrees, adjust the temperature setting using a screwdriver. **3**

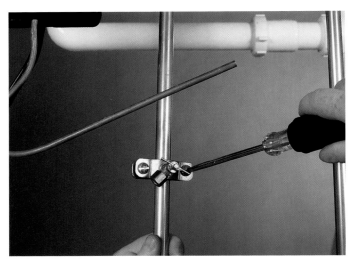

1 Install the self-piercing saddle valve on the cold-water copper riser. You can still use the valve on brass or galvanized pipes if you shut down the system first.

2 Feed the threaded shank of the heater through the sink hole, and install the mounting nut from above (inset). Tighten the jamb nut from below.

3 Make the water connections, and test the unit. You can adjust the water temperature by turning the adjusting screw on the face of the heater.

Ice Makers

Many refrigerator manufacturers now include automatic ice makers or chilled water dispensers as standard equipment. You can also retrofit ice makers on an existing refrigerator. In either case, you must get water from the sink to the refrigerator.

Ice-maker installation kits you find in home centers and hardware stores include a self-piercing saddle valve, such as the one shown here. However, before buying one check the refrigerator manufacturer's directions. Some companies recommend that you use a standard shutoff valve with a ⅜-inch to ¼-inch reducing coupling instead of a self-piercing saddle valve.

Making the Connections

Drill holes through the bottom of base cabinets that stand between the sink plumbing and the refrigerator. The tubing should be placed so that it will not be damaged by stored items or closing drawers. Install the self-piercing saddle valve in the cold-water riser. **1** Pull the refrigerator out from the wall, and remove the bottom access panel. **2** The plumbing connection should be located in one of the corners. There will be a plastic tube running from the connection point up to the freezer. Use a compression fitting to connect the tubing to the ice-maker nipple. **3** Reinstall the access panel, and gently place the tube behind the appliance. Do not put kinks in the plumbing line.

Hooking Up an Ice Maker

Difficulty Level: 🦇🦇

Tools & Materials: ❖ Ice-maker installation kit ❖ ¼-inch copper or plastic tubing ❖ Fixture shutoff valve (optional) ❖ Flat-blade screwdriver ❖ Groove-joint pliers ❖ Adjustable or open-end wrenches ❖ Tubing cutter (optional)

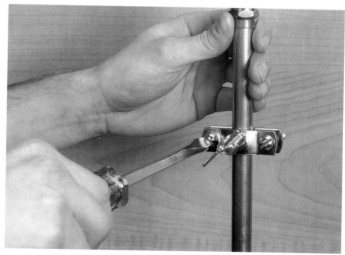

1 Install the self-piercing saddle valve in the cold-water riser. Some manufacturers require a standard shutoff valve for this project.

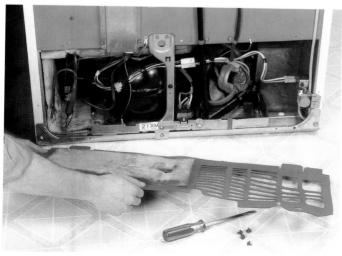

2 Locate and remove the screws that hold the access panel in place. It is usually located in the back of the refrigerator near the floor.

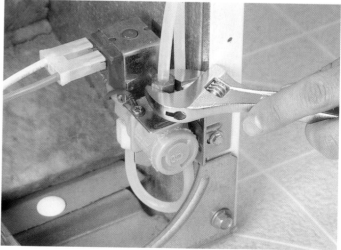

3 Use compression fittings to connect the ¼-in. tubing to the saddle valve under the sink and to the ice maker's nipple. Replace the access panel.

Resource Guide

Andersen Corporation
100 Fourth Ave. North
Bayport, MN 55003-1096
888-888-7020
www.andersencorp.com
The Andersen Corporation is a major window manufacturer that offers a full range of residential window and skylight sizes and styles.

Jenn-Air
Maytag Customer Service
240 Edwards St.
Cleveland, TN 37311
800-688-1100
www.jennair.com
Jenn-Air is a part of the Maytag Corporation that offers a wide range of kitchen appliances.

Armstrong World Industries
Attn: Customer Response Center
P.O. Box 3001
Lancaster, PA 17604
800-233-3823
www.armstrong.com
Armstrong World Industries is a manufacturer of cabinets, flooring, and ceiling materials.

Kohler
444 Highland Dr.
Kohler, Wisconsin 53044
800-456-4537
www.kohlerco.com
Kohler is a major manufacturer of kitchen and bath fixtures. They offer a wide variety of kitchen sinks, faucets, and kitchen accessories.

Faber
P.O. Box 435
Wayland, MA 01778
508-358-5353
www.faberonline.com
Faber specializes in range hoods in many shapes and sizes. The company offers information on selecting and sizing ventilation systems.

KraftMaid Cabinetry, Inc.
P.O. Box 1055
Middlefield, OH 44062
888-562-7744
www.kraftmaid.com
Kraftmaid Cabinetry manufactures an extensive line of built-to-order cabinets. The company offers a variety of finishes and storage options.

Frigidaire
P.O. Box 212378
Martinez, GA 30917
800-374-4432
www.frigidaire.com
Frigidaire is a manufacturer of many home appliances, including ranges, cooktops, range hoods, dishwashers, washers, and dryers.

National Association of Remodeling Industry(NARI)
780 Lee St., Ste. 200
Des Plaines, IL 60016
800-611-6274
www.nari.org
NARI offers homeowners help in selecting and working with professional remodeling contractors.

General Electric
GE Customer Relations
P.O. Box 22108
Memphis, TN 38122
800-626-2000
www.geappliances.com
General Electric produces a wide variety of appliances, including refrigerators, dishwashers, and ovens.

National Kitchen and Bath Association(NKBA)
687 Willow Grove St.
Hackettstown, NJ 07840
www.nkba.org
800-652-2776
NKBA, a national trade organization, offers remodeling information to professionals and homeowners.

This list of manufacturers and associations is meant to be a general guide to additional industry and product-related sources. It is not intended as a listing of products and manufacturers represented by the photographs in this book.

Rejuvenation
Sales and Service
2550 NW Nicolai St.
Portland, OR 97210
888-401-1900
www.rejuvenation.com
Rejuvenation is a manufacturer of light-ing fixtures that range from vintage to modern designs.

Sears Cabinet Refacing
Sears National Customer Relations
3333 Beverly Rd.
Hoffman Estates, IL 60179
800-469-4663
www.sears.com
Sears Home Service division provides cabinet refacing and other contractor services for the entire house.

Sub-Zero Freezer Company
P.O. Box 44130
Madison, WI 53744-4130
800-222-7820
www.subzero.com
Sub-Zero makes built-in refrigerators and freezers for both home and indus-trial use. They are available in many different styles.

Thermador
5551 McFadden Ave.
Huntington Beach, CA 92649
800-656-9226
www.thermador.com
Thermador offers a broad line of kitchen appliances, including built-in ovens, electric and gas cooktops, and traditional ranges.

Tile Council of America, Inc.
100 Clemson Research Blvd.
Anderson, SC 29625
864-646-8453
www.tileusa.com
TCA is committed to improving the tile installation industry. They offer litera-ture on selecting and installing tile.

Velux-America, Inc.
P.O. Box 5001
1418 Evan Pond Rd.
Greenwood, SC 29648
800-888-3589
www.velux.com
Velux is an international manufacturer of skylights, roof windows, and solar energy systems.

Wellborn Cabinet, Inc.
P.O. Box 1210
Ashland, AL 36251
800-762-4475
www.wellborn.com
Wellborn Cabinet sells a wide variety of kitchen, bath, and entertainment cabinetry in a variety of styles, finishes, and price ranges.

Wilsonart International
P.O. Box 6110
Temple, TX 76503-6110
800-433-3222
www.wilsonart.com
Wilsonart is a manufacturer of solid-surfacing materials, laminates, and adhesives for cabinets, countertops, floors, and fixtures.

Wolf Appliance Company, LLC
P.O. Box 44848
Madison, WI 53744
800-222-7820
www.wolfappliance.com
Wolf, a division of Sub-Zero, offers professional style cooking appliances, including ranges, cooktops, ovens, grills, and warming drawers.

York Wallcoverings, Inc.
750 Linden Ave.
York, PA 17404
800-375-9675
www.yorkwall.com
York Wallcoverings offers an extensive line of wallpapers and borders, as well as advice and decorating tips.

Glossary

Accent lighting Lighting that emphasizes a particular area or object.

Ambient lighting Lighting that illuminates an area or room.

Appliance garage Countertop storage for small appliances.

Baking center An area near an oven(s) and a refrigerator that contains a countertop for rolling out dough, and storage for baking supplies and utensils.

Backsplash The finish material that covers the wall behind a countertop. The backsplash can be attached to the countertop or separate from it.

Base cabinet A cabinet that rests on the floor and supports a countertop.

Bearing wall A wall that supports the structure above it. Joists rest on the top plate of a bearing wall. See *Joist*.

Building codes The legal standards and methods that must be followed during any construction project.

Butcher block A counter or tabletop material composed of strips of hardwood, often rock maple, laminated together and sealed against moisture.

Carousel shelves Revolving shelves that are usually installed in corner cabinets.

Caulking Any one of a number of compounds used to fill cracks and seams.

Chalk line A device used to mark a straight line on a surface. Stretch the chalk-covered cord taut just above the surface. Pull the cord up in the center and release to leave a chalk mark on the surface.

Chair rail A decorative wall molding installed midway between the floor and ceiling. Traditionally, chair rails protected walls from damage from chair backs.

Circuit The electrical path that connects one or more outlets (receptacles) and/or lighting fixtures to a single circuit breaker or fuse.

Circuit breaker A device that closes an electrical circuit when demand exceeds safe limits or during a short circuit.

Cleanup center The area of a kitchen where the sink, waste-disposal unit, trash compactor, dishwasher, and related accessories are grouped for easy access and efficient use.

Convection oven An oven in which heat is circulated by a small fan rather than radiated from a burner or element.

Cooking center The kitchen area where the cooktop, oven(s), and food preparation surfaces, appliances, and utensils are grouped.

Coped joint Two pieces of molding that are joined by cutting the end of one with a coping saw to fit over the contours of the other.

Copper tubing Seamless tubing that is 99.9 percent copper.

Countertop The work surface of a counter, island, or peninsula, usually 36 inches high. Common countertop materials include plastic laminate, ceramic tile, slate, and solid surfacing.

Cove lights Lights that reflect upward, sometimes located on top of wall cabinets.

Crown molding A decorative molding usually installed where the wall and ceiling meet.

Drywall Sheets of gypsum sandwiched between backing paper and a smooth-finish front surface paper. Also called wallboard and, improperly, Sheetrock (a trade name).

Ductwork Sheet-metal passages that carry heated or cooled air, or exhaust air in a ventilation system.

Exhaust fans A fan used in a ventilation system that pulls air from a kitchen.

Fish tape A long, flexible metal tape used to pull wires through existing walls.

Floating floor A floor material that is glued together on it's tongue-and-groove edges but is not attached to the subfloor.

Fluorescent lights A type of light containing a phosphor that attracts ultraviolet light and then converts it into visible light.

Framed cabinets Cabinets with a full frame across the face of the cabinet box.

Frameless cabinets European-style cabinets without a face frame.

Framing The skeleton structure of the studs and joists that support walls, ceilings, and floors. See *Joist, Stud*.

Furring Strips of wood attached to a wall to provide support and attachment points for a covering such as hardboard paneling.

Gardening center A kitchen area used for cutting, arranging, and planting flowers.

General lighting Light that illuminates the entire room.

GFCI Stands for ground-fault circuit interrupter. A type of electrical receptacle that reacts to an abnormal condition in a fraction of a second.

Great rooms Open spaces where cooking, dining, and areas for relaxing flow into one another.

Grout A mixture of Portland cement and water—and sometimes sand—used to fill the gaps between ceramic tiles.

Halogen lights High-tech incandescent lights that require special fixtures.

Home equity loans A loan that is based on the equity you have in your house. Home equity loans generally have longer terms and lower interest than personal loans.

Header A horizontal structural member used to span an opening in the framing, such as for a window or door, and to transfer the structural load across the opening.

Incandescent lights Lights that heat a tungsten filament to incandescence in order to give off light.

Island A base cabinet and countertop unit that stands independent from walls, so that there is access from all four sides.

Jamb The vertical (side) and horizontal (top) pieces that cover the wall thickness in a door or window opening.

Joist A floor or ceiling support member that rests on the top plates of bearing walls.

Joint compound The plaster material used to fill small holes and seams in drywall.

Joint tape Paper or synthetic mesh tape about 3 inches wide that is used to reinforce joint compound that is used on the seams between drywall panels.

Kitchen fans Fans that remove grease, moisture, smoke, and heat from the kitchen.

Knockdown cabinets Cabinets that are shipped flat and assembled on the building site.

Laminate floors Floors whose structural core is covered with a plastic laminate wear layer.

Lazy Susan Axis-mounted shelves that revolve. Also called carousel shelves.

Low-voltage lights Lights that operate on 12 to 50 volts rather than the standard 120 volts.

Magnetic-induction cooktops Cooktops that transfer energy from under the surface directly to the cooking vessel without heating the burner.

Microwave oven An quick-cooking appliance that uses high-frequency electromagnetic radiation to cook food.

NKBA National Kitchen and Bath Association, an educational trade organization of the kitchen industry that, among other things, tests and certifies kitchen designers.

Non-bearing wall An interior wall that provides no structural support for any portion of the house.

Pantry A storage room or large cabinet for packaged foods.

Particleboard A material composed of wood chips and coarse fibers bonded with adhesive into large sheets from ½ to 1½ inches thick. It is commonly used as the support for countertops and for cabinet construction.

Partition wall A wall built to separate certain parts of the kitchen, for example, a dining area from the work area.

Patching plaster A type of plaster mix used to fill holes and cracks prior to painting.

Peninsula A countertop, with or without a base cabinet, that is connected at one end to a wall or another countertop and extends outward, providing access on three sides.

Plastic laminate A hard-surface, thin material made from melamine under high pressure and used for the finished surfaces of countertops, cabinets, flooring, and furniture.

Plaster A pastelike material used on ceilings and walls that hardens as it dries.

Rail A horizontal member that runs between two vertical supports, such as the rails on a cabinet or door.

Range hood A ventilator set above a cooktop or the burners of a range.

Recessed light fixtures Light fixtures that are installed into ceilings, soffits, or cabinets and are flush with the surrounding area.

Refacing Replacing the doors and drawers on cabinets and covering the face frames with a matching material.

Roof windows A skylight that also serves as a way to exit a building in an emergency.

Secondary work center An area of the kitchen where extra activity is done, such as laundry or baking.

Semi-custom cabinets Cabinets that are available in specific sizes but with a wide variety of options.

Sheetrock See *Drywall*.

Shim A thin wedge-like insert used to adjust the spacing between adjacent materials.

Shutoff valves Supply valves that control the flow of water or gas to specific fixtures or appliances.

Sliders Sliding doors are made up of large, framed glass panels. In most cases, one door slides and the other is stationary.

Skylight A roof-mounted window that allows natural light into a building.

Soffit A short wall or filler piece between the top front edge of a wall cabinet and the ceiling above it.

Solid-surface countertop A countertop material made of acrylic plastic and fine-ground synthetic particles, sometimes made to look like natural stone.

Stiles The vertical parts of a framework, such as a sash or a door.

Stock cabinets Cabinets that are in stock or available quickly when ordered from a retail outlet.

Stud A vertical framing member of a wall.

Sunrooms Also known as a solarium, a sunny room that has many windows or is enclosed by glass panels for maximum sunlight.

Task lighting Light aimed directly onto a work area, such as a sink or a cooktop.

Track lighting Lights that are attached to the ceiling by a track and can be easily moved and adjusted.

Traffic pattern The pattern of movement people use in a kitchen.

Under-cabinet light fixtures Light fixtures that are installed on the undersides of cabinets for task lighting.

Underlayment Sheet material—usually plywood—placed over a subfloor to provide a smooth, even surface for new flooring.

Vapor retarder A material used to prevent water vapor from moving from one area into another or into a building material.

Ventilation The process of removing or supplying air to a certain space.

Wainscoting Paneling that extends 36 to 42 inches or so upward from the floor level, over the finished wall surface. It is often finished with a horizontal strip of molding mounted at the proper height and protruding enough to prevent the top of a chair back from touching a wall surface.

Wall cabinet A cabinet, usually 12 inches deep, that's mounted on the wall a minimum of 15 inches above a countertop.

Wallboard See *Drywall*.

Work triangle The area bounded by the lines that connect the sink, range, and refrigerator. In theory, the sum of the lines in the triangle should not exceed 26 feet.

Index

Metric Conversion

Length

1 inch	25.4 mm
1 foot	0.3048 m
1 yard	0.9144 m
1 mile	1.61 km

Area

1 square inch	645 mm^2
1 square foot	0.0929 m^2
1 square yard	0.8361 m^2
1 acre	4046.86 m^2
1 square mile	2.59 km^2

Volume

1 cubic inch	16.3870 cm^3
1 cubic foot	0.03 m^3
1 cubic yard	0.77 m^3

Common Lumber Equivalents

Sizes: Metric cross sections are so close to
their U.S. sizes, as noted below, that for most
purposes they may be considered equivalents.

Dimensional	1 × 2	19 × 38 mm
lumber	1 × 4	19 × 89 mm
	2 × 2	38 × 38 mm
	2 × 4	38 × 89 mm
	2 × 6	38 × 140 mm
	2 × 8	38 × 184 mm
	2 × 10	38 × 235 mm
	2 × 12	38 × 286 mm
Sheet	4 × 8 ft.	1200 × 2400 mm
sizes	4 × 10 ft.	1200 × 3000 mm
Sheet	¼ in.	6 mm
thicknesses	⅜ in.	9 mm
	½ in.	12 mm
	¾ in.	19 mm
Stud/joist	16 in. o.c.	400 mm o.c.
spacing	24 in. o.c.	600 mm o.c.

Capacity

1 fluid ounce	29.57 mL
1 pint	473.18 mL
1 quart	1.14 L
1 gallon	3.79 L

Temperature

(Celsius = Fahrenheit – 32 × ⁵⁄₉)

°F	°C
0	–18
10	–12.22
20	–6.67
30	–1.11
32	0
40	4.44
50	10.00
60	15.56
70	21.11
80	26.67
90	32.22
100	37.78

Photo Credits

Project sequences by Freeze Frame Studio except where noted.

page 1: Brian Vanden Brink **page 6:** Mark Samu, designer: Jim DeLuca, A.I.A. **page 7:** Brian Vanden Brink, designer: Morning Star Marble Company **page 8:** *top* Jessie Walker, designer: Gail Drury/Drury Design. *bottom left* Mark Samu. *bottom right* Brian Vanden Brink **page 9:** Tim Street-Porter/Beateworks.com **pages 10–11:** Anne Gummerson, architect: Wood-Mode Cabinetry, designer: Kenwood Kitchens **page12:** *top* courtesy of Kraftmaid. *bottom* Melabee M Miller, designer & fine arts consultant: Elizabeth Guest **page 13:** courtesy of Kraftmaid **page 14:** Mark Samu, designer: Jim DeLuca, A.I.A. **page 15:** *top* courtesy of Kraftmaid. *bottom* Mark Lohman **page 16:** Mark Samu, designer: William Spadero Designs **page 17:** *bottom* courtesy of American Olean **page 18:** *top* Tria Giovan. *bottom* Mark Samu, courtesy of Hearst Publications **page 19:** *top left* Mark Samu, stylist: Margaret McNicholas. *top right & bottom* courtesy of KraftMaid **page 20:** *left* Mark Samu, designer: Rick Shaver. *right top & bottom* courtesy of Merillat **page 21:** *top* courtesy of KraftMaid. *bottom* davidduncanlivingston.com **page 22:** Mark Lohman. *bottom* davidduncanlivingston.com **page 23:** *top* Mark Samu, designer: Van Florio, A.I.A. *bottom* Mark Samu, designer: Rick Shaver Design **page 24:** Mark Lohman **page 25:** *top* courtesy of Wolf. *bottom* davidduncanlivingston.com **page 26:** *top* Tria Giovan. *bottom* Mark Lohman **page 27:** davidduncanlivingston.com, designer: Ken Burghardt **page 28:** Mark Lohman **page 29:** *top & bottom* davidduncanlivingston.com **page 30:** *top & bottom* davidduncanlivingston.com. *middle* Mark Samu, stylist: Margaret McNichols **page 31:** Mark Lohman **page 32:** *top & bottom* davidduncanlivingston.com **page 33:** davidduncanlivingston.com **page 34:** Lisa Masson Studio **page 35:** *all* davidduncanlivingston.com **page 36:** *top* davidduncanlivingston.com. *bottom* Phillip H. Ennis Photography, designer: Nancy Mullen/MDM Kitchens **page 37:** courtesy of KraftMaid **pages 38–39:** courtesy of Armstrong Floors **page 40:** davidduncanlivingston.com **page 41:** courtesy of Rejuvenation **page 42:** *top* Mark Samu, designer: Kitchen Designs by Ken Kelly. *bottom* Anne Gummerson **page 43:** Anne Gummerson, designer: Richstone Custom Homes **page 44:** Tony Giammarino **page 45:** Tony Giammarino, architect: Susan Kipp Construction **page 46:** Phillip Ennis Photography, architect: Lim Chang **page 48:** *top* Mark Lohman. *bottom* Mark Samu, designer: Jim DeLuca, A.I.A. **page 49:** Mark Samu, courtesy of Hearst Specials **pages 50–51:** Nancy Hill, designer: Kitchens by Deanne **page 52:** courtesy of Kraftmaid **page 53:** Anne Gummerson, designer & builder: Ilex **page 54:** Brian Vanden Brink, architects: Weston & Hewitson **page 55:** *top* davidduncanliv-

ingston.com., designer: Ken Burghardt. *bottom* Brian Vanden Brink, architect: John Morris, project architect: John Gillespie **page 56:** Anne Gummerson, architect: Sarah Schweizer, designer: Richard Rice/Mill Valley Kitchens **page 57:** *top* Melabee M Miller Photography, designer: Mark Cobucci/Dovetail Designs. *bottom* Anne Gummerson, architect: Laura Thomas/Melville Thomas Architects **page 59:** Anne Gummerson, architect: Sarah Schweizer, designer: Arnot & Associates, table design: Henry Fox/Fox Brothers **page 60:** davidduncanlivingston.com **page 61:** *top* Mark Samu, designer: Jim DeLuca, A.I.A. *bottom* davidduncanlivingston.com **page 62:** top Tony Giammarino. *bottom* Tria Giovan **page 63:** Tria Giovan **page 64:** davidduncanlivingston.com, designer: Lamperti Associates **page 65:** *top* davidduncanlivingston.com., designer: Robert Nebolon. *bottom* Mark Samu, designer: Kitchen Designs by Ken Kelly **page 66:** Nancy Hill, designer: Rooms of England by Pamela **page 67:** *top* davidduncanlivingston.com *bottom* Tony Giammarino **page 68:** Melabee M Miller Photography, cabinets by Merillat **page 69:** Brian Vanden Brink, architect: Thom Rouselle **page 70:** *top* courtesy of Wilsonart *bottom* courtesy of Kraftmaid **page 71:** Jessie Walker, designer: Dave Hagerman **pages 72–73:** Mark Samu, designer: Kitchen Designs by Ken Kelly **page 74:** Jessie Walker, designer: Dave McFadden **page 75:** *top* Jessie Walker, designer: Dave McFadden *bottom* Brian Vanden Brink, architect: Peter Rose **page 76:** Tim Street-Porter/Beateworks.com architect: Larry Totah **page 77:** *top* Jessie Walker, *bottom* Jessie Walker, architect: Thomas L. Bosworth **page 78:** Jessie Walker, designer: Mastro-Sklar **page 79:** *all* Mark Lohman **page 80:** Brian Vanden Brink **page 81:** *top right* Brian Vanden Brink *bottom* Philip Clayton-Thompson **page 84:** Brian Vanden Brink, architect: Ted Wengren **page 87:** Tony Giammarino, designer: Bruce Bierman Designs **page 89:** Brian Vanden Brink, architect: Winston Scott **page 94:** Mark Samu, designer: Kitchen Designs by Ken Kelly **page 95:** *top* Mark Samu, courtesy of Hearst Specials. *bottom* Brian Vanden Brink, architect: Rob Whitten **page 96:** courtesy of Kraftmaid **page 99:** Melabee M Miller, designer: Joan Picone/European Country Kitchens Photography **pages 104–105:** Mark Samu, courtesy of Hearst Specials **page 106:** Brian Vanden Brink, architect: Mark Hutker & Associates **page 107:** Brad Simmons Photography, designer: Phyllis Craver/Fine Designs **page 108:** Jessie Walker, architectural designer: Avis Gray **pages 110–111:** Melabee M Miller Photography, cabinets by Merillat **page 117:** John Parsekian **page 120:** *top* Anne Gummerson, architect: Laura Thomas/Melville-Thomas Architects. *bottom* Brian Vanden Brink, architect: Rob Whitten **page 121:** *top* Brian Vanden Brink, architect: Rob

Whitten. *bottom left* Jessie Walker, designer: Kelly Hutchinson. *bottom right* Brian Vanden Brink, architect: Bob McNight **page 123:** *top right* John Parsekian. *bottom right* Clarke Barre **page 129–131:** courtesy of Velux America **page 130:** *left top to bottom, & right bottom* courtesy of Velux America **page 132:** *top left* Brian Vanden Brink, architect Mike Homer. *top right* davidduncanlivingston.com. *bottom* Brian Vanden Brink, architect: Mark Hutker & Associates **page 133:** *top* Brian Vanden Brink, architect: Jeremiah Eck. *bottom left* Jessie Walker, designer: Betsy McGann/Artistic Kitchen Designs of Oak Brook. *bottom right* Brian Vanden Brink **pages 136–137, 141:** Brian C. Nieves **page 146:** *bottom left* Brian C. Nieves. *bottom right* John Parsekian **page 147:** *top* Clarke Barre. *bottom four* Brian C. Nieves **page 151:** Lisa Masson, designer & builder: Hopkins & Porter **page 152:** Merle Henkenius **pages 153 & 158:** John Parsekian **page 160:** *sequence* John Parsekian **page 161:** top Grey Crawford **page 164:** *top left* courtesy of York Wallcoverings. *top right* John Schwartz, designer: Sharon L. Sherman. *bottom* Philip Clayton-Thompson **page 165:** *top* Jessie Walker, designer: Star Norini-Johnson/Distinctive Kitchen Designs. *bottom* John Schwartz, designer: Steve Kinon, CKD for Ulrich, Inc. **pages 168–169:** Brian C. Nieves **page 170:** *top* Brian Vanden Brink, architect: Dominic Mercadante. *bottom left* Mark Samu. *bottom right* Melabee M Miller, designer: Ellen Brounstein **page 171:** *top* courtesy of Lindal Cedar Homes. *bottom* Brian Vanden Brink, builder: Axel Berg **page 172:** Mark Samu/Montllor Box A.I.A. **pages 176–177:** Mark Samu **page 179:** John Parsekian **page 186:** *top row* davidduncanlivingston.com. *bottom* Brian Vanden Brink, architects: Van Dam & Renner **page 187:** *top left & right* courtesy of Armstrong Floors. *bottom* Brian Vanden Brink, architect: Van Dam & Renner **page 188:** courtesy of American Olean **pages 189, 192, 194–195:** John Parsekian **pages 198–199:** Randall Perry **pages 200–203:** John Parsekian. **page 204:** *top* Brian Vanden Brink. *bottom* Jessie Walker, architect: Richard Becker **page 205:** *top left* Tony Giammarino. *top right* davidduncanlivingston.com. *bottom left* Mark Samu, courtesy of Hearst Specials. *bottom right* Melabee M Miller Photography, designer: Mike Boyette/Boyette Kitchens & Baths **page 208:** courtesy of Sears Cabinet Refacing **page 214:** John Parsekian **page 216:** *top left & right* davidduncanlivingston.com. *bottom* Mark Lohman **page 217:** *top left* davidduncanlivingston.com. *top right* courtesy of Wellborn. *bottom* Gary David Gold, CH **page 219:** courtesy of Corian **pages 222–225:** John Parsekian **page 226:** *top* courtesy of Corian **page 240:** *top left* courtesy of General Electric. *top right* courtesy of Sub-Zero. *bottom* courtesy of Jenn-Air **page 241:** *top left & right* davidduncanlivingston.com. *bottom* courtesy of Wolf

Sources

Photographers
Beateworks.com, Los Angeles, CA; 310/558-1100. *Brian Vanden Brink*, Rockport, ME; 207/236-4035. *Philip Clayton-Thompson*, Portland, OR; 503/234-4883. *Phillip H. Ennis Photography*, Freeport, NY; 516/379-4273. *Tony Giammarino*, Richmond, VA; 804/320-9709. *Tria Giovan*, New York, NY; 212/533-6612. *Anne Gummerson*, Baltimore, MD 410/276-6936. *Nancy Hill*, Ridgefield, CT; 203/431-7655. *David Duncan Livingston*, Mill Valley, CA;

415/383-0898, davidduncanlivingston.com. *Freeze Frame Studio*, Hackensack, NJ; 201/343-1233. *Mark Lohman*, Los Angeles, CA; 323/933-3359. *Lisa Masson Studio*, Annapolis, MD; 410/990-1777, lisamassonphotography.com. *Melabee M Miller*, Hillside, NJ; 908/527-9121. *Mark Samu*, Saratoga Springs, NY; 212/754-0415. *Brad Simmons Photography*, Perryville, KY; 859/332-8400. *Jessie Walker Associates*, Glencoe, IL; 847/835-0522.

Kitchen Designers & Architects
Richard Becker, 847/433-6600. *Mike Boyette, Boyette Kitchens & Baths*, Bloomfield, NJ; 973/784-2841. *Mark Cobucci, Dovetail Designs*, Bergenfield, NJ; 201/385-7681. *Avis Gray*, 970/726-7155. *Elizabeth Guest*, Stanton, NJ; 908/236-0503. *Dave Hagerman*, 517/882-2599. *Kelly Hutchinson*, 847/295-4905. *Mastro-Sklar*, 312/919-7912. *Dave McFadden*, 630/469-7429. *Joan Picone, European Country Kitchens*, Far Hills, NJ; 908/781-1554.

Have a home improvement, decorating, or gardening project? Look for these and other fine Creative Homeowner books wherever books are sold.

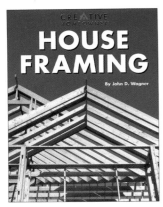

Designed to walk you through the framing basics. Over 400 illustrations. 208 pp.; 8¹/₂"×10⁷/₈"
BOOK#: 277655

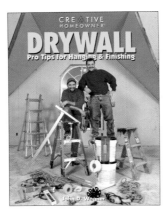

A complete guide covering all aspects of drywall. Over 250 color illustrations. 144 pp.; 8¹/₂"×10⁷/₈"
BOOK #: 278315

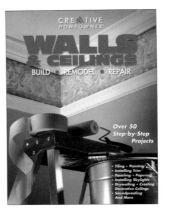

Comprehensive guide to interior surfaces. Over 460 color photos. 160 pp.; 8¹/₂"×10⁷/₈"
BOOK #: 277708

Everything you need to know about setting ceramic tile. Over 450 photos. 160 pp.; 8¹/₂"×10⁷/₈"
BOOK#: 277524

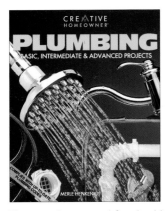

The complete manual for plumbing projects. Over 750 color photos and illustrations. 272 pp.; 8¹/₂"×10⁷/₈"
BOOK#: 278210

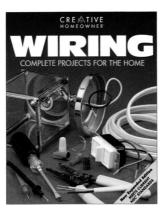

Best-selling house-wiring manual. Over 700 color photos and illustrations. 256 pp.; 8¹/₂"×10⁷/₈"
BOOK #: 278237

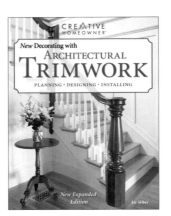

Transform a room with trimwork. Over 550 color photos and illustrations. 240 pp.; 8¹/₂"×10⁷/₈"
BOOK #: 277500

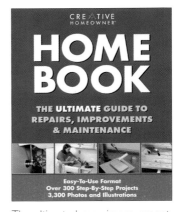

The ultimate home improvement reference manual. Over 300 step-by-step projects. 608 pp.; 9"×10⁷/₈"
BOOK#: 267855

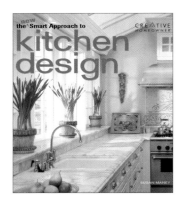

How to create kitchen style like a pro. Over 150 color photographs. 176 pp.; 9"×10"
BOOK #: 279946

All you need to know about designing a bath. Over 150 color photos. 176 pp.; 9"×10"
BOOK #: 279234

An impressive guide to garden design and plant selection. More than 950 photos. 384 pp.; 9"×10"
BOOK #: 274610

Lavishly illustrated with portraits of over 100 flowering plants; more than 500 photos. 208 pp.; 9"×10"
BOOK #: 274032

For more information and to order direct, visit our Web site at www.creativehomeowner.com